Are Canonizations Infallible?

Are Canonizations
INFALLIBLE?

REVISITING
A DISPUTED QUESTION

ESSAYS BY

Phillip Campbell • Fr. Thomas Crean, O.P.
Roberto de Mattei • William Matthew Diem
Christopher Ferrara • Msgr. Brunero Gherardini
Fr. John Hunwicke • Peter A. Kwasniewski
John R.T. Lamont • Joseph Shaw
Fr. Jean-François Thomas, S.J.
José Antonio Ureta

EDITED BY

Peter A. Kwasniewski

AROUCA
PRESS

ISBN 978-1-989905-65-4 (cloth)
ISBN 978-1-989905-64-7 (paperback)

Arouca Press
PO Box 55003
Bridgeport PO
Waterloo, ON N2J 3G0
Canada
www.aroucapress.com
Send inquiries to info@aroucapress.com

CONTENTS

EDITOR'S PREFACE

FOR A LONG TIME NOW, THE MAJORITY POSI-
tion among Catholic theologians has been that canonizations conducted
by a pope should be considered infallible and/or inerrant. A casual
online search quickly leads to copious documentation of this view. It is
not, however, the only view that has been held (as the use of the word
"majority" itself implies), and there are compelling reasons to revive the
minority position, or at least to give its adherents a fair opportunity
to make their case. It should not be forgotten that the Immaculate
Conception of the Blessed Virgin Mary was *not* held by four great
doctors of the Church—St. Bernard, St. Albert, St. Thomas, and St.
Bonaventure; neither was it the consensus of the masters for most of
the thirteenth century. While they probably *would* have assented to
the doctrine had it been proposed to them with Scotus's explanation
(distinguishing priority of time and priority of nature in the first
instant of Mary's existence), it remains true that faithful Catholics
living at the time of those doctors would have been materially in error
by following the majority position. A lesson that may be drawn from
this episode is that we should be content to adopt the consensus of
good and holy theologians from centuries past *until and unless* there
is a compelling reason to depart from that consensus.

The reasons for reviving the minority position may be divided into
those that have already been part of the debate for centuries and those
that are peculiar to the ecclesial situation in which we find ourselves
today—such as the concerns that arise from the total overhaul of the
processes of beatification and canonization in 1983 and from reservations about the canonizability of certain controversial figures. As several authors herein discuss, the meaning and use of the word "infallible"
has also developed over time, with 1870 as a watershed moment, and
participants in the debates have not always taken care to contextualize
their sources, distinguishing between pre-1870 and post-1870 frame-
works. If there is one thing the contents of this volume demonstrate,
it is that the historical, doctrinal, liturgical, and moral aspects of canonization are more complex than many realize. Thus, even those who,

having considered opposing arguments, still believe they can or must defend inerrantism will nonetheless be in a position to exhibit a greater nuance and modesty than is customarily found in the (neo)scholastic shallows of discourse in which far too many playfully splash.

The authors who agreed to participate in this joint project do not necessarily hold one and the same opinion on the matters under discussion, although it would be fair to say that nearly all of them reject the widespread idea that canonizations conducted by a pope are always and everywhere infallible and must be considered and accepted as such by the faithful. A central goal of this collection is to advance arguments for why it would be acceptable and could (at least under certain circumstances) be compulsory to distance oneself from the inerrantist view. As will be apparent, the authors do not dismiss the majority view out of hand, but test its foundations and applications to see if it may have been assumed too hastily as the only view possible or as the one that has so much plausibility that it practically excludes the contrary. It may be pointed out here that a major source for the infallibilist position, Prospero Lambertini's four-volume treatise *De servorum Dei beatificatione et de beatorum canonizatione* — authored while he was still a cardinal in the Roman Curia — is too often cited in secondary literature as the work of "Benedict XIV," which might mislead readers into thinking that Lambertini's opinions as a private theologian wear the mantle of papal authority. In a subject that precisely concerns the papal magisterium, this honorary "papalization" of a non-papal source — which would undoubtedly be innocent in most contexts — acquires more gravity and should be avoided. In any case, Lambertini is frequently and thoroughly discussed in these pages.

In chapters 1 and 2, Fr. Jean-François Thomas and José Antonio Ureta furnish an overview of canonizations in the Church and set the stage for our debated question. In chapter 3, Phillip Campbell provides a short history of the *promotor fidei* or "devil's advocate" — a role eviscerated by John Paul II in 1983, with implications that are traced out by several authors later on. The next four chapters may be considered the theological heart of the book, as three formidable Thomistic scholars discuss the correct interpretation of the Angelic Doctor's teaching. In chapter 4, William Matthew Diem carefully examines the texts of Aquinas and the historical context before and after. Arguing against infallibility simply speaking, Diem maintains that even if the Church could err in canonization — in the sense that she could canonize one who is not in heaven — she cannot canonize one who manifestly did not lead a holy life, and therefore the faithful will not have grounds to deny any particular canonization without temerity. In chapter 5, Fr. Thomas Crean succinctly presents, *more Thomistico*, the principal arguments for and against the inerrantist position, concluding in favor of inerrantism, albeit in a minimalist sense. Chapter 6 is Diem's rejoinder to Fr. Crean. In chapter 7, the late Msgr. Brunero Gherardini — eminent theologian of the Roman School, Dean of the Faculty of Theology at the Lateran, long-time editor of *Divinitas*, and a collaborator with the Congregation for the Causes of Saints — proposes a tightly-argued case against the infallibility of canonizations. Chapters 8 through 15 — written by John Lamont, Fr. John Hunwicke, Christopher Ferrara, Roberto de Mattei, Joseph Shaw, and myself — advance a variety of arguments against the view that all papal canonizations are infallible and in favor of the view that at least some such canonizations may be erroneous and invalid owing to defects in authority, intention, process, form, or matter. An appendix offers choice paragraphs from Prospero Lambertini on the precise norms for the right evaluation of papal sanctity.

Inevitably, some overlap will be found among the contributors. Yet each author brings distinct facts, observations, and arguments to the conversation, and each offers a unique perspective or angle. Together they vigorously reanimate a debate that has lain dormant for too long. We have published this book as a service to the truth — as a spur to a more intensive theological engagement with a *quaestio disputata* that should not be prematurely treated as definitively solved. If the essays here provide a more compelling (because more realistic) account of what canonization is and is not, what it involves, implies, and excludes; if they offer new insights or dismantle old assumptions; if they disturb easy certainties or reassure troubled consciences, then they will have amply served their purpose, to the greater glory of God and the veneration of His undoubted saints, especially the all-holy and immaculate Virgin.

The famous question in St. Thomas Aquinas's *Quaestiones Quod-libetales,* a true *locus classicus* — debated, according to Gauthier's hypothesis, in Advent of 1257, and thus a relatively early work of the master's, written right after the *Commentary on the Sentences*[1] — is referred to in scholarly literature in two different ways. Some refer to *Quodlibet* IX, q. 8, while others refer to *Quodlibet* IX, art. 16. The discrepancy arises from two competing ways of enumerating the items. The quodlibet contains sixteen individual questions, with the one on canonization being the very last (hence, "art. 16" if numbered consecutively). Other sources, however, group the material into eight thematically-unified "questions" with varying numbers of articles (q. 1 has a single article, q. 2 has three, q. 3 has one, q. 4 has five, q. 5 has two, q. 6, has one, q. 7 has two, and q. 8 has one — the one on canonization).

Chapters 5 and 6 are published here for the first time, and chapters 1, 2, and 7 for the first time in English translation (from French, Portuguese, and Italian respectively). Chapter 4 appeared in the journal *Nova et Vetera.* The remaining chapters were published online as indicated in the first note of each. To avoid clutter in the footnotes, internet sources have been referred to very simply by author, title of piece, title of website, and date. A Google search will turn up any of these in a split second, and if they have "gone missing," the Wayback Machine of the Internet Archive will deliver the goods. No attempt has been made to impose a single system of footnote conventions; each chapter is, however, internally consistent, according to the author's preferences.

Peter A. Kwasniewski, Ph.D.

June 24, 2021

Nativity of St. John the Baptist

---

1 See Jean-Pierre Torrell, O. P., *Saint Thomas Aquinas*, vol. 1: *The Person and His Work*, trans. Robert Royal (Washington, DC: Catholic University of America Press, 1996), 211; cf. René-Antoine Gauthier's introduction to the Leonine critical edition (t. XXV.1–2) of the *Quaestiones de quolibet*, also published in 1996.

The Church Triumphant and the Rules of Canonization Today†

FR. JEAN-FRANÇOIS THOMAS

FATHER THOMAS, COULD YOU REMIND US WHAT a saint is, and especially a saint canonized by the Church?

Holiness is part of Revelation. Only God is holy — thrice-holy — in the strict sense. We proclaim this by reciting or singing the *Sanctus* during Mass. Nevertheless, in the Old Testament, certain figures are already recognized as haloed by holiness. St. Robert Bellarmine traces the beginnings of canonization to the description in the Book of Ecclesiasticus (chapters 44–51) of the holiness of the patriarchs, prophets, and kings of Israel: Enoch, Noah, Abraham, Isaac, Jacob, Moses, Aaron, Joshua, Samuel, David, etc. From the very beginning of the Church, while it was being persecuted, the veneration of the martyrs developed, in addition to that of the Blessed Virgin, St. John the Baptist, and the Apostles. Of course, there was no legal [official] canonization at that time, any more than there would be during the first millennium for the confessor saints. Their holiness had been publicly manifested and recognized thanks to their faith and perseverance. The ratification of it was from the local church, not even by the voice of the hierarchy: *vox populi, vox Dei.*

When persecutions ceased, the *cultus* of the saints entered a new stage: that of "inventions and translations," that is, the discovery, exhumation, and recognition of the bodies of holy men and women and the relocation of their relics to more dignified burial places and into sanctuaries of churches. They were the first to be recognized for their virtues and to be proposed as models of Christian life to

---

† This interview appeared in French in two parts at *Paix Liturgique*, Letter 779 (January 13, 2021) and Letter 781 (January 25, 2021) and is published here in English for the first time, with the permission of Mr. Christian Marquant; the translation is by a Benedictine Oblate.

the community of the faithful. At that time, all of the baptized were "saints" because, through their filial adoption, they shared in the divine holiness, as St. Paul reminds us in his letter to the Corinthians: "To the church of God which is in Corinth, to those sanctified in Christ Jesus, who are called saints . . . " (1 Cor 1:2), and again: "Paul, an apostle of Jesus Christ, by the will of God, and Timothy his brother, to the church of God which is at Corinth, and to all the saints throughout Achaia" (2 Cor 1:1). St. Cyprian speaks of "the Gospel of Christ which makes martyrs," showing that holiness is first of all giving one's life as a witness for the Master, according to the words of Christ: "Greater love hath no man than this, that a man lay down his life for his friends. Ye are my friends if ye do whatsoever I command you" (Jn 15:13). It was no longer enough to be baptized [in order to be considered a "saint"], but one had to shed one's blood as a witness to the true faith. The martyr knows that he is unworthy of being the image of Christ, which is why the title of "martyr" was originally reserved for the Savior alone, as can be read in the *Letters of the Churches of Lyons* or in those of the faithful of Smyrna reporting the martyrdom of the first Christians. If the Holy Mysteries were then celebrated on the tombs of the martyrs, it was precisely to show the indissoluble link between the sacrifice of the Cross and the sacrifice of the disciples. St. Maximus of Turin, in his sermon 77, emphasizes that "those who died to glorify His [Christ's] death must rest in the mystery of His sacrament."

Next, when the period of systematic or sporadic persecutions ceased, more and more non-martyr confessors would become models for the putting into practice of the cardinal and theological virtues. The first were often monks, who, instead of shedding their blood, go through a kind of spiritual death by renouncing everything. The *Acts of the Martyrs* was followed by the *Sayings* of the Desert Fathers of Egypt and of Palestine in particular: St. Paul the Hermit, St. Anthony the Great, the father of monasticism, and then too, in the West, men like St. Martin of Tours. Their lives were written down, often by writers who were themselves saints — for example, we have the life of St. Anthony by St. Athanasius. Two aspects of these exceptional lives are highlighted: first of all, asceticism, because these monks are "athletes of God," and then also the thaumaturgical or miracle-working dimension, because they healed while they were alive and continued to do so after their death.

As for formal and official canonizations, these appeared only gradually and later on, first under the control of bishops, then sometimes with the consent and approval of the Roman Pontiff, starting in the sixth century and in a more solemn way in 993 with the proclamation of the sanctity of Ulrich of Augsburg by Pope John XV. The term "canonization" was not used until the beginning of the eleventh century. Pope Alexander III, in 1171, called the king of Sweden to order by telling him that only the pope could authorize the *cultus* of a potential saint. This papal privilege was officially ratified by the Fourth Lateran Council in 1215 under Pope Innocent III and published in the *Decretals* of Pope Gregory IX by St. Raymond of Peñafort. Nevertheless, many exceptions remained until the seventeenth century, when, with the reform movement of the Council of Trent, everything was put in order, and in the eighteenth century when the rules were definitively fixed by Pope Benedict XIV. Thus the saints were first recognized as such by small communities, then by local churches, and finally by the universal Church. In all cases, martyrs and confessors are raised to the altars primarily as models for the faithful. They imitated Our Lord in the most perfect way possible: they show us Christ to imitate.

There are recognized saints, lesser-known saints, anonymous saints, highly celebrated saints, and forgotten saints. Are they pleased about being honored? Do they have a little more glory in heaven because of a Mass, a feast day, a candle in front of their statue?

It would be problematic and contradictory to imagine saints who have consecrated their lives to God, who have effaced themselves before Him, suddenly deriving personal glory from the veneration of which they are the object! They are all about renunciation, and desire to be — even in Paradise and the Church triumphant — effective channels of God's presence to the Church militant. The veneration they receive is pleasing to them only insofar as it is a glorification of the divine work in them. They are not idols and pagan deities concerned with their self-image and jealous of each other. As you point out, most saints are forgotten, unrecognized, but they are not forgotten in heaven, and saints popular on earth do not parade themselves proudly in the Kingdom. Sanctity, moreover, is not limited to those who have been canonized. All of the elect are saints and only a few have been declared as such by the Church, precisely because they lived the virtues in a more visible way or because, by miraculous signs, they illuminated the faith of believers. The most common sanctity appears ordinary and people don't notice it.

How many saints are officially recognized as such? At least 6,000, even though lists are difficult to draw up, particularly regarding those who lived before the thirteenth century. *The Roman Martyrology*, which lists the names of martyrs and confessors celebrated each day, has seen additions over time, but also removals and disappearances. Without saying that there is a "trend" in the choice of the most appreciated saints for an era, there are in any case political elements, in the broad sense of the term, in certain canonizations or in the disaffection of which others are victims. Nevertheless, devotion remains a human thing, so it can vary in intensity or even vanish. This does not affect the saints themselves who, as we have seen, are not preoccupied with their personal glory.

Sometimes, certain ones had an extremely popular *cultus* for centuries, until their sanctity was questioned. A famous example is that of Charlemagne, canonized on Christmas 1165 in Aachen by Paschal III. That canonization was rejected by the Church in 1179 at the Third Lateran Council because Paschal III was considered an antipope elected under pressure from Emperor Frederick Barbarossa who was occupying Rome and needed the figure of Charlemagne to establish his authority. However, the *cultus* of St. Charlemagne spread throughout Europe until the sixteenth century and his remains were enshrined in precious reliquaries. Charles V wanted to make him the patron saint of the kingdom of France. St. Joan of Arc told Charles VII that St. Louis IX and St. Charlemagne were on their knees in prayer before God to intercede for him. Louis XI fixed St. Charlemagne's day on January 28 and made it a day off of work. In 1661, the Sorbonne chose him as its patron saint. Even Benedict XIV thought that Charlemagne could be venerated as a Blessed in certain local churches. It was not until 1850, under Pope Pius IX, that the *cultus* was limited to its strict minimum, without being suppressed or prohibited. Only the heavenly court can tell us whether Charlemagne is a member. This is an example of a very political canonization, pronounced by an antipope, condemned by a council, treated with caution by many pontiffs — and yet, to this day, a *cultus* of the great emperor who was given the title of "defender and helper of the holy Church in all her needs" survives. This also sheds light on the infallibility of canonizations, a complex question that we will address later.

Apart from these exceptional cases, it is true that many saints remain in the shadows here below, even if their lives are rich in instruction. Without mentioning Marian devotion and the veneration of St. Joseph, only a few are popular all over the world — for example, St. Anthony of Padua, St. Rita of Cascia, St. John Vianney, St. Thérèse of Lisieux. Others are very well known but do not necessarily have their statue or stained-glass window in most churches: St. Augustine of Hippo, St. Thomas Aquinas, even St. Francis of Assisi and many others. There are also some saints who have a widespread devotion although little or nothing is known about their biography: St. Christopher is a famous case. The temptation was, after the Second Vatican Council, to officially dismiss such as these and put them in the closet. This had happened before with Pope Pius V who, in order to respond more effectively to the Protestant attacks, had ordered very precise historical work on the *cultus* of the saints, a requirement that was reinforced in the seventeenth century with the creation of the Society of Bollandists (named after John Bolland, a Flemish Jesuit) which, even until now, is dedicated to the "scientific" study of the life and *cultus* of the saints.

Honoring all these saints — the famous, the unknown, the forgotten — brings us closer to the heavenly court and prepares us interiorly to join it, if we imitate the virtues of those who are thus raised to the altars. The candle placed before the statue, the pious image in the missal, the prayer recited, participation in a procession of the relics or the veneration of the latter, the visit to a shrine where the canonized person lived, a novena addressed to God through the intercession of one of His faithful servants: all these are effective means of imitating Our Lord, through the channel of His saints who are instruments of sanctification. Therefore, their glory is only that of God. For many centuries, Christians did not celebrate their own birthday but celebrated their patron saint, a beautiful way of forgetting oneself and opening doors to the holiness to which every baptized person is called.

Why does the Church make the final decision that a particular saint can be honored?

The Church is always very careful, with the virtue of prudence, like the wise virgins of the Gospel. She makes her provision of oil for the faithful. In every generation, the faithful have need of recourse, of support, of models. Since she can govern herself thanks to this virtue of prudence, she proposes examples that can help each one to conduct himself in a virtuous way. The thousand-year-old experience of faith shows that martyrs and confessors have been helpers, in their lifetime and after their death, for each generation of the baptized. Therefore, the Church does not hesitate to offer to everyone these precious icons of the perfect holiness which is Christ our Savior. She is not concerned primarily with miracles, even though these are normally necessary to make a saint, but rather with the *life* of the latter, looking at how such a life, often very distant in the past, can enlighten our Christian practice right now and for generations to come. It is true, however, that when canonization processes were almost non-existent or were simpler, the saints probably corresponded more to the ordinary situations of the faithful, because the privilege [of canonization] did not belong exclusively to the great religious orders, to high clergy, to princes, as will tend to happen from the Middle Ages onwards for political and financial reasons (since processes are expensive).

For the past fifty years, on the other hand, our period has witnessed a surfeit of beatifications and canonizations based on questionable choices and following a sometimes very simplified process. There is the risk of forgetting that the recognition of sanctity is first of all for the benefit of the faithful, not to please a religious order or to support opinions of ecclesiastical policy that may well change over time. While martyrdom is a sufficient reason to recognize the holiness, even late in coming, of a baptized person, when considering the category of confessors it is preferable to be extremely prudent and not to give in to the fashions of the time. Canonization is not an honorary decoration, not something "due." It must be the culmination at the end of a judicious process and of a complete and irreproachable investigation.

Protestants and Modernists say that only Jesus Christ should be venerated, that the cult of the saints is a kind of idolatry. What is the answer?

France has a rich history of sanctity because it is one of the countries, if not *the* country, with the most beatified or canonized Catholics. The geography of our provinces was formed around many villages named after saints who were the evangelizers of the region during late antiquity and the entirety of the Middle Ages. The revolutionaries in the eighteenth century were not mistaken in systematically renaming these towns and villages, which were for them symbols of obscurantism, as for example when Saint-Denis was renamed Franciade.[1] In a certain way, France is an immense reliquary, both because of the number of saints who rest there and are venerated there, and because of the names of places. All who fought against this over the centuries were not mistaken: the Protestants, the first iconoclasts in France, destroyed reliquaries and relics, and burned pilgrimage shrines; then the French Revolution completed the sacrilege by attacking relics and confiscating the precious metals and gems of the reliquaries for its war effort; not to mention — which is really the last straw! — that a portion of the clergy itself, in the wake of the Second Vatican Council, decided that all these superstitions no longer made sense and, having become effectively Protestant, removed reliquaries from churches or sold them to the highest bidder. A cultural heritage curator told me thirty years ago that, in the region for which he was then responsible, the post-Vatican II destructions had without doubt been more significant than those that took place during the French Revolution itself. In short, the *cultus* of the saints has been attacked several times in our country

---

1 Here and below, Fr. Thomas means they were not mistaken in seeing the *cultus* of saints as an integral part of the Christian Faith and civilization that they sought to overthrow. If the establishment of secular modernity was to take place, it had to proceed by way of iconoclasm and the cancellation of the saints. —*Ed.*

since the sixteenth century. And yet, in spite of this, it is still alive! The desecrators all have one thing in common: in fighting this *cultus*, they are uncultured. In fact, from the very beginning, the Church was concerned with collecting the least of the mortal remains of a martyr or a confessor. In the *Acts of St. Cyprian*, it is reported that during his martyrdom in Carthage on September 14, 258, St. Cyprian, kneeling in front of his executioner, was surrounded by cloths placed by the faithful who wished to preserve his blood shed for Christ.

Faced with Protestant iconoclasm, the Council of Trent wanted to establish in a definitive way the nature of the *cultus* due to the saints. It recalled the distinction between *latria*, the adoration reserved for God, and *dulia*, the honor shown to the saints. The word *dulia* comes from the Greek *doulos*, meaning slave, servant. It is therefore the veneration given to the servants of God. The Blessed Virgin, by her very nature, receives a higher degree of veneration called *hyperdulia*. Thus *cultus* is a reality that contains several aspects, since this word can have many meanings: worship of ancestors, worship of great men, worship of saints, divine worship. It should be noted in passing that even the atheist and anti-Christian Republic has developed its own *cultus* of relics, without however any link to God, by annexing the church of Sainte-Geneviève in Paris, built under Louis XV, in order to transform it into a Panthéon for the men it considers illustrious and who, for the most part, are not likely to be regarded as such in eternal life.[2] Of course, strictly speaking, the only worship deserving the name without qualification is that which recognizes the perfection and omnipotence of God: *latria*. The cults of *dulia* and *hyperdulia* derive their legitimacy from that primary *cultus*, since they involve creatures who have tried to imitate God as perfectly as possible. Between *latria* and *dulia*, we are talking about a difference not of degree but of kind. On the other hand, in the *cultus* of *dulia*, there are degrees: the *cultus* of the saint in heaven is more valuable than the *cultus* of his relics on earth, because the first allows one to advance in the virtues through imitation and by his intercession, while the second is only an act of veneration that should be directed

---

2   Among those whose remains are interred in the Panthéon are Voltaire, Rousseau, Victor Hugo, and Émile Zola. —*Ed.*

to the first. In fact, the two must be held together: veneration, a testimony of respect, and invocation, a request for intercession to receive a particular grace.

Most French Catholics are unaware of a very interesting detail that shows, once again, that the Republic is not far from a contradiction: the *cultus* of *dulia* and *hyperdulia* is registered, by the Ministry of Culture, in the inventory of the "immaterial cultural heritage" (as are, for example, the sardine fishing in Saint-Gilles-Croix-de-Vie, French culinary dishes, or the festival of the deity Ganesh on the Île-de-France). As for modern society, it does not hesitate to idolize the "stars" of the moment: soccer players, actors, singers, and other "artists," while despising the manifestations of the *cultus* of the saints that would only be a remainder of the obscurantism fortunately overcome by the minds of the Enlightenment. Such a shift turns us into garden gnomes before the giants of faith from the medieval period, the golden age of *hyperdulia* and *dulia*.

Let us cling to the saints as the Church invites us to do at each Mass in the Roman Canon and during the Litany of Saints, even in the prayers for those in their last agony. The saints accompany us until our last breath. They pull us and push us towards heaven.

Should the saints serve as models for us in everything, or should we "screen" their lives? Do we have the right to have favorite saints? And also to invoke "specialized" saints—for example, Saint Anthony when we have lost something, or Saint Blaise when we have a sore throat? Doesn't that sound like an unenlightened religion?

The "screening" has already been done, once the Church has decided to authorize the public veneration of a saint. The faithful are therefore not required to conduct their own personal investigation. That said, it is normal to feel closer to some saints than to others and to remember certain aspects of their lives more than other aspects. That isn't to say that each person makes his own market and then his own menu, but each person is free to attach himself to the models of Christian virtue with whom he feels more connected. This doesn't mean that he despises or rejects the others, but simply that no one can venerate *all* the saints in the same way, because there are just too many of them, thousands, and they are often part of a particular culture and time, even if the Church always tries, especially in the past, to choose universal, and therefore Catholic, examples. In any case, we honor all the elect in heaven at least once a year, on All Saints' Day. In the presence of this garden, we can then gather an armful of flowers, to use the expression of St. Augustine in one of his sermons on the martyr St. Lawrence: "In the garden of the Lord there are not only the roses of the martyrs, but the lilies of the virgins, the ivy of the married couples, the violets of the widows… Let us learn, then, without shedding our blood, without facing the sufferings of martyrdom, how a Christian must imitate Jesus Christ." It is certain that most of the faithful will feel more attracted to a miracle-working saint than to a saint who has dedicated his life to the defense of doctrine. Here, the delicate problem of our "self-interest" comes into play when we offer *dulia* or *hyperdulia*. Our intentions are not always very pure; sometimes they are even tinged with superstition, especially if deeper prayer and conversion of heart do not accompany our devotion.

Nevertheless, the saints, who spent their lives, long or short, doing good, do not cease to be interested in us after their death, and all of them spend their heaven being channels of divine grace for the Church militant. We shouldn't be afraid to disturb them, to pester them with our requests, presented with humility but with persistence. Hence, for example, the spiritual effectiveness of novenas through the intercession of a saint. Many of them have "specialties," in fact: they are the miracle-working saints, who were often miracle-workers in their own lifetime, performing this or that miracle which became famous and built their reputation as "specialists." It's sometimes difficult to separate reality from gilded legend. It doesn't matter, because God receives all prayers that are sincere. Even if a saint was invoked who did not exist, God can still grant the believer what he asked, in view of the purity of his request.

How does one become a canonized saint, and in what stages? What are the rules of canonization today? Has the procedure evolved over the course of history? It's said that it is much less difficult to be canonized now than it was in the past.

When, in the twelfth century, Pope Alexander III decided that all recognitions of sanctity should be ratified by Rome, inquiries for the canonization process were developed. The beatification stage didn't yet exist, but since the search for information, the compilation of files, and the Roman response extended over a period of time, many bishops continued until the seventeenth century to carry out translations of relics on their own initiative. The popes, in order to safeguard their authority and to limit abuses, granted (while waiting for the official canonization) the right to a local *cultus*, which was called beatification. To this day, beatifications authorize only a restricted *cultus*: a diocese, a religious order, but not a universal *cultus*. The first beatification with the Roman seal was that of Saint Francis de Sales in 1662.

The decisive and "modern" phase was the step-by-step setting up of investigations for a process by the Holy Inquisition and the *Licet Heli* decree of 1213. It was necessary to prove the "reputation" of the one who was considered a saint, just as it was necessary to prove that a heretic was really guilty; hence the setting up of a "trial" in the modern sense of the term, with, in particular, a defense lawyer and a prosecution lawyer, the so-called "devil's advocate" (more correctly, *promotor fidei*). So the investigations were, from that time on, quite complex. Everything was fixed, in a very detailed and legal way, by Cardinal Prospero Lambertini, who reigned as Pope Benedict XIV from 1740 to 1758. Previously Archbishop of Bologna, this distinguished jurist in both civil and canon law wrote a treatise *On the Beatification of the Servants of God and the Canonization of the Blessed*, published in four volumes from 1734 to 1738. At the same time, he served the cause of the saints as an advocate and then as Promoter of the Faith in the Roman curia, thus establishing four essential criteria for the process of beatification and canonization[3]: the reputation for holiness or thaumaturgical gift, as we mentioned before; martyrdom; the heroic practice of the virtues; finally, the existence of a miracle. The procedure that he put in place when he ascended the See of Peter was maintained until 1983 with the publication of a new *Code of Canon Law* that replaced, sometimes in an unfortunate way, that of 1917.

---

3   That is, at least one of these criteria had to be present in order to proceed.

What was the old procedure? It began with a triple process conducted by a tribunal appointed by a local bishop: research and study of the writings of the potential saint, in order to verify the orthodoxy of her faith; a collection of information and testimonies to ratify what we just mentioned: heroic virtues, martyrdom, or a miracle; and a process in the case of an absence of [longstanding] *cultus*, which involves exhumation of the remains and visiting the places where she lived.[4] After this diocesan process, the sealed results were sent to the competent Roman dicastery, the Sacred Congregation of Rites created in 1588 by Sixtus V. There, they were carefully examined by two theologian-reviewers who passed on their conclusion to the Promoter of the Faith, the "devil's advocate." Then the cardinal members of the Sacred Congregation would meet to decide the fate of the extensive dossier: to reject it or to submit it for papal approval. If the pope gave his signature for introducing the cause, an Apostolic Process took place, on the same model as the diocesan process, based on remissorial letters appointing judges and giving them all the powers necessary for the investigation. When all the documents in the file were collected, they were handed over to a commission of five cardinals who decided on the validity of that stage. Then a Relator wrote the *Positio*, a summary of everything that could contribute to the beatification or canonization. This text, together with the *Animadversiones* of the "devil's advocate" and the comments of the Advocate of the Cause, was transmitted to a Cardinal Ponent, the Relator, who presented it in three sessions: (1) the antepreparatory one, before the prelates and consultors; (2) the preparatory one, before all the members of the Sacred Congregation; and (3) the general one, bringing together the same people, in the presence of the Supreme Pontiff. If the latter signed off, the Servant of God became "venerable" (for example, Pius XII

---

4 As will be explained below, this absence of *cultus* does not refer to a wholesale lack of popular veneration (since such veneration is one of the most important testimonies to the holiness of any proposed saint), but rather to a relative lack compared with the veneration that has been offered to a proposed saint for many centuries or over a wide area, which is the basis of equipollent canonization. For example, not every martyr of Elizabethan England received popular veneration, but even such a one could later be investigated, his relics recovered, his life examined, etc. This would be a process in the absence of *cultus*.

is a Venerable...). Next comes the recognition of miracles — at least two for a beatification, and then two new ones, which had occurred since the beatification, for a canonization. The latter required going through the system of three delegations at the end of which the pope could sign the decree *de tuto* for the canonization announced by a decretal letter. It should be added that a diocesan process couldn't be undertaken until at least thirty years after the death of the Servant of God, in order to avoid emotional reactions, excessive admiration, dubious cases, and human, all-too-human, manipulations.

Needless to say, as with all the rest of the content of faith and tradition, the conciliar reform after Vatican II applied itself to "simplifying" the procedures. This took place in several successive phases, beginning with Paul VI who, in 1969, abolished the double diocesan and apostolic process, keeping only the first, with the introduction of the cause, the decree *de tuto*, and the three sessions of cardinals. This gave the green light for an *aggiornamento* of the way holiness and miracles were regarded. The work was completed by John Paul II publishing, in his words, "the last conciliar document" in 1983, namely the new edition of the *Code of Canon Law*. At the same time, he signed the Apostolic Constitution *Divinus Perfectionis Magister* on the subject of causes of canonization. From then on, only one miracle was necessary for a beatification, except for a martyr, and only one other for a canonization, but it didn't necessarily have to be a cure. For example, when Francis canonized John XXIII, he specified that the miracle selected was that of the convocation of the Second Vatican Council.[5] Another innovation in the reformed process is that miracles are examined by three groups: "experts" (e.g., doctors), theologians, and the cardinals of the dicastery. Similarly, the *Positio* tends to become central, a veritable summation rather than a résumé of the salient facts of the candidate's life.

All of the above is valid for one of the types of canonization mentioned before — the one "by way of absence of *cultus*." On the other

---

5 If Francis actually said this, it was surely meant to be tongue-in-cheek on his part, since there is obviously nothing miraculous about convening an ecumenical council. Other reports say that a second miracle was simply waived in recognition of John XXIII's popularity and the claim that a number of purported miracles had already been submitted to the Vatican. — *Ed.*

hand, there is another type called canonization *per viam cultus* or equipollent. The latter requires no procedure, no newly-established miracle, and is the result of a papal decision that is not arbitrary as long as the following criteria, also established by Benedict XIV, are respected: the longstanding existence of a *cultus* towards the Servant of God, constant attestation of the person's virtues reported by historians and sources worthy of faith, and a reputation for the working of miracles, past and present. As early as the sixteenth century, saints were officially recognized as such in this manner: for example, St. Bruno the Carthusian in 1623. Since the nineteenth century, among the "equipollent" saints we find SS. Cyril and Methodius and St. Albert the Great. Benedict XVI used this form of canonization for St. Hildegard of Bingen. Francis has made extensive use of it—for example, for St. Angela of Foligno and St. Peter Faber. By making too much use of it, such canonization risks becoming a second-rate canonization.

Furthermore, the contemporary problem is, generally, to have multiplied beatifications and canonizations to excess. John Paul II canonized 482 saints and beatified more than 1,300 people. Francis, while his pontificate is not over, has canonized 899 people and beatified 1,226, and even then, these figures may not be up-to-date. By comparison, Pius XII (reigned 1939–1958) canonized 33 saints and beatified 163! It seems that the simplification of procedures has opened the door to a kind of one-upmanship. As we have seen, the purpose of canonizations is always to propose *particular models of virtue* and not to crown all those who have been just. The multiplication of possible models runs the risk of making the procedure look very relative. Moreover, there have been cases of very rapid canonizations in recent decades, forgetting the wise decision of Benedict XIV, which prescribed a period of at least thirty years after the death of the person concerned. The reforms undertaken since 1969 with regard to the process may also diminish the requirements of the criteria for the recognition of sanctity. It is difficult to know or to affirm this without having access to the files, but what is outwardly seen could lead to the conclusion that it is easier to be canonized today. In any case, the necessary distance and caution are much reduced.

Does the Church, at least nowadays, intend to exercise its infallibility by canonizing?

This is indeed a pressing question today, since until a few decades ago it hardly occurred to the faithful to ask it. The acts of a pope were all received with confidence, clothed as they were with an authority that — although not always attached to the infallibility of a solemn declaration — appeared to be trustworthy because it was faithful to the whole Tradition of the Church. Things began to go wrong with the reform of beatifications and canonizations undertaken by Paul VI and then completed by John Paul II. The simplification and speed of the processes, the multiplication of canonizations, and the raising to the altars of disputed persons partly undermined the natural adherence of many of the faithful.

We have seen that, in the past, certain canonizations, more political than religious, were questioned and these saints were put in the closet, if not in purgatory. Paul VI was certainly the pope who looked with the most suspicion on canonizations carried out before the thirteenth century, namely, when they didn't depend on the Holy See. At the same time that collegiality, synodality, and the increased autonomy of the "particular churches" were becoming common refrains, the pope was questioning the validity of the canonizations of the first thirteen centuries of the Church's history! Thus, having created yet another commission to review the presence of saints in the liturgical calendar, he eliminated many of them for lack of historical sources, including some very popular ones who had been venerated for centuries, such as St. Catherine of Alexandria, St. Christopher, and St. Valentine. Therefore, "science" replaced the argument of the ages and of a *cultus* dating back to the greatest antiquity of the Church. He didn't go so far as to "decanonize" these saints, simply because such a process has never existed in the Church, even for those saints about whom there is a sudden doubt about virtues or usefulness. Removing a saint is not an act of infallibility, since it is reversible. John Paul II restored the rights of St. Catherine of Alexandria, so to speak, by seeing that her memorial was reinserted into the missal of Paul VI. St. Pius V, moreover, had also removed from the calendar saints who were too unhistorical — saints, for the most part, reinstated into the *Missale*

Romanum by his successors. This means that the popes themselves don't seem to be very sure of the infallibility of the canonizations of their predecessors.

The reason for this is simple: there is no official document specifying the infallibility of canonizations. Put simply, although most canonists and theologians have considered and still consider the papal authority to canonize as infallible, nevertheless those scholars, however respectable they may be, are not infallible themselves, and their opinion, though worthy of consideration, doesn't have the force of law.

It would be necessary to take up the whole complex significance of papal infallibility to understand the matter more clearly. That theologians hold canonizations to be truths connected to the Faith doesn't necessarily mean that each and every act of canonization is infallible. Since the dogma of papal infallibility was proclaimed one hundred and fifty years ago, the tendency has been to manipulate and distort it, either by denying it, relativizing it, or claiming that it applies to everything the pope teaches. The argument of those who hold canonization as infallible is that this act is "definitive and irreformable." In fact, Church history proves that the way in which canonizations have been viewed is much less certain, since, if no questioning were possible, no pontiff could have reversed the choices of his predecessors. Certainly, none has "decanonized" anyone, but more than one has done a "filtration" of saints. However, what is infallible does not permit any choice, even temporary. It is or it is not. When interpretations begin to flourish, we are no longer in the presence of a fixed dogma or an accepted article of faith.

In conclusion, let us repeat that, either way, none of the faithful is obliged to have veneration for all the saints. What is important is to be attached to some of them, so as to be led in our turn into the Church triumphant.

2

The Cult of Saints in the Catholic Church†

JOSÉ ANTONIO URETA

THE EXAMPLE OF THE SAINTS IS SUCH AS TO stimulate the faithful in piety and to excite them to the practice of virtues that the saints exercise in an outstanding way. Indeed, many were the souls throughout history who were converted due to reading the lives of the saints.

DIFFERENCE BETWEEN HOLINESS AND PROTESTANT "JUSTIFICATION BY FAITH"

Strictly speaking, only God is holy. Holiness is the property of His Being that He reveals in the Holy Scriptures: it consists in the fact that God, in His omnipotence, glory, and majesty, is infinitely above all that is not Himself, which requires from man an attitude of worship and a desire to imitate Him in His perfections. But holiness is also one of the essential notes of the Catholic Church that allow us to recognize it as the true Church of our Lord Jesus Christ. This means that, being the Mystical Body of Christ, the Catholic Church has the supernatural means to bring man out of sin and unite him to God. It also means that she will never be lacking in her bosom souls who witness to this supernatural strength. In other words, saints.

Holiness in man is the effect of sanctifying grace and consists in participating in the holiness of God. It is inseparable from the theological virtues — faith, hope, and charity — and when it reaches its fullness it also elevates the moral virtues to a heroic degree, especially the cardinal virtues of prudence, justice, temperance and fortitude.

---

† Original article: "O culto dos santos na Igreja Católica," in *Revista Catolicismo* 759 (March 2014), online at www.catolicismo.com.br. Translated by a Benedictine Oblate.

Herein lies one of the great differences between the Catholic Church and the Protestant sects. The heresy of "justification by faith alone" (*sola fides*) leads adherents of Protestantism to assume that baptism does not entirely wash away the stain of original sin, which is why even the most heroic acts of man would be objectionable in God's eyes. Man is saved, according to them, only because his rottenness is outwardly covered by faith in the salvific death of Jesus, but inwardly the baptized Christian would remain a sinner. Our Lord's teachings, on the contrary, assert that the "old man" is completely renewed within by grace and, though still subject to the lure of evil — called concupiscence — he is able to love God above all things and his neighbor as himself. And, owing to his union with God, he is capable of doing good and even heroic works, earning merit for himself and for his brothers through the communion of the saints.

The state of total union with God to which man is called can be attained only after death, when he sees God face to face, with no possibility of turning away from Him. But this state of beatitude is already prefigured by the intimate union with God of souls who, in this life, generously correspond to the calls of divine grace. It is this holiness that the Church recognizes and presents as an example by canonizing some of her children, to show that sanctification is not just a theoretical possibility, but something within the reach of all who are in a state of grace — or even of sinners who wash their souls through the sacrament of Confession.

THE CULTS OF *DULIA* AND *HYPERDULIA*

Consistent with what has been said, the Church not only presents us with the saints as models, but encourages the faithful to venerate them and ask for their intercession before God, as they already enjoy eternal life and, in the heavenly court, they are friends of God. The effectiveness of the intercession of the saints is based on the intensity of friendship existing between them and God, and in virtue of the merits they acquired in their sojourn on Earth. This veneration of saints is called the "cult of *dulia*," which is altogether distinct from the "cult of *latria*," the worship/adoration reserved for God alone.

The cult of *dulia* is an indirect way of praising Him for the work of sanctification that He wrought in these saints and for the examples of virtue they displayed when they resided among us.

In the veneration of creatures, that which is due to Our Lady stands out because she is the Mother of God, having a relationship with her divine Son closer than that enjoyed by any other saint, and is the universal Mediatrix between Him and us; the cult she deserves and receives from us is therefore called *hyperdulia*. Our relationships with the saints are not limited, however, to the fact that we admire their example and ask their intercession. We form one Mystical Body with them in the communion of saints, and we tend, all together, to the same purpose, which is to know, love, and serve God and to participate fully in the divine life in heaven.

THE DEVELOPMENT OF THE CULT OF SAINTS IN HISTORY

In addition to the Apostles, the first saints venerated were the martyrs, whose bodies people collected and arranged in the catacombs so as to transform their tombs into altars on which Holy Mass was celebrated. Bishops would then place them in the official catalogue of martyrs.[1] Starting in the fourth century, those Christians who, although not having shed their blood for Jesus Christ, had "confessed" his Name before men and passed through multiple trials, began to be included in this veneration as well. At the request of the faithful, the bishops authorized the placing of these figures, too, in the diptychs.

Although every believer has the right to pray to people he knew and admired who died in the "odor of holiness," the Church realized that it should reserve institutional veneration only for those people for whom there were well-founded reasons to believe they were in heaven and who had offered a true example to the faithful here on Earth. Around the year 1000, the popes were committed to having the virtues and miracles of God's servants — believers who practiced outstanding virtues, whose veneration had surpassed the boundaries of a diocese — analyzed in regional synods, and their veneration approved collectively.

---

1   The most famous of such catalogues is referred to as *The Roman Martyrology*, traditionally recited after the Office of Prime.

A constitution by Pope Alexander III (1159–1181) removed the bishops' right to authorize veneration of a servant of God in their dioceses. However, that decision became fully effective only in the first decades of the seventeenth century through a decree of Pope Urban VIII (1623–1644), which reserved the process for causes of beatification and canonization to the Holy See alone. From that time onwards, a more precise distinction between "blesseds" (*beati*) and "saints" (*sancti*) was introduced. The first are depicted with a halo of diffuse light around their head, to signify that their veneration is permitted only in a particular set of dioceses or in a religious order. Beatification is the stage prior to canonization. Canonized saints, on the other hand, are depicted with a defined halo and their veneration is authorized for the whole Church in all countries.

Two types of causes for canonization began, at that time, to be handled by the popes. First, "formal canonizations," so called because, after a long process of studying the candidate's life, they are the object of a formal judgment,[2] with the intervention of the so-called "devil's advocate" (that is, an expert in charge of raising objections to the canonization), proceeding to a rigorous analysis of the miracles that would certify if it is God's will that this person be canonized. Second, "equipollent (or equivalent) canonizations," where the judgment is limited to confirming the immemorial character of the veneration rendered by the faithful to a servant of God and prescribes it for the whole Church.

The canonization judgment involves three realities logically arising from each other: 1) that the servant of God enjoys the beatific vision in heaven; 2) that he deserved to achieve this glory by his union with God and for the heroic virtues he practiced, which are an example to the faithful; 3) that the Church must venerate the saint and ask for his intercession, thanking God for granting us the boon of his life.

SIMPLIFIED PROCESSES AND EXPONENTIAL INCREASE OF CANONIZATIONS: POSTCONCILIAR NOVELTIES

In view of the foregoing, it is understandable that the Church was very restrained in the past in authorizing the inscription, in the

---

2   The word in Portuguese is *sentença*, which could also be rendered decree, verdict.

catalog of saints, of servants of God who died in the odor of holiness and were revered by the faithful. It was considered, with St. Thomas Aquinas,[3] that although all the baptized are called to holiness, there were few "saints of the altar," because of the weakness introduced into our nature by original sin and the sovereign character of God's mercy, who chooses whomever He will to raise above the common state. In turn, the exemplarity of the saints, in order to attract attention, presupposed something extraordinary — quite out of the ordinary. And it was for this reason that, despite heaven being populated by servants of God, only a few were raised to the glory of the altars. Multiplying the saints — it was thought — would end up diminishing their exemplarity in the mind of the common faithful.

In contrast, the popes after the Second Vatican Council decided, as it were, to make holiness available to the whole world, in accordance with the Council's insistence on the universal call to holiness. In this way, Pope John Paul II alone raised 482 saints to the honor of the altars — that is, a greater number than all of his predecessors put together. And Pope Francis, even in the first ceremony, canonized the 813 martyrs of the city of Otranto, slaughtered by Muslims in 1480, and two Latin American nuns, practically doubling in one act John Paul II's number of saints.

To facilitate this exponential increase in the number of beatified and canonized servants of God, John Paul II carried out a radical reform of the rules of the processes involved in canonization — reducing the period of waiting for the opening of cases from fifty to only five years; reducing from two to one the miracles required for beatification and then, once more, for canonization; eliminating the "devil's advocate" and assigning to the Promoter himself the task of raising the objections; allowing the aforementioned Promoter to make a selection of witnesses, with the ability to discard people who wished to report negative events about the person in question. Many experts and countless faithful were deeply perplexed by this simplification of procedures, which no longer offer the same guarantees of scientific and religious rigor as the classic procedures had done.

---

3 *Summa theologiae* I, q. 23, a. 7, ad 3.

FALLIBILITY OR INFALLIBILITY OF CANONIZATIONS

This relaxation of rigor in the processes reanimated a very old theological debate that had diminished considerably in intensity in the course of the twentieth century: Is the solemn judgment of canonization an infallible act of the pope? Yes or no?

There is a general consensus that beatifications may end up concerning people who are not in heaven or who do not deserve to be venerated. The argument is that the beatification decrees are merely permissive and not impositive, in addition to the fact that the veneration authorized is restricted to a defined area and not universal. But as far as canonizations are concerned, most theologians deem them to be infallible. However, the Church's Magisterium has never pronounced itself definitively on the question. Accordingly — this must be emphasized — it is a matter on which a theologian, having weighty reasons, may differ from the common opinion, which is favorable to the thesis of the infallibility of canonizations. In fact, there has never ceased to exist a minority that denies this thesis or raises serious doubts about it. Medieval writers of great authority, such as Pope Innocent IV and the Cardinal of Susa (known as Ostiensis), or the canonist Joannes Andreæ, from Bologna, admitted the possibility of error in canonizations. In the sixteenth century, the greatest and best commentator on St. Thomas Aquinas, the famous Cardinal Cajetan, was of the same opinion, as were his confreres in the Dominican Order, the Cardinal Tommaso Badia (who had been one of Luther's contradictors at the Diet of Worms) and the provincial of Tuscany, Fra Niccolò Michelozzi.

According to this current of thought, there are three main theological objections to the infallibility of canonizations: 1) since public Revelation[4] ended with the death of the last Apostle and the Church does not enjoy the charism of inspiration, it cannot add new truths to the deposit of faith; 2) it is a dogma of faith that no one can know with certainty, without a private revelation, whether or not he is in a

---

4 God can be known with certainty by the light of natural reason. However, He wanted to give us a supernatural knowledge of Himself and of His divine purposes in regard to truths inaccessible to human reason — for example, the Holy Trinity — through public Revelation, which was fully realized and completed in the person of Our Lord Jesus Christ and is contained in the Holy Scriptures and in the oral Tradition received from the Apostles.

state of grace, and even less can a third party who observes the life of a person from without; 3) the Church bases its judgment on fallible human witnesses, therefore her conclusion can be mistaken.

The majority current that defends the thesis of the infallibility of canonizations does not respond to these three arguments as such, but affirms that the help of the Holy Spirit promised by Our Lord to the Church makes up for the deficiencies of a merely human examination. And it adds that if the Church proposed a false saint to the faithful for veneration, she would be offering an erroneous model of moral life and, therefore, a misapplication of the truths of the faith.

APPEARANCE OF THE CONCEPT OF "SECONDARY OBJECT" OF INFALLIBILITY

This argument on behalf of infallibility was indirectly reinforced due to the debates raised in seventeenth-century France by the condemnation by Pope Innocent X (1644–1655) of five heretical theses from the book *Augustinus* by Cornelius Jansen (1585–1638). Jansen's followers, invited to recant, said they had no problem rejecting these heresies — just that, contrary to what the pope said, such errors were not to be found in the incriminated book. Faced with this refusal, three years later Pope Alexander VII (1655–1667), successor of the previous pope, declared solemnly that the five theses *did* figure in the writings of Jansen, and he asked the Archbishop of Paris to demand from the Jansenists a formal acceptance of this decision. The latter asked if they should give it an assent of divine faith, or just human faith (if it were an assent of human faith, they thought they could subscribe to the formula but continue to believe that the book did not contain the heresies pointed out). Assisted by the famous Fénelon, the archbishop declared that the due assent was neither divine faith nor human faith, but an intermediary assent he called "ecclesiastical faith," because of the Holy Spirit's assistance to the Church.

As a result, in theology treatises there appeared the concept of the "secondary object of infallibility" — that is, that the Church is infallible not only in what has been formally or virtually revealed by God (the so-called "primary object of infallibility"), but also in those non-revealed truths necessary so that the revealed deposit of faith can be preserved in its entirety, fittingly explained, and effectively defended. Examples would be a philosophical truth such as that reason is capable of knowing the truth (without which the idea of "revealed truth" becomes meaningless), or the fact that the pope points out heresies contained in a work the reading of which would be corrosive to the faith of the faithful (as in the case of Jansen's *Augustinus*).

In view of the appearance of this concept of "secondary object of infallibility," writers of treatises soon began, almost systematically, to include canonization judgments in the Church's secondary object of infallibility. All the more so as Pope Benedict XIV (1740–1758) — who was formerly a renowned canonist and "devil's advocate" of various causes — had previously written, before ascending to the pontifical throne, a book in which he affirmed, neither more nor less, the following: "Whoever dared to maintain that the pope was wrong in this or that canonization or that this or that canonized saint should not be venerated, if he is not a heretic, at least should be called reckless, one who scandalizes the whole Church, reviles the saints, favors heretics who deny the authority of the Church in the canonization of the saints, and, at the same time, opens the way for infidels to mock the faithful, supports an erroneous proposition, and deserves the most serious reproaches"!

THE OBJECT OF INFALLIBILITY LEFT IN ABEYANCE AT THE FIRST VATICAN COUNCIL

During the First Vatican Council, which defined papal infallibility as a dogma of the Catholic faith, there was disagreement among the council fathers as to the extent of the object of infallibility. While for some it was limited to Revelation *stricto sensu* — that is, to truths formally or virtually revealed and capable of being proclaimed as dogmas of faith and imposed on the faithful to be believed with divine faith — for others, influenced by the debate raised around Jansen's *Augustinus*, the object of infallibility also extended to truths unrevealed but necessary for the preservation, explanation, and defense of the deposit of faith.

During the debate, it was even proposed that it be explicitly stated that the pope is infallible in canonizations and in the approval of universal laws and of the rules of religious orders; but the proposal was rejected by the majority.[5] In any case, at the suggestion of Pope Pius IX — who viewed with concern the Franco-Prussian War of 1870 and the consequent risk of the Council coming to be postponed without the proclamation of the dogma of pontifical infallibility — the Secretariat of the Council, called the Deputation of Faith, suspended the debate on the object of infallibility and drafted a formula that did not settle the issue. The formula says that the pope is infallible "in matters of *fides et mores*," an expression hallowed in theology to indicate the *depositum fidei*, but adding that his infallible definitions must be "accepted" by the faithful as irreformable. If the formula had said that they should be "believed" — a term used in Catholic theology exclusively for assent due to divinely revealed truths — it would, in fact, have limited the extent of infallibility exclusively to its primary object, Divine Revelation.[6] Explaining this detail, Msgr. Vincent Ferrer Gasser, secretary of the Deputation of Faith, declared in the conciliar hall: "It is of faith that the pope is infallible in the primary object; infallibility in the secondary object remains at the level of theological certainty," that is, at the level of those doctrines on which the Magisterium has not pronounced itself explicitly or definitively, but that, according to the more or less unanimous opinion of theologians, cannot be denied without jeopardizing a revealed truth.

Given that the secondary object's being covered by the charism of infallibility of the Church is not itself an object of faith, even less is the thesis that canonizations are infallible. The Magisterium has not yet defined what degree of connection there must be between the deposit of faith and a non-revealed truth (such as a canonization) so that the latter is part of the secondary object of infallibility. There

---

5   Cfr. Umberto Betti, *Dottrina della costituzione dommatica "Pastor Æternus,"* in *De doctrina Concilii Vaticani Primi* (Città del Vaticano: Libreria Editrice Vaticana, 1969), 356.

6   With regard to the supernatural virtue of faith, theology distinguishes between the truths revealed by God, assent to which is based directly on faith in the authority of God's Word — doctrines *de fide credenda* — and the truths proposed by the Church as irreformable, though not revealed, whose assent is based on faith in the assistance of the Holy Spirit to the Magisterium and on the Catholic doctrine of the infallibility of the Magisterium — doctrines *de fide tenenda*.

is only unanimity that the connection between the deposit of faith and an unrevealed truth must be intimate and necessary so that the deposit of faith can be properly preserved, explained, and defended. But there is no consensus on the fact that this organic nexus actually exists in the case of canonizations. In other words, it is a dogma of faith that men go to heaven if they die in a state of grace; the problem is to know if, in order to believe in this dogma, it will be *necessary* to believe also that people canonized enjoy eternal blessedness and intercede for us with God. Or if, on the contrary, it happens as it does with the cult of relics: we know that some relics may be false, but God — the ultimate end of all our prayers — does not fail to accept our act of devotion on that account.

THE EBB OF MAJORITY OPINION FROM THE START OF THE TWENTIETH CENTURY

A growing number of theologians, from the 1930s onwards, began respectfully to contest the theology manuals' nearly-unanimous favoring of the infallibility of canonizations. The first treatise writer to do so was Msgr. Bernard Bartmann in a manual that was translated into several languages and very much used in seminaries before the Second Vatican Council. This highly-regarded theologian took up again the difficulties that the supposed infallibility of canonizations had posed for theology ever since the Middle Ages — that is, that the Church cannot add "new truths" to the deposit of faith, that no one can know without a revelation whether another is in a state of grace, and, moreover, that the human witnesses are fallible. Msgr. Bartmann also highlights the fact that supporters of the infallibility of canonizations, in the absence of a decisive theological argument, rest on a "bundle of clues" whose number tries to make up for the weakness of each argument taken in isolation. Regarding this topic, the German theologian concludes with the following words:

> The acts of canonization cannot be accepted except with a general and ecclesiastical faith and not with divine faith. The faithful do not, without a doubt, make a special act of faith in the canonization; they believe in it through an act of general faith, an act by which they accept as a whole the worship of the Church. If, in the body of saints, there is

sometimes a "false" saint . . . the relative veneration rendered
to him ultimately reverts to God. A king is honored through
a false ambassador, and God, too, through a false saint.[7]

THE OBJECTIONS AND RESERVATIONS OF MSGR. GHERARDINI

More recently, another renowned theologian who respectfully
raised objections and reservations to the thesis of the infallibility of
canonizations was Msgr. Brunero Gherardini, for many years dean
of the Lateran University's Faculty of Theology, which until the Second Vatican Council had been the bastion of the so-called "Roman
school of theology," clearly conservative in orientation. In an article
for the magazine *Divinitas*, later reproduced in *Chiesa Viva* under
the title "Canonizations and Infallibility,"[8] the illustrious Florentine
priest preliminarily observes that supporters of the infallibility of
canonizations make a "reasoning from absurdity,"[9] that is, it would
be intolerable for canonizations not to be infallible because this would
have deleterious repercussions on the life of the Church. And he adds
that many authors today dispute the force of that argument.

Going to the heart of the problem, Msgr. Gherardini's premise is
that canonization does not define any revealed truth and, therefore,
in theological language, it is a proclamation *"non immediate de fide"*;
it is not part of what St. Thomas calls *"iis quae ad fidem pertinent."*[10]
Nor does it have such an intimate connection with some revealed
truth that canonization is transformed into an implicitly and indirectly revealed truth. If the canonization itself is not *de fide*, still less
is the declaration that such a person is a blessed in heaven. It would
be on the plane of "ecclesiastical faith"; but it turns out that the
assistance of the Holy Spirit promised by Our Lord to His Church
is restricted to a very precisely delimited exercise, which excludes
canonization's equivalency to a dogmatic definition. The fact that it
is said and repeated that canonization must be assimilated to a "dogmatic fact" (such as the condemnation of *Augustinus*) is not a valid

---

7 *Précis de Théologie dogmatique* (Mulhouse: Éditions Salvator, 1947), 1:57–59.
8 Published herein as chapter 7.
9 Here meaning a *reductio ad absurdum*: proving the truth by showing that
a false consequence results from denying it.
10 not immediately concerning the faith; the things that belong to the faith.

argument: what is gratuitously asserted can be gratuitously denied.

The astute Florentine theologian adds another embarrassing argument for supporters of the infallibility of canonizations — an infallibility they simultaneously deny to beatifications. The reasoning from absurdity mentioned above does not explain, says Msgr. Gherardini, why the charism of infallibility would be valid for canonizations and not for beatifications. The Church is not a sum of private churches, since even the smallest and most hidden Catholic community underground in China *is* the Catholic Church. Therefore, a decision concerning a portion of the flock, such as the authorization of a blessed's veneration, reaches the entire Church and has, of itself, a universal extension. What, then, asks Msgr. Gherardini, is the meaning of the distinction between canonization and beatification, based on the idea that the second is local and the first universal?[11]

A CONSULTANT TO THE CONGREGATION FOR THE CAUSE OF SAINTS WEIGHS IN

Almost simultaneously, Fr. Daniel Ols, O. P., sometime professor at the Pontifical University of Saint Thomas Aquinas, the Angelicum (Rome), and consultant to the Congregation for the Causes of Saints, wrote a booklet entitled *Theological Foundations of the Cult of Saints*,[12] in which he places himself openly in the current that defends the non-infallibility of canonizations. He claims that canonization contains two aspects: on the one hand, the dogmatically definable affirmation that a person practicing Christian virtue goes to heaven; on the other hand, the application of that statement to a particular person. Well, says Fr. Ols, if it can be easily demonstrated that the general proposition is contained in Revelation, "it is also evident that the *fact* that 'Tizio' or 'Caio' lived holy lives is not contained therein, either explicitly or implicitly." And, unlike the condemnation of the errors in a book — for it is necessary for the preservation of the faith of the faithful that they know with certainty that such-and-such heresies are to be found in it — in the

---

11   In other words, if the part can be in error, and the part is inseparable from the whole, the whole can also be in error.

12   Available at www.scribd.com/doc/47381315/OLS-Fond-Amen-Ti-Teologici -Del-Culto-Dei-Santi.

case of canonizations there would be no mortal harm to the faith if the Church makes a mistake. Venerating someone who is in hell is not as serious as following Luther or another heretic.[13] Therefore, the matter of canonization does not seem fit to be a matter of infallibility, concludes Fr. Ols. To this theological argument, Fr. Ols adds another, of a sociological nature: if the reason for the infallibility of canonizations is to avoid the risk of presenting a false model of sanctity, then what happens with blesseds who are far better known and far more popular — even in places far from where their veneration is officially permitted — than a great number of canonized saints? Why, given that these blesseds are also being taken as models of sanctity, shouldn't beatifications also be included in the charism of infallibility? Refuting the argument of the defenders of the infallibility thesis that the content of the decrees of canonization prove that the popes intend to engage their infallibility in them, Fr. Ols points out that, between such decrees and the formulas that have been used for the proclamation of a dogma (for example, of the Immaculate Conception or of the Assumption of Our Lady), there is a substantial difference: in the proclamation of a dogma, the pope explicitly says that the declared truth must be believed with divine faith by the faithful as being a revealed truth whose denial, even if interior, entails loss of faith and automatic excommunication from the Holy Church — that is, he dispenses a condemnatory document; while in the decree of canonization, the pope states merely that the person in question is enrolled in the catalogue of saints and should be venerated by the universal Church, but says nothing about imposing such belief on the faithful in their internal forum.[14] He only threatens with ecclesiastical penalties, in the external forum, whoever speaks out publicly against the canonization; but this is a frequent formula in

---

13   That is, if an object of veneration were believed be in heaven because the available signs of his life pointed to sanctity, but owing to some unknown or unknowable fault his soul was in fact in hell, the one venerating would not be misled, because he would still be drawn to what is known or presented as positive and therefore worthy of emulation. Following a known heretic, on the other hand, necessarily involves one in his errors.

14   In other words, imposing it on them as a personal obligation without the embrace of which they would be excluded from the Church and lose their salvation.

many other decrees and bulls where no doctrinal connotation is to be found and which clearly do not involve infallibility.

Both Msgr. Gherardini and Fr. Ols — and other scholars before them — also adduce the argument that the Church withdrew from the calendar and suppressed the worship of several figures whose very existence, with the advance of historical research, is no longer certain today. The power of the keys does not authorize the pope (they comment) to place as a saint in the reality of history someone who did not live as a saint, and even less someone who did not even live, because he was never born!

Finally, in certain traditionalist environments that feel obliged to support the infallibilist thesis common in preconciliar theology manuals, two studies by Fr. Michel Gleize of the Fraternity of Saint Pius X are in circulation that reveal the deficiencies of the current processes of canonization and, what is more, the change that took place in the very concept of holiness, as well as the collegiate character that has been given to the processes, with ample participation by dioceses. In the opinion of the Lefebvrist priest, that would entail the non-infallibility of the decree resulting from such processes, by a deficiency in the pope's will to define — an indispensable condition for an *ex cathedra* definition.

SAINT THOMAS AQUINAS'S SAPIENTIAL POSITION ON THE QUESTION

Given that the official Magisterium has not definitively ruled on the fallibility or infallibility of canonizations and that there is a certain divergence among theologians — a disagreement, by the way, that is increasing, given the number of theologians who are swelling the ranks of the current that was until recently a minority — the best attitude the faithful can take, until the Church pronounces on the question, is to follow the common-sense solution proposed by St. Thomas Aquinas in his *Quodlibetal Questions*, a set of disputations on various issues held by the Angelic Doctor at the universities where he taught.

Addressing the question "On whether all the canonized saints are in glory or are any of them in hell,"[15] the Angelic Doctor answers

---

15 *Quodlibetal Question* IX, q. 8.

it is certain that it is impossible for the Church to err in matters of faith, but it is possible that she err in the judgment of particular facts, because of false witnesses. Canonization, the saint continues, is "halfway" between the two preceding cases, since the honor accorded to the saints is *in a way* a profession of faith (insofar as it concerns the truth that people who die in God's friendship enjoy eternal glory). So it is piously to be believed (*pie credendum est*) that in these cases, too, the judgment of the Church does not err.

Fr. Ols highlights the precision of the terms used by St. Thomas. When talking about matters of faith, he says "it is certain that it is impossible" for the Church to err; in the canonizations, only "*pie credendum est*," an expression always used by Saint Thomas when "there is not and cannot exist [matter] for an infallible teaching because it lacks foundation in Revelation." It is therefore a question of adopting, in the face of canonizations, the same attitude assumed towards the doctrinal teachings of the ordinary Magisterium not covered by the charism of infallibility: they are given a religious assent, as they come from pastors assisted by the Holy Spirit, but the possibility of occasional error is admitted, until the doctrine taught is (in due course) extraordinarily defined or it becomes obvious that it *is* a doctrine that was taught always, everywhere, and by everyone. In a case where there are serious reasons for inferring that some teaching is contrary to Tradition, the believer is authorized to suspend his interior assent and, at times, his obsequious exterior silence, in order to express his reservations. In the current state of the Magisterium's development regarding the secondary object of infallibility, nothing prevents us from proceeding in the same way in the face of controversial canonizations.

3

History and Role of the "Devil's Advocate"†

PHILLIP CAMPBELL

MOST PEOPLE HAVE HEARD THE PHRASE "DEV-il's advocate." Colloquially, a devil's advocate is a person who argues against a position he favors for the purpose of testing the argument for weaknesses. If you have ever devised a plan of action and then mentally run through all the ways it could potentially go wrong, you have played the role of the devil's advocate. We do this to reinforce the strength of an argument by taking an opponent's view of it.

Within the Catholic Church, the "devil's advocate" was an official of immense importance in the process of canonization, whose correct and formal title was the *Promotor Fidei*, Promoter of the Faith. The office is first attested during the pontificate of Leo X (1513–1521) and was formally established by Sixtus V in 1587 as part of the reforms of the Counter-Reformation. The duty of the *Promotor Fidei* was to oversee every aspect of the beatification and canonization process for procedural integrity. This encompassed a variety of duties: ensuring that no person received the honors of sainthood rashly, that proper juridical form was observed, and that every potential weakness or objection to the saint's canonization was raised and evaluated in order that only those who were truly worthy would be raised to the dignity of the altars. Since the *Promotor Fidei* took a juridical position *against* the canonization of any given saint, it was joked that he was taking the devil's part in the proceedings, hence the common appellation *advocatus diaboli*. This essay will examine the historical origins, office, and rationale behind the *advocatus diaboli*, as well as the consequences attendant upon the abolition of this office by John Paul II in 1983.

---

† First published at the blog *Unam Sanctam Catholicam*, July 11, 2013. Revised by the author for its inclusion herein.

HISTORICAL DEVELOPMENT OF THE LEGAL ASPECTS OF CANONIZATION

The first mention of anything like an *advocatus diaboli* was during the preliminary studies on the beatification of St. Lawrence Justinian under the pontificate of Leo X. As part of the preparatory work on the cause, Leo appointed a theologian specifically tasked with challenging the evidence of St. Lawrence's sanctity. St. Lawrence was beatified under Leo's successor Clement VII in 1524, the first *beatus* whose virtues had been formally scrutinized by an *advocatus diaboli*. In 1587 the office became official under Sixtus V with the title *Promotor Fidei* as a member of the Sacred Congregation of Rites. In 1708 the *Promotor Fidei* was elevated to become the most important office in the Congregation.

But focusing solely on the establishment of the office and its institutional development gives us only a partial picture, for even Leo X was drawing on a much older legal tradition when he called for an *advocatus diaboli* in the case of St. Lawrence Justinian. The rationale behind Tridentine-era popes' enthusiastic embrace of the office is bound up with the larger historical development of the *cultus* of the saints.

In the first millennium of the Church, the *cultus* of a local saint was promulgated by the authority of the bishop of the diocese in which the saint had lived or worked. Renowned saints of the magnitude of St. Augustine of Hippo or St. Isidore of Seville attracted devotion outside their respective dioceses and became honored by the Church universal without any formal canonization process. This can be viewed as a kind of informal canonization by acclamation — although it is important to note that even at this early stage the public veneration of a saint was still subject to local ecclesiastical oversight.

For historical reasons that go beyond the scope of this essay, these local canonizations increasingly fell short of the standards expected by the Church during the latter part of the first millennium. The patchwork, slipshod nature of these local canonizations aroused the attention of the papacy. Beginning in the late Carolingian era, the popes began exercising a more direct role in canonizations, reviewing bishops' determinations or chastising them for raising people to the altars too rashly — sometimes even overriding their decisions and ordering the locally canonized saint to be struck from the calendar, as Pope Alexander III did in 1173. It was this same pontiff who centralized canonizations under the exclusive authority of the Holy See by a papal bull promulgated in 1170. This was the beginning of the "modern" canonization process as we now know it.

Why did the Holy See insist on taking over the canonization process at this time? The immediate cause of Alexander III's bull of 1170 was a botched local canonization in which a bishop allowed the veneration of a man who had been killed in a drunken fight. The pope scolded the careless bishop, warning that "for the future you will not presume to pay him reverence, as, even though miracles were worked through him, it would not allow you to revere him as a saint unless with the authority of the Roman Church."[1] But these sorts of interventions must be understood in the context of broader currents within the Church. The assumption of all canonizations by the Holy See took place concurrently with the canonist movement of the eleventh to the thirteenth centuries. The canonist movement was a largely legal revolution in the Church's governance. Freed from the dominion of secular rulers following the Investiture Controversy, the Church embarked upon the difficult but important process of streamlining its administration based on traditional precedents, which meant bringing centuries of disparate practices from all corners of Christendom into harmony and deducing general legal principles from them. This monumental process of gathering and codifying centuries of canonical tradition was headed by such canonists as Anselm of Lucca (c. 1083), Roland Bandinelli (later Alexander III), and most famously Gratian (c. 1150).

The subsequent revival in the study of canon law was pioneered by disciples of such men, known as the Decretists. The Decretist revival lasted into the mid-thirteenth century and was characterized by a desire to apply regularized legal norms to every aspect of the Church's governance. The development of the canonization procedure at this time reflected a desire to move canonization away from

---

1 Camillo Beccari, "Beatification and Canonization," in *The Catholic Encyclopedia* (New York: Robert Appleton Company, 1907), www.newadvent.org/cathen/02364b.htm. See also Gregory IX, *Decretales*, III, "De reliquiis et veneratione sanctorum."

the realms of hearsay and popular piety towards a firm, legal footing that lent the process more credibility, thus safeguarding the integrity of the Faith. The development of legal norms for canonization can be characterized as law applied to saint-making.

A similar legal development paralleled the assumption of canonizations by the Holy See: the emergence of the Courts of the Inquisition, first episcopal and then papal. If canonization was law applied to saint-making, the inquisitorial courts were law applied to dealing with heresy. Because of this emphasis on legal procedure, it made sense that both the Inquisition and the canonization procedure were viewed in terms of a trial. The alleged saint was the defendant, and his sanctity must be defended against possible accusations. While the exact canonical procedures for canonizations between the twelfth century and the Tridentine period are not known with surety, it is certain that they were viewed in terms of a trial. This is exemplified in the surviving records, such as those surrounding the canonization of St. Dominic in 1234. Witnesses were interviewed, depositions taken, "evidence" carefully cataloged, and "testimonies" noted.

ESTABLISHMENT AND ROLE OF THE *PROMOTOR FIDEI*

Although the office of the *Promotor Fidei* (*advocatus diaboli*) did not exist in the time of St. Dominic, we can already see the fundamental principles in place that would later be adopted by the *Promotor Fidei*. In Dominic's canonization we see the testimony of many witnesses to the saint's holiness, but we also see witnesses who could potentially debunk the claims of Dominic's sanctity. For example, St. Dominic's confessor was interviewed, and while of course the specific content of Dominic's confessions was not recounted, the inquisitors wished to know if St. Dominic had ever committed a mortal sin. The confessor, a Brother Bonaventure of Verona, stated that he did not believe that Dominic had ever committed a mortal sin.[2] Brother William of Montferrat, who spent a considerable amount of time in the company of Dominic, was asked whether he ever saw St. Dominic deviate from the Rule. He replied in the negative.[3]

---

2   Bologna Canonization Hearings of Dominic Guzman, Testimony of Bonaventure of Verona, 5.
3   Ibid., Testimony of William of Montferrat, 12.

We can see here an example of the "trial mentality" that developed in medieval canonizations: witnesses might give testimony in favor of the sanctity of a *beatus*, but those witnesses must be cross-examined. Yes, you witnessed a miracle, but did you witness any deviation from the Rule? Yes, you witnessed extreme acts of virtue, but were you aware of any occasion on which the person in question could have sinned? Ever? While canonizations were weighted in favor of the candidate, we nevertheless see the presence of a vigorous "prosecution," a line of questioning that probes for weak points in the defense. In this sense the canonizations bear a strong resemblance to inquisitorial hearings, which is not surprising since the two institutions developed simultaneously. There was sometimes a crossover between the two: at Dominic's canonization hearings, the ecclesiastics in charge of hearing testimonies were also inquisitors.

During the age of the Protestant Revolt, the Church's doctrines of the communion of saints and the *cultus* of the saints were called into question, as well as the practices that had developed out of these cults (veneration of relics, for example). Following the lead of certain Renaissance Humanists such as Erasmus — who had mocked the veneration of relics and considered much of the fifteenth-century *cultus* of the saints questionable — the Protestant Reformers launched an all-out attack upon the Catholic veneration of the saints. Although theological and biblical arguments were put forth, many of the Reformers, including Luther, objected on what we might call "methodological grounds": relics were not properly authenticated, local cults were often of questionable historicity, the *acta* and *vitae* of many popular saints were mostly legendary, the deeds of many saints were not sufficiently verified. Given the literacy of the age, coupled with its advancements in science and medicine, the Tridentine Church deemed that a more thorough scrutiny of the lives and deeds of alleged saints was appropriate. Hence in 1587, Pope Sixtus V created the office of the *Promotor Fidei*, which took many of the prosecutorial practices that had already emerged in medieval canonizations and concentrated them in the hands of a single individual.

What was to be the role of the new *Promotor Fidei*? Back when Pope Gregory IX opened the commission of inquiry into the sanctity of St. Dominic, the pope had stated that the purpose of the investigations was to ensure that the Church was "eager to affirm certainties and slow to credit doubtful matters."[4] This was the conceptual framework behind the establishment of the *Promotor Fidei*. Following the trial model established in the Middle Ages, the Church appoints its own "prosecutor" to try to disprove the sanctity of alleged saints. The power entrusted to the *Promotor Fidei* was very weighty, as he served as a kind of gatekeeper over the Church's calendar of *sancti*. His importance grew in the post-Tridentine period, such that in 1708 he became the most important official in the Sacred Congregation of Rites. His job was to scrutinize everything relating to the saint's life and deeds. The 1913 *Catholic Encyclopedia* sums up his role as:

> ... to prevent any rash decisions concerning miracles or virtues of the candidates for the honors of the altar. All documents of beatification and canonization processes must be submitted to his examination, and the difficulties and doubts he raises over the virtues and miracles are laid before the congregation and must be satisfactorily answered before any further steps can be taken in the processes. It is his duty to suggest natural explanations for alleged miracles, and even to bring forward human and selfish motives for deeds that have been accounted heroic virtues.... His duty requires him to prepare in writing all possible arguments, even at times seemingly slight, against the raising of any one to the honors of the altar. The interest and honor of the Church are concerned in preventing any one from receiving those honors whose death is not juridically proved to have been precious in the sight of God.[5]

Any documents or processes not submitted to the scrutiny of the *Promotor Fidei* became null and void by that very fact. Because of his duty to suggest alternate explanations for alleged miracles and

---

4 The Decree of Gregory IX Instituting the Commission of Inquiry, Rome, July 13, 1233.

5 William Fanning, "*Promotor Fidei*," in *The Catholic Encyclopedia*, vol. 12 (New York: Robert Appleton Company, 1911), www.newadvent.org/cathen/12454a. htm. See also Richard Burtsell, "*Advocatus Diaboli*," in *The Catholic Encyclopedia*, vol. 1 (New York: Robert Appleton Company, 1907), www.newadvent. org/cathen/01168b.htm.

virtues, he was nicknamed the "devil's advocate" (*advocatus diaboli*). He thus served as a filter to screen out candidates whose sanctity was not beyond doubt, or who were perhaps being canonized out of rashness, popular appeal, or the fickle moods of the day. The thinking was that if the deeds of a saint were truly miraculous, they would stand up to every kind of scrutiny — indeed, they *must* stand up to scrutiny if they are to be placed before the faithful and the world as witnesses to the reality of God's grace.

Every action of the saint was to be scrutinized, even ones that were seemingly harmless. The definitive post-Tridentine work on how canonization proceedings are to be carried out was written by Prospero Lambertini, who was *Promotor Fidei* for twenty years and later became Pope Benedict XIV (1740–1758). His classic work *De servorum Dei beatificatione et de beatorum canonizatione* laid down the principles that were followed in canonization proceedings until the post-Vatican II era. In this work we see examples of the seemingly slight questions the *Promotor Fidei* would raise in objection to a candidate's sanctity — for instance, whether a candidate who committed much of his thoughts or deeds to writing might be guilty of vanity:

> There have been servants of God, as we have seen, who, at the command of their superiors, committed their own lives to writing, giving therein an account not only of their own praiseworthy actions, but likewise of the various gifts and graces bestowed on them by God. And there are others, again, who, though they have not published such things, have yet communicated them by word of mouth to their confessors, their companions, or others. In this state of things, then, a doubt is raised whether they have been guilty of the sin of self-conceit or vainglory. Certainly there are not wanting examples of saints who have done this and the like [he goes on to cite the examples of St. Paul, St. Ignatius Loyola, and other saints who were prolific writers].... If anyone should suppose from these and such like examples that every one may, without the fault of boasting and vainglory, set forth his own praiseworthy actions, he would deceive himself... Every one, therefore, sees that it is necessary to be acquainted with some rules, in order to pass a correct judgment, so often as examination is made into the causes of such servants of

God as have committed to writing, or related to others, their own great and noble actions; a judgment, I mean, as to this point, whether their doing so is to be ascribed to virtue or to vice, the vice, namely, of vainglory, which is reproved by the Apostle in his Epistle to the Galatians.[6]

This passage demonstrates the level of scrutiny to which candidates were subjected. It may have occurred to us to ask whether a candidate for sainthood had any serious character defects; Lambertini goes a step further, suggesting we should inquire about selfish motives even in their good deeds, such as writing. How many people would think to question the integrity of a candidate for sainthood based on the fact that he wrote a lot? But Lambertini — and Church Tradition following him — insist that every act and motive must be questioned, no matter how slight. While no saint is absolutely perfect, the *Promotor Fidei*'s job was to ensure that those raised to the sacred dignity of sainthood were as perfect as possible. It was an incredibly high standard.

It might be supposed that such a scrutiny into the motives of saintly individuals would be contrary to faith, a kind of pessimistic impiety. After all, St. Paul tells us that charity "believes all things" (1 Cor 13:7) and that we should rejoice in the good lives of holy men and women rather than scrutinize them searching for flaws. It is true that love must "believe all things," but we are also admonished to temper our credulity: "Test all things; hold fast to that which is good" (1 Thess 5:21). In other words, measure all things against the standard of Christ, retain everything that measures up, and then believe those things that remain. Recall the *Catholic Encyclopedia*'s statement that "the interest and honor of the Church are concerned" in questions of canonizations. The faith of the Christian people and the integrity of the Church's message is weakened if non-suitable candidates are raised to the altars.

Understood properly, then, it would actually be a sin against faith *not* to scrutinize the lives of candidates. To fail to ask sufficient questions about their sanctity would be to compromise the certitude of faith in the eyes of the faithful. This is why Lambertini quotes Fr.

---

6 Prospero Lambertini, *De servorum Dei*, "On Heroic Virtues," 1:3, 8.

Bartoli, biographer of St. Robert Bellarmine, saying that the desirable end in any canonization is "the edification of His Church, for the glory of His name"7 and why Pope Alexander III chastises a bishop in 1173 for allowing a man unsuitably scrutinized to be honored as a saint, as we have seen.

ABOLITION OF THE *PROMOTOR FIDEI* AND CONSEQUENCES

The *Promotor Fidei* had many responsibilities, but in essence his job was to ensure that canonizations remained matters of objective fact. That is why four miracles were traditionally required as well. This gave demonstrable evidence that the saint was among the blessed, for "no man could do such signs unless God were with Him" (Jn 3:2). In consequence of these norms, canonizations were rare events; from 1900 to 1978, only 98 saints were canonized. As we shall see, this pales in comparison to the number of post-1978 canonizations.

By the twentieth century, some had begun to claim that the process for getting saints canonized was too cumbersome. A few reforms were made during the pontificate of Pius XI, such as establishing a special department for the study of "historical" causes, as distinct from the department which studied the theological aspects of a candidate's life. But bishops continued to complain that the process was too burdensome and repeatedly asked the pope for a more streamlined approach, something less bureaucratic which would nevertheless still preserve the integrity of the investigative process. Pope Paul VI subsequently created the Congregation for the Causes of Saints in 1969, making it distinct from the Sacred Congregation of Rites (which thereafter became the Congregation for Divine Worship). This was a first step.

The all-encompassing reform came during the pontificate of John Paul II, who in 1983 issued the constitution *Divinus Perfectionis Magister* which overhauled the entire canonization process as it had been known since the Tridentine era, abrogating all previous law on the process and laying down new norms. Under John Paul II's reforms, the role of the *Promotor Fidei* is replaced by a Secretary, whose job is mainly that of a chairman to ensure that procedure is followed. The theological

---

7 Lambertini, *De Servorum Dei*, "On Heroic Virtues," 1:21 and Gregory IX, *Decretales*, III, "De reliquiis et veneratione sanctorum."

writings of a saint are examined by theological censors who look for theological errors in the works. Others, called Relators, prepare reports documenting virtues, and a medical board documents alleged miracles.

What of the *Promotor Fidei*? Contrary to popular belief, his office has not been abolished altogether, although John Paul II altered it to such a degree that it is no longer recognizable as being the same office as the one established by Sixtus V. In Chapter 2 of *Divinus Perfectionis Magister*, John Paul II says:

> The Sacred Congregation is to have one Promoter of the Faith or Prelate Theologian. His responsibility is: 1. to preside over the meeting of the theologians, with the right to vote; 2. to prepare the report on the meeting itself; 3. to be present as an expert at the meeting of the Cardinals and Bishops, although without the right to vote.[8]

We can see that in *Divinus Perfectionis Magister* the "trial" nature of the canonization process has been abolished. Instead of a candidate being on trial and having to face accusations by the *Promotor Fidei* as the Church's "prosecutor," the procedure now takes the form of a committee meeting where experts present reports. Glaring problems with a candidate's life or miracles still must be accounted for, but the inquisitorial aspect of the procedure has been eliminated. As an example of this, compare the old system, where the *Promotor Fidei* was charged not only to preside and prepare a report, but actively to seek out naturalistic causes for miracles and selfish motives in the candidate's life. His job was not only to point out problems, but to seek them out systematically. Furthermore, the canonization process could not move forward until every one of the *Promotor Fidei*'s objections were answered to his satisfaction, giving him an effective veto power on the whole canonization.

In the modern procedure, the *Promotor Fidei* does not actively seek out problems and no longer has veto power over the process; his influence is reduced to presenting a report and being on hand as an "expert" whose opinion may be solicited. There is nothing in the modern procedure whereby the *Promotor Fidei* submits a list of objections that *must* be answered by the Postulators. Nor is there

---

8 John Paul II, *Divinus Perfectionis Magister*, II, 10:1–3.

any mandate for the *Promotor Fidei* to personally approve all evidence and documentation in the procedure on pain of nullity. With the removal of the prosecutorial role of the *Promotor Fidei* and the reduction of his authority, the nature of the proceedings is fundamentally transformed: instead of a forum set up to argue for or against a candidate's virtues, the Congregation for the Causes of Saints now becomes more of a committee that collects favorable testimonies of candidates and issues reports on them. The corresponding reduction of necessary miracles from four to two further decreases the burden of proof in favor of the candidate.

The result is that the modern Congregation has been unfavorably compared to a "saint-making factory." Above we noted that there were 98 canonizations from 1900 to 1978, an average of 1.2 per year. When we come to John Paul II's pontificate, the Church canonized 482 saints from 1978 to 2005, an average of 17.7 per year, *almost a 1000% increase*. This increase is unprecedented; it is not merely that John Paul II canonized more saints than all of his twentieth-century predecessors, he canonized more saints than all popes combined going back to 1588.[9]

The Church still may and at times does employ hostile witnesses to try to find fault with candidates, but very commonly these specialists are not Catholic, have no background in theology, and present objections of a very worldly nature. For example, atheists Aroup Chatterjee and Christopher Hitchens were asked to testify against Mother Teresa in her 2002 hearings. Their objections were absurd: Chatterjee objected that Mother Teresa damaged the reputation of Calcutta and that her charity was not effective in reducing the sum total of poverty in the region. Such worldly objections were noted and then studiously ignored by the Congregation. Meanwhile, problems that truly did have a bearing on Catholic theology — like Mother Teresa's practice of praying with pagans, encouraging Hindus to be better Hindus, her syncretist statements that all religions worship the same God, and the extremely questionable nature of her miracle — were

---

9 In the estimation of Cardinal José Saraiva Martins: see "Why John Paul II Proclaimed So Many Saints," *ZENIT*, April 4, 2006, www.ewtn.com/catholicism/library/why-john-paul-ii-proclaimed-so-many-saints-5988.

never addressed.[10] Such objections were not addressed because there was nobody designated to bring forward potentially damning evidence against the candidate. She was duly beatified without these issues ever being resolved.

While it can be argued that these reforms and the basic elimination of the *Promotor Fidei* in his traditional role do not necessarily mean the integrity of the process is compromised, it is undeniable that John Paul II eliminated safeguards that had been put in place by previous popes for the very purpose of preserving "the interest and honor of the Church" and "for the edification of His Church, for the glory of His name." Therefore, there is a strong argument to be made that in eliminating these safeguards the modern Magisterium has indeed compromised the soundness of the process.

Another troubling aspect of the modern Magisterium's approach is the rationale that underlies the massive increase in canonizations. Rather than proclaiming saints because they were in fact objectively and manifestly saintly, the modern canonizations seem to have an ulterior motive: to showcase the universal call to holiness taught at Vatican II. In commenting upon the many canonizations of John Paul II, Cardinal Martins stated that the pope viewed his canonizations in the context of a "fulfillment" of the vision of the Council:

> The first reason the pope gave [for so many canonizations] was that he, by beatifying so many Servants of God, did no more than implement the Second Vatican Council, which vigorously reaffirmed that holiness is the essential note of the Church... Therefore, John Paul II said, holiness is what is most important in the Church, according to the Second Vatican Council. Then no one should be surprised by the fact that the pope wished to propose so many models of holiness to Christians, to the People of God.
>
> The second reason is the extraordinary ecumenical importance of holiness. In *Novo Millennio Ineunte*, the pope said that the holiness of the saints, blesseds, and martyrs is perhaps the most convincing ecumenism, these are his words, because holiness, he said with even stronger words, has its

---

10   For the problems with Mother Teresa's miracle, see "Should Mother Teresa be Canonized?," *Unam Sanctam Catholicam*, September 4, 2007.

ultimate foundation in Christ, in whom the Church is not divided. Therefore, the ecumenism we all want calls for many saints, so that the convincing ecumenism of holiness is placed in the candelabrum of the holiness of the Church.[11]

Who knows whether Cardinal Martins really spoke John Paul's mind on this or not—but if so, the comments are telling. The argument seems to be not that there are more saintly men and women, but that the modern ecclesial vision *demands* that there be more of them. Yet we know holiness is not affirmed by removing the safeguards put in place by Tradition, safeguards whose very existence ensured that only true models of holiness were proposed. One cannot make more orange juice by simply pouring more water into the pitcher. What we have with the modern Magisterium's approach is essentially pouring more water into the pitcher. The addition technically increases volume, but the content of the resulting mixture is not as pure.

The Cardinal's statement about ecumenism is more interesting, because the Cardinal basically admits an ulterior motive in the modern canonizations, that "the ecumenism we want calls for many saints"—and therefore we must have more saints! Where does this leave us? While the *Promotor Fidei* ensured that canonizations remained an objective matter, the subsuming of canonization to the "needs" of the modern Church has effectively subjectivized the procedure. A canonization is no longer about whether a candidate truly meets the Church's standard of holiness, but is now about what role models the modern Church "needs" at any given time to promote its particular vision. This is not entirely unprecedented; one might recall the hasty canonization of St. Thomas Becket because the Church of the time "needed" a martyr in its struggle against royal domination. While such things certainly happened in the past, today they have been institutionalized in the very methodology of the proceedings themselves, which is of much greater import.

Are modern canonizations to be questioned? The traditional opinion of most theologians has tended towards the infallibility of canonizations, at least in their final determination—that is to say, the fact of a canonization was considered certain, but not necessarily the

---

11   http://www.ewtn.com/library/MARY/zmanysaints.HTM.

integrity of the evidence, procedure, or methodology, which were all matters of human prudence. If so, what we are witnessing today is not saints who are not really saintly, but saints whose level of sanctity is much lower than that expected by previous generations, and less able to withstand the scrutiny of detractors. Whereas nobody could doubt the miracles at Lourdes (which even converted atheists), not even the husband of the woman Mother Teresa healed believes in the legitimacy of the miracle, nor do the doctors. Yet, because of the loss of the *Promotor Fidei*'s role, these objections do not ultimately need to be resolved. The process allows them to be ignored. In the old days, the *Promotor Fidei* would attack or scrutinize even the good deeds of a candidate; now, even questionable issues are disregarded.

Incidentally, in the fall of 1965 when some bishops began calling for the canonization of John XXIII only three years after his death, the effort was blocked by the powerful Cardinal Suenens and by Pope Paul VI himself, on the premise that it was rash to propose a candidate for canonization so soon after his death.[12]

Does the Church need models of holiness? Absolutely. How do we get them? By cultivating a spiritual atmosphere in our parishes and homes that nourishes real saints, so that we actually have an objective increase in the number of saintly people. We cannot get more saints by making it easier to proclaim saints. We cannot make more juice by adding water to it.

---

12   Roberto de Mattei, *The Second Vatican Council: An Unwritten History* (Fitzwilliam, NH: Loreto Publications, 2010), 459.

4

The Infallibility of Canonizations: A Revisionist History of the Arguments†

WILLIAM MATTHEW DIEM

THE MODERN CONSENSUS AND THE *PRIMA FACIE* PROBLEM

Since the publication of *De servorum Dei beatificatione et beatorum canonizatione* by Prospero Lorenzo Lambertini (later Pope Benedict XIV), a general consensus has emerged that formal canonizations of the saints are infallible papal acts.[1] Indeed it is so commonly held that the *New Catholic Encyclopedia* simply asserts, without any note of either controversy or explanation, that canonizations are infallible declarations.[2] More precisely, it is commonly held that, in canonizations, the pope infallibly teaches that the one canonized is now in heaven.[3]

---

1 See Prospero Lorenzo Lambertini, *De servorum Dei beatificatione et beatorum canonizatione*, esp. bk. I, chs. 43–45 (Venice: Antonius Foglierini, 1744), 195–212. Especially noteworthy treatments of the history and arguments of this position are found in Eric W. Kemp, *Canonization and Authority in the Western Church* (London: Oxford University Press, 1948), and Max Schenk, *Die Unfehlbarkeit des Papstes in der Heiligsprechung: Ein Beitrag zur Erhellung der theologiegeschichtlichen Seite der Frage* (Freiburg: Paulusverlag, 1965). It is worth noting that there was a competing tradition still present in the eighteenth century; see, for example, Lamindus Pritanius (Ludovico Antonio Muratori), *De ingeniorum moderatione in religionis negotio*, bk. I, ch. 17 (Venice: Johannis Baptistae Pasquali, 1752), 75–78.

2 P. Molinari and G. B. O'Donnell, "Canonization of Saints (History and Procedure)," in *New Catholic Encyclopedia*, 2nd ed., vol. 3 (Detroit, MI: Thomson/ Gale, 2003), 66: "The bull of canonization infallibly declares the exemplariness of the saint's life and recognizes his or her role as a heavenly intercessor." It is, however, worth noting the restraint concerning the object of this declaration.

3 As an early example of this now common opinion, see Camillo Beccari, "Beatification and Canonization," in *The Catholic Encyclopedia*, vol. 2 (New York: Robert Appleton, 1907), 367: "What is the object of this infallible judgment of the pope? . . . My own opinion is that nothing else is defined than that the person canonized is in heaven."

---

† First published in *Nova et Vetera* English ed. 17.3 (2019): 653–82; reproduced here with the journal's permission.

Yet, this position faces a rather significant objection. As Avery Cardinal Dulles notes, "it is difficult to see how [formal canonizations and the approval of religious institutes] fit under the object of infallibility as defined in the two Vatican councils."[4] What he means is this: the two Vatican councils connect the Church's infallibility directly to the guarding and expounding of the deposit of faith handed down from the apostles. Hence Vatican II in *Lumen Gentium* teaches, "this infallibility with which the Divine Redeemer willed His Church to be endowed in defining doctrine of faith and morals, extends as far as the deposit of Revelation extends, which must be religiously guarded and faithfully expounded."[5] So much is uncontroversial: the Church's infallibility is linked directly to her office as guardian and teacher of public revelation.

Now, we should note another uncontroversial point: that this infallible teaching authority extends not only to what has been

4 Avery Cardinal Dulles, *Magisterium: Teacher and Guardian of the Faith* (Ave Maria, FL: Sapientia, 2010), 78. He then quotes the Lutheran–Roman Catholic Dialogue, "Teaching Authority and Infallibility in the Church: Common Statement," *Theological Studies* 40 (1979): 113–66, at 149: "The Church has the power to recognize authentic Christian holiness, yet canonization of its nature would not seem to convey infallible certitude that the holiness in question was actually present in the life of this or that historical individual." This problem had been raised in the eighteenth century by Muratori, *De ingeniorum moderatione*, bk. I, ch. 17 (p. 76); see Schenk, *Die Unfehlbarkeit*, 61.

5 Second Vatican Council, *Lumen Gentium*, §25 (unless otherwise noted, translations of the documents of Vatican II come from the Vatican's website as reproduced in Denzinger-Hünermann [DH], 43rd ed., English ed. R. Fastiggi and A. E. Nash [San Francisco: Ignatius, 2012]). Similarly, see Vatican I, *Dei Filius*, ch. 4, §13: "Neque enim fidei doctrina, quam Deus revelavit, velut philosophicum inventum proposita est humanis ingeniis perficienda, sed tamquam divinum depositum Christi Sponsae tradita, fideliter custodienda et infallibiliter declaranda [for the doctrine of the faith that God has revealed has not been proposed like a philosophical system to be perfected by human ingenuity; rather it has been committed to the spouse of Christ as a divine trust to be faithfully kept and infallibly declared]" (trans. J. Neuner and J. Dupuis, as found in DH, no. 3020). See also Vatican I, *Pastor Aeternus*, ch. 4, §6, "Neque enim Petri successoribus Spiritus Sanctus promissus est, ut eo revelante novam doctrinam patefacerent, sed ut eo assistente traditam per Apostolos revelationem seu fidei depositum sancte custodirent et fideliter exponerent [for the Holy Spirit was not promised to the successors of Peter that they might disclose a new doctrine by his revelation, but rather that, with his assistance, they might reverently guard and faithfully explain the revelation or deposit of faith that was handed down through the apostles]" (trans. Neuner and Dupuis, in DH, no. 3070).

directly revealed in public revelation — the primary or direct objects of infallibility — but extends also to those things that are necessarily connected with revealed truth by either a logical or a historical necessity. Defenders of the infallibility of canonizations — well aware that Christ revealed nothing about the fate of particular post-apostolic individuals — thus place canonizations among these secondary or indirect objects of infallibility. Hence, for example, Ludwig Ott writes, "to the secondary objects of infallibility belong . . . the canonization of saints, that is the final judgment that a member of the Church has been assumed into eternal bliss and may be the object of general veneration."[6] But what necessary connection is there between a particular historical individual's beatitude and the Faith? As Dulles notes, "it is not easy to see how the fact that this or that saint possessed heroic virtue is either a necessary condition or a necessary consequence of Christian faith."[7]

Now to complete the difficulties, we can consider the two lines of data that are examined leading up to a formal canonization and on which the determination of sainthood is ultimately made. Since the beginning of the practice of formal canonizations by the popes,[8]

---

6 Ludwig Ott, *Fundamentals of Catholic Dogma*, trans. Patrick Lynch (Rockford, IL: TAN, 1974), 299. Similarly Adolphe Tanquerey lists canonizations among the "indirect" objects of infallibility, noting that this thesis is the *communis et vera sententia* in *Synopsis Theologiae Dogmaticae*, 16th ed. (Rome and Paris: Typis Societatis Sancti Joannis Evangelistae, 1919), vol. 1, 546–47 (no. 842).

7 Dulles, *Magisterium*, 91.

8 The first formal, papal canonization — so far as we can tell — was of St. Ulric of Augsburg by John XV in 993; see Kemp, *Canonization and Authority*, 57. For the point that a determination of sanctity must be based on these two lines of evidence, see Innocent III's bull of canonization of St. Homobonus in 1199: "duo tamen, virtus videlicet morum et virtus signorum, opera scilicet pietatis in vita et miraculorum signa post mortem, ut quis reputetur sanctus in militanti Ecclesia requiruntur." He draws particular attention to the insufficiency of miracles alone: "frequenter angelus Satanae se in lucis angelum transfigurat et quidam faciunt opera sua bona, ut videantur ab hominibus, quidam etiam coruscant miraculis quorum tamen vita merito reprobatur (sicut de magis legitur Pharaonis), et etiam Antichristus, qui electos etiam, si fieri potest, inducet miraculis suis in errorem, ad id nec opera sufficiunt sola nec signa, sed cum illis praecedentibus ista succedunt, verum nobis praebent indicium sanctitatis" (*PL*, 214:483–84). See also Innocent IV, *Apparatus in quinque libros decretalium*, bk.

two lines of investigation have been carried out to determine sanctity:
The first is an examination of the person's life, and the second is an
examination of miracles attributed to the person's intercession.

To the first of these, we must note that, while a thorough investigation of a person's life may give very good reason to determine that
a person was holy and is now in glory, it is ultimately inconclusive
insofar as we cannot read another person's soul.[9] What's more, not
even the individual can know his own state of grace with absolute
certainty — the sentiment is clear in Paul: "I am not aware of anything
against myself, but I am not thereby acquitted. It is the Lord who
judges me" (1 Cor 4:4). Trent is explicit: "For as no pious person
ought to doubt the mercy of God, the merit of Christ and the virtue and efficacy of the sacraments, so each one, when he considers
himself and his own weakness and indisposition, may have fear and
apprehension concerning his own grace, since no one can know with
the certainty of faith, which cannot be subject to error, that he has
obtained the grace of God."[10] Note carefully the distinction, in Trent,
between those things on the one hand that are matters of divine
revelation — the mercy of God, the merits of Christ, the efficacy of
the sacraments — and on the other, those particular matters of fact
that revelation does not touch — one's own response to these things.
The former are certain as matters of faith; the latter are necessarily
uncertain. Hence the problem: if even the individual himself cannot
be absolutely certain of his own sanctity at any given moment, how

---

III, rub. 45, ch. 1, in *Audivimus*, which makes the same point — "non sufficiunt
miracula sine vite excelentia [miracles do not suffice without excellence of life]"
(since even Pharoah's magicians worked wonders) — but on the other hand,
the Church must not canonize persons of good life without miracles "quia in
secreto potuerunt laxiorem vitam ducere [for they could have led less rigorous
lives in secret]" (unless otherwise noted, all translations of non-magisterial texts
are my own). See also Aquinas, *Quodlibet* IX, a. 8, ad 1, and arg. 2 (produced
in note 35); though, unlike these prior two, Aquinas's only expressed concern
with either miracles or lives is that they be unreliably reported, not that they
actually be diabolical or deceptive.

9   1 Cor 2:11: "For what person knows a man's thoughts except the spirit of
the man which is in him?"

10   Council of Trent, *Decree on Justification* (1547), ch. 9 (trans. Rev. Fr. H.
J. Schroeder in *The Canons and Decrees of the Council of Trent* [Rockford, IL:
TAN, 1978]).

can the pope determine — through an examination of the records of his life — the state in which an individual died years prior?[11]

But here the defenders of infallibility will point to the second sort of evidence: our human investigations may lead us only to a likely belief that a person died in grace and is now in heaven, but God, doubtless, knows the person's state with certainty, and can confirm the individual's salvation through miracles worked through his intercession. Thus the divine testimony of miracles supplies that certainty wanting from our investigation of his life. This, however, brings us back to the original problem: even if the miracles in question are perfectly clear divine testimony of God's favor toward the individual, the Church emphatically does not claim to teach the content of so-called private or special revelations infallibly. Vatican I writes, "for the Holy Spirit was not promised to the successors of Peter that they might disclose a new doctrine by his revelation, but rather that, with his assistance, they might reverently guard and faithfully explain the revelation or deposit of faith that was handed down through the apostles."[12]

Having laid out the *prima facie* case against the infallibility of canonization, I would like to examine the principal arguments adduced in its favor. Ott provides the very form of all the strongest arguments in a single line: "If the Church could err in her opinion [about saints], consequences would arise which would be incompatible with the sanctity of the Church."[13] This is the fundamental argument. But which consequences specifically?

In light of space I must restrict myself to examining the arguments of two figures. These two are, however, the most important in the tradition, as between them they established — so far as I can tell — all of the strongest arguments in favor of the infallibility of canonizations. And at least one of the two is explicitly cited by

---

11 On this point, consider also Gregory the Great, *Epistles*, bk. VII, Epistle 25 (to Gregoria).

12 Vatican I, *Pastor Aeternus*, ch. 4, §6. Vatican II sums up the teaching nicely in *Dei Verbum*, §10: "Quod quidem Magisterium non supra verbum Dei est, sed eidem ministrat, docens nonnisi quod traditum est . . . [This teaching office is not above the Word of God, but serves it, teaching only what has been handed on]" (DH, no. 4214).

13 Ott, *Fundamentals*, 299.

almost every subsequent theologian who treats the topic.[14] Thus, for example, all four of the arguments provided by Lambertini in favor of the infallibility of canonizations are explicitly drawn from these two figures.[15] I speak of Melchior Cano and Thomas Aquinas. Because his arguments present fewer interpretational difficulties, I propose to treat Cano first. I will argue that his proofs do not successfully arrive at a simple infallibility in canonizations — that is, they do not prove that one canonized is certainly in heaven. Turning then to Aquinas, I will argue two further points: first, that, despite ambiguities in the text, reading Aquinas's arguments to establish a simple infallibility of canonizations renders his arguments invalid, and second, that placing those arguments in their historical context gives us compelling reason to conclude, *pace* Lambertini, that Aquinas never intended them to prove such a simple infallibility. Finally, I will argue that the arguments marshaled by these authors do prove a divine guarantee in canonization, but a more subtle guarantee than simple infallibility.

MELCHIOR CANO

In his *De locis theologicis*, Melchior Cano (d. 1560) explicitly defends the infallibility of formal canonizations under the heading of conciliar authority.[16] While Cano notes that individually his arguments may be inconclusive, nonetheless he thinks that joined together they are decisive.[17] He offers three arguments, all of which echo through the tradition.

---

14 Kemp notes: "Cano's discussion is important because he and St. Thomas are the two theologians most frequently quoted by later writers" (*Canonization and Authority*, 157).

15 In *De beatificatione et canonizatione*, bk. I, ch. 43 (pp. 198–99), Lambertini produces a total of four arguments in favor of the infallibility of canonizations. The first he identifies in both Thomas and Cano; the second and third he takes from Thomas; the fourth is drawn from Cano.

16 Melchior Cano, *De locis theologicis*, bk. V, ch. 5, no. 43 (Salanticae: Mathias Gastius, 1558), 195–96.

17 Cano, *De locis theologicis*, bk. V, ch. 5, no. 43 (p. 196). Note that Cano does offer a prior argument that is also often cited, *viz.*, that he does injury to a martyr who prays for him. But this is offered not as an argument that canonizations are infallible, but that the denial of a canonization is a crime deserving strict ecclesiastical censure.

Cano's first argument is that, if we could call even one canonization into question, then we could call all the saints into question, even doctors like Jerome, Ambrose, and Augustine. In fact, we could, without any crime, condemn them with the devils, beat them down with maledictions, and vex them with contumelies—a prospect from which all the faithful will recoil in horror. If the Church could err in placing a man in the catalog of saints, "it would not be terribly absurd to eject from the Church the cults of all the saints consecrated since Clement [i.e., Pope Clement I, the last pope of the apostolic era]. Who could say something more stupid or imprudent?"[18]

Once we strip away the polemics, this is ultimately an argument from the practice of the Church. Francisco Suárez (d. 1617) takes this argument and develops it by appealing to a threefold division of practices he takes from Augustine.[19] Augustine noted (*Letter* 54, ch.

---

18   Cano, *De locis*, bk. V, ch. 5, no. 43: "Mox etiam, si unum aliquod huius generis decretum in quaestionem veniat, certe Hieronymi, Ambrosii, Augustini ac reliquorum sanctitatem sine crimine in quaestionem vocare poterimus: atque adeo asserere illos cum daemonibus condemnatos, ita posses eos maledictis, ac vexare contumeliis, quae omnia aures sane fidelium perhorrescunt. Quod si viris iustis in divorum catalogum reponendis ecclesia errat, nimirum non esset valde absurdum, divorum omnium cultum ab ecclesia explodere eorum, qui post Clementem consecrati sunt. Quo quid aut stultius aut imprudentius dici potest? [Also, if one of these decrees should come into question, then certainly we could call the sanctity of Jerome, Ambrose, Augustine, and the rest into question without crime; and place them, condemned, among the demons, so you could vex them with curses and contumelies, from which all the ears of the faithful rightly recoil in horror. For if the Church could err in placing the just in the catalog of the godly, doubtless it would hardly be absurd to throw out of the Church the cult of all the saints who have been consecrated after Clement. Who can say something more stupid or imprudent?]" (p. 195).

19   Francisco Suárez, *Defensio fidei catholicae et apostolicae adversus anglicanae sectae errors*, bk. II, ch. 8, no. 9 (Conimbricae: Apud Didicum Gomez de Loureyro, Academiae Typographum, 1613), 167–68. His concluding line here is: "Ergo quando universa Ecclesia Catholica de aliquius Sancti felicitate non dubitat, et in illius cultu concordat, non licet viro Catholico, et prudenti disputare, quin ita faciendum sit [Therefore when the universal Catholic Church does not doubt the blessedness of some saint and is of one accord in his cult, it is not permissible for the Catholic and prudent man to dispute whether one should do so]." He presents another version of this argument in *Opus de triplici virtute theologica: fide, spe, et charitate*, tract I (*De fide*), disp. 5, sect. 8, n. 8: "Item, non licet fidelibus dubitare de gloria Sancti canonizati: id enim sub praecisa obligatione praecipiunt Pontifices in ipsa canonizatione: ergo oportet, ut illi praecepto

5) that there are three sorts of practice in the Church: first, those that are prescribed in Scripture, and these we cannot doubt ought to be practiced; second, those things done differently in different parts of the Church, and these we ought to practice so long as they are not contrary to faith and morals; third, those practices observed by the whole Church, and of these—among which Suárez places the *cultus* of each saint—he remarks that it would be most insolent madness to doubt whether we ought to observe and do them.

Robert Bellarmine (d. 1621) likewise adopted and refined Cano's argument: "If one were permitted to doubt whether a canonized saint were holy, one would be permitted to doubt whether he should be venerated: but this is false." The reason it is false is given in the line from Augustine we just saw quoted by Suárez: "it is most insolent to dispute whether it should be done as the whole Church does." Thus since "we are bound to obey the pontiffs indicating the feast day of some saint; [and since one cannot] act against conscience: therefore we cannot doubt whether he is to be venerated who is canonized by the Church."[20]

---

non possit subesse error, alias deficeret Deus in re maxime necessaria Ecclesiae, quod est contra providentiam, et promissiones eius [It is not permissible for the faithful to doubt the glory of a canonized saint. For the Pontiffs command it under a 'specific obligation' {i.e., an obligation that binds in conscience} in the canonization itself: therefore it is necessary that that command not be able to be in error, otherwise God would fail in a thing most necessary for the Church, which would be contrary to his providence and promises]" ([Lugduni: Sumptibus Iacobi Cardon et Petri Cauellat, 1621], 104).

20   Robert Bellarmine, *Disputationes de controversiis christianae fidei: de ecclesia triumphante sive de gloria et cultu sanctorum*, bk. I (*De sanctorum beatitudine*), ch. 9: "Primo: Quia si liceret dubitare, an sanctus canonizatus sit sanctus, liceret etiam dubitare, an sit colendus: at hac est falsum. Siquidem s. Augustinus in epist. 118 [according to the current enumeration of Augustine's letters this is actually Epistle 54] dicit insolentissimae insaniae esse disputare, an sit faciendum, quod tota Ecclesia facit. Item ex Bernardo in epist. 174 ad canonicos Lugdunenses, ubi loquens de colendis festis in honorem sanctorum, dicit: Ego quae accepi ab Ecclesia, securus teneo et trado. Praeterea: Omnes veteres, sine ulla dubitatione sanctos coluerunt, et colendos asseruerunt. Denique tenemur obedire pontifici in licenti diem festum alicujus sancti; nec tamen possumus contra conscientiam aliquid agere: ergo non possumus dubitare, an sit colendus ille, qui ab Ecclesia est canonizatus" (in *Roberti Cardinalis Bellarmini Opera Omnia*, 2nd ed. [Milan: Edente Natale Battezzati, 1858], 178).

As Bellarmine produces it, I think this argument is remarkably strong. If we were permitted to doubt the sanctity of some saint, we could be bound in conscience not to venerate him. But we are bound to venerate him because that veneration is a practice of the whole Church, and in the case of a formal canonization it is a practice enjoined on the Church by the pope precisely as an obligation. Thus if we could doubt the sanctity of some saint, we would be forced either to reject a practice enjoined on us by the Church or to act against conscience.

Having noted the strength of the argument, I will for the moment point out but one further thing, namely, the force of the conclusion: Bellarmine concludes that one is not permitted to doubt that the saint is in fact a saint. The quotation from Augustine (marshaled by both Suárez and Bellarmine) concludes only that one is not permitted to doubt the practice of the Church. Even Cano's argument proved only that one could not doubt any particular decree of canonization.

Cano's second argument is that the matter of who is to be venerated is a question of morals, and therefore the Church would err in teaching morals if it erred in canonization. In a line that has been frequently quoted over the intervening centuries, he asserts, "it makes no difference whether you venerate a devil or a condemned man."[21]

---

21 Cano, *De locis*, bk. V, ch. 5, no. 43: "Item multum refert ad communes ecclesiae mores scire, quos debeas religione colere: quare, si in illis erraret ecclesia, in moribus quoque graviter falleretur. Nec differt diabolum colas, an hominem condemnatum. Atque si ecclesia abstinentiae legem fogaret, quae vel rationi vel Evangelio adversa esset, turpiter ab illa profecto erraretur: turpiter ergo etiam errabit in doctrina morum, si legem ferat de colendo divo, quem colere si divus non est, et cum ratione et cum Evangelio pugnat [It matters a good deal for the common conduct of the Church to know whom you ought to worship with religious observance. Which is why, if the Church erred in those things, it would also be gravely deceived in conduct. It does not matter whether you worship a devil or a condemned man. And if the Church should give a law of abstinence which was against either reason or the Gospel, it would certainly err shamefully in so doing, therefore so also would it shamefully err in the moral doctrine, if it proposed a law honoring as a saint someone whose being so honored contradicts reason and the Gospel, if he is not a saint]" (p. 195). Again Suárez repeats the argument in *De fide*, bk. II, ch. 8, no. 8: "Secundo infertur, non posse errare Pontificem in Sanctorum canonizatione, ut recte docuit D. Thom. quodlib. 9. art. Ultimo, Anton. et Cano, supra, et Bellarm. lib. 1. de Sanctorum beatitudinem, cap. 5; . . . Ratio vero est: quia haec est pars quaedam materia moralis, et valde

55

Again, Bellarmine puts it in its most nuanced form by appealing to the communion of saints; he notes that, if the Church could err in canonizations, "those who are not saints would be defrauded of the suffrage of the living," while "the living would be defrauded of the intercession of the saints, for they would often invoke the damned for the blessed"; in fact, "the Church would often ask for itself malediction in place of benediction, since in prayers to the saints it asks, that just as God glorified them in heaven, so he grant us grace on earth."[22] This would be a nasty sort of irony if this were prayed of a condemned soul. Bellarmine closes here by qualifying the force of the conclusion: "Although the Church would not ask the malediction but materially, nonetheless it seems absurd." We will return to this argument below.

Finally, Cano makes another argument that will be repeated many times down to the present day: not even once has the Church been

---

necessaria, ut Ecclesia non erret in cultu, et adoratione religionis; alias contingere posse, ut coleret hominem damnatum, et ad illum preces funderet; quod est etiam contra puritatem, et sanctitatem Ecclesiae [Second, it is concluded that the Pontiff cannot err in the canonization of the saints, as Saint Thomas (in QL IX, final article), Antoninus, Cano (above), Bellarmine (Bk. 1 On the Beatitude of the Saints) rightly taught.... The reason is that this is a certain part of moral matters, and certainly necessary, namely that the Church not err in religious worship and adoration. Otherwise, it could happen that the Church honor a damned man and offer prayers to him, which is certainly against the purity and sanctity of the Church]" (p. 104). Lambertini quotes this passage of Cano and joins it to Aquinas's second *sed contra* in *De beatificatione et canonizatione*, bk. I, ch. 43, no. 9 (p. 198). Notice that Cano does not explain precisely in which respect devil worship and veneration of a condemned soul are morally equivalent; this ambiguity, left unresolved by Cano though not by Bellarmine, proves significant, as we will see when we return to this point further on.

22 Bellarmine, *De sanctorum beatitudine*, "Secundo: Ex incommodis duobus; nam in primis fraudarentur non sancti suffragiis vivorum; nam pro canonizatis non licet orare. Ut enim Augustinus dicit, serm. 17. de verbis apostoli: Injuriam facit martyri qui orat pro martyre; et idem intelligendum de omnibus sanctis canonizatis, docet Innocentius, cap. *Cum Marthae*, de celebrat. Missarum: at si in hoc Ecclesia erraret, defraudaret eum, qui habetur sanctus, et non est, quicumque non oraret pro eo. Deinde fraudarentur etiam viventes intercessionibus sanctorum, invocarent enim saepe damnatos pro beatis, si Ecclesia in hoc erraret. Praeterea Ecclesia peteret sibi maledictionem pro benedictione, cum in orationibus sanctorum petit, ut sicut illos Deus glorificavit in coelis, sic nobis gratiam largiatur in terris. Et quamvis eam maledictionem non peteret nisi materialiter, tamen hoc ipsum absurdum videtur" (pp. 438–39).

shown to have erred in these judgments.²³ The most obvious problem with such an argument is that, if canonizations are not infallible — particularly if they are not infallible because we have no direct access to the matter of fact they are claimed to establish — then there is in principle no way for us to find an error (unless the Church herself admit an error — but even then, all we would know is that there was some error; we would not know whether it was in the canonization or in the retraction). In other words the theory that canonizations are infallible is in principle unfalsifiable from direct observation.²⁴ I will consider this argument dispensed with.

THOMAS AQUINAS

Thomas Aquinas (d. 1274) is generally considered the first theologian to have directly considered the question of the infallibility of canonizations, and the arguments he produced are — with those of Cano — frequently and explicitly cited in the subsequent literature; Lambertini styles him the *dux omnium qui pugnant pro summi Pontifici infallibilitate* (the leader of all those who fight for the infallibility of the Supreme Pontiff).²⁵ His treatment is found in *Quodlibet* IX,

23   Cano, *De locis*, bk. V, ch. 5, no. 43: "Ne igitur tantus error in ecclesia sit, Deus peculiariter providere credendus est, ne ecclesia, quamlibet hominum testimonia sequatur, in sanctorum canonizatione erret. Cuius peculiarissimae providentiae abunde magnum argumentum est, quod nunquam infirmata est fides ab humanis testibus semel in huiusmodi iudiciis suscepta. Quod in causis civilibus saepe accredit [Lest there be such error in the Church, it is to be believed that God specifically provides that, whatever human testimony it follow, the Church not err in the canonization of the saints. It is a great argument for this most particular providence that the faith derived from human witnesses in such judgments has never, even once, been disproven, although that often happens in civil cases]" (195–96). This is quoted by Lambertini, in presenting his fourth argument in favor of the infallibility of canonizations, in *De beatificatione et canonizatione*, bk. I, ch. 43, no. 14 (p. 199).

24   It is worth noting that, even granting that we can determine that there has never been an error, the argument is still inconclusive. Thus, for example, Muratori follows Cano in holding that there has never actually been an error in canonization, although he admits the possibility that the Church could err in a canonization. Muratori, *De ingeniorum moderatione*, bk. I, ch. 17 (p. 77).

25   Lambertini, *De beatificatione et canonizatione*, 197 (this formulation is a condensation of what Lambertini writes in bk. I, ch. 43, no. 4: "Pugnant vero pro Summi Pontificis infallibilitate caeteri mox referendi. Dux nempe omnium est Sanctus Thomas Quodlibet 9 art 16 ut infra latius exponetur [But others,

q. 8, where he asks whether all the saints who have been canonized by the Church are in glory or whether some are in hell.

Before considering Aquinas, however, it may be desirable to consider his immediate context. While Aquinas was at the University of Paris, Bonaventure (d. 1274) held a series of disputed questions on evangelical perfection, and in the course of these, he defended mendicant poverty against the attacks of William of Saint-Amour, a defense found in his *De perfectione evangelica*, q. 2.[26] The series of questions was held in the fall of 1255,[27] during Aquinas's first Paris regency,[28] and shortly before Aquinas wrote *Quodlibet* IX.[29] Part of Bonaventure's defense is that the lives of the saints record that

---

who are to be referred to soon, fight for the infallibility of the Supreme Pontiff. Indeed the leader of them all is Saint Thomas, QL IX, a. 16 as will be discussed at greater length below]"). As one noteworthy example of how Aquinas is read on this point, consider Reginald Garrigou-Lagrange, *Reality: A Synthesis of Thomistic Thought*, ch. 43, where he somewhat facilely cites *Quodlibet* IX to establish that Aquinas holds that the Church's infallible teaching authority extends even to dogmatic facts: "In his [Aquinas's] treatise on faith [here, in note 90, he cites *ST* II-II, q. 1, a. 10, and *Quodlibet* IX, a. 16] he finds in the Church a doctrinal authority that is plenary and infallible, extending even, as in canonizing her saints, not merely to dogmatic truths, but also to dogmatic facts" (trans. Patrick Cummins [St. Louis, MO: Herder, 1953]).

26 In St. Bonaventure, *Opera Omnia*, ed. Collegii S. Bonaventura, vol. 5 (Florence: Quaracchi, 1891). There is a possibility of confusion as this second question circulated separately under the title *De paupertate*. The specific passage we are concerned with is in the afterword to the article, "Replicatio adversus objectiones postea factas," sect. 4 "dubia," obj. 1 (p. 152). As a note, this dispute — being inherently polemical in purpose — gives life to the controversy. Aquinas's disputed questions are generally sanitized, recording only the most concise form of the strongest arguments. Bonaventure here records his objectors' every argument — with all their warts — to head off every evasion. The reader cannot but feel the vigor and vibrancy of the intellectual community that was the Latin Quarter in the thirteenth century.

27 See Jay M. Hammond, "Bonaventure's *Legenda Major*," in *A Companion to Bonaventure*, ed. Jay Hammond, Wayne Hellman, Jared Goff (Leiden and Boston: Brill, 2013), 453–508, at 472.

28 1252–1259. See Jean-Pierre Torrell, *St. Thomas Aquinas*, vol. 1, *The Person and His Work*, trans. Robert Royal (Washington, DC: Catholic University of America Press, 1996), 36–39, 96.

29 Torrell summarizes the various opinions concerning the date of the disputed questions, *Thomas Aquinas*, 1:210–11; cf. 61. René Gauthier (editor of the Leonine edition) dates it to Advent 1257, two years after Bonaventure's *De perfectione evangelica*.

several of the saints (including, among many others, Francis and a fourth-century Roman named Alexius) chose to give up their wealth and live off alms.[30] His adversaries called a number of assertions related to this argument into question, holding that it was dubious and uncertain that Alexius begged or that Francis worked miracles—and even if Francis did work miracles, so too have many evil men. In his reply, Bonaventure argues first that the lives of the saints, as they are recorded in the *legenda*, are models of Christian virtue, that is, that the written lives of the saints are worthy moral guides,[31] and second that to deny that the miracles of the saints are sound evidence of their holiness is to accuse the Church of being a fool, by credulously accepting such signs as divine indications of sanctity.[32]

---

30 A whole series of *exempla* drawn from lives of the saints are given as arguments *sed contra*: Bonaventure, *De perfectione*, q. 2, a. 2, sc 16–23 (pp. 138–39).

31 Bonaventure, *De perfectione*, "Replicatio adversus objectiones postea factas," sect. 4 "dubia," ad 1: "Nam si in dubium revocetur, quod legitur in legenda sancti Alexii et legenda beati Francisci; pari ratione in dubium venit quidquid legitur in legendis aliorum Sanctorum: ergo omnia exempla virtutum et gesta Sanctorum iam revocantur in dubium. Sed dubia imitari vel credere periculosum est; ac per hoc perit fides, devotio et reverentia, quae habetur in Sanctis, si in dubium revocentur cetera, quae narrantur de ipsis [For if the things we read in the *legenda* of Saint Alexius and blessed Francis were called into doubt, by the same token whatever we read in the *legenda* of any other saint comes into doubt: and therefore all the examples of the virtues and the deeds of the saints are called into doubt. But such hesitation (to imitate or to believe) is dangerous, and through such hesitation, the faith, devotion, and reverence which is had for the saints would be destroyed, if the other things that are narrated about them were called into doubt]."

32 Bonaventure, *De perfectione*, "Replicatio adversus objectiones postea factas," sect. 4 "dubia," ad 1: "Si miracula, quae fecerunt non sunt testimonia efficacia ad sanctitatem eorum astruendam, stultizat hodie Ecclesia, quae propter testimonia miraculorum sanctos canonizat [If the miracles which they worked are not testimony sufficient for establishing their sanctity, then the Church today, which canonizes saints on account of the testimony of miracles, acts a fool]." While some have taken this to be an implicit argument for the infallibility of canonizations (e.g., Schenk, *Die Unfehlbarkeit*, 14), it would be a rather weak argument—as Donald S. Prudlo rightly notes (*Certain Sainthood: Canonization and the Origins of Papal Infallibility in the Medieval Church* [Ithaca, NY: Cornell University Press, 2015], 126). But it need not be taken to speak of infallibility at all. And if it is not so taken then it is a strong argument. The argument is a *reductio*, and the impossibility it argues from is that the Church play the fool, by accepting identifiably fraudulent miracles as evidence of sanctity (what the objector was

What is important is that neither of these arguments needs to be read as implying that the Church infallibly teaches that saints are in heaven.[33] The first treats only their lives as known in the *legenda*. The second need only be taken to assert that it is censurable to imply that the Church has credulously accepted identifiably fraudulent miracles as a sign of sanctity.

Thus the timely and very practical context of Aquinas's speculative question, "whether all the saints who have been canonized by the Church are in glory, or whether some of them are in hell?" He considers two objections: first (as we already argued), that no one can be certain of another's state, just as he cannot be certain of his own;[34] second, that a judgment formed from a fallible middle is itself able to

---

implying). The impossibility is not that the Church err, but that it err in a way that makes it a fool. There is quite a bit that falls between being a credulous fool and being infallible. All Bonaventure's argument implies, then, is that the Church is not the former. And so read, the argument is strong and is open to none of the accusations of naiveté that could be brought against it were it implying infallibility.
33   Note that while shortly thereafter he writes, "est horribilissimum et incredibilissimum, quod Deus permitteret sic errare universaliter populum sanctum suum . . . " he has moved on to a new argument (this is labeled the "ad 2" by the editors) and is referring to error in ecclesiastical approval of religious orders, not to canonizations of saints, *pace* Prudlo (*Certain Sainthood*, 125). Moreover, while Prudlo cites Schenk as the source of this last quotation — and asserts that Schenk agrees with Tanner, Turrianus, and others that Bonaventure is here speaking of canonizations (*Certain Sainthood*, 126, fn. 10), the explicit purpose of the section in Schenk (*Unfehlbarkeit*, 12–14) is to show, rightly, that this passage (which the cited authors evidently were paraphrasing) is not actually speaking of canonizations but of the approval of religious orders. Prudlo falls into precisely the misunderstanding of these passages that his secondary source was quoting them in order to refute, and he is simply wrong to assert that Schenk concurs with Turrianus and Tanner.
34   Aquinas, *Quodlibet* IX, q. 8, arg. 1: "Nullus enim potest esse ita certus de statu alicuius sicut ipsemet, quia *quae sunt hominis* nemo nouit *nisi spiritus hominis qui in ipso est*, ut dicitur I Corinthiorum II [v. 11]; set homo non potest esse certus de se ipso utrum sit in statu salutis: Ecclesiastes IX [v. 1]: Nemo scit utrum sit dignus odio vel amore; ergo multo minus Papa scit; ergo potest in canonizando errare [For no one can be so certain of someone's state as the man himself, for no one knows the things of man but the spirit of the man which is in him, as it is said in I Cor 2:11, but man cannot be certain of himself whether he is in a state of salvation — Ecclesiastes 9:1: No one knows whether he is worthy of hate or love. Therefore much less does the Pope know, and therefore he can err in canonizing]" (Leonine ed., vol. 25/1–2).

err, but the Church relies on fallible human testimony in examining both the saint's life and miracles.[35] Aquinas's replies to both amount to asserting that God guides the pontiff and the Church, thus obviating the objections.[36] In neither of the replies does he attempt to prove that God does in fact guide the Church in these matters. That was the work of the corpus. Although they seem to assert more, all that the replies actually prove is that, *if* God guides the Church in canonization, then the objections are irrelevant. (It is worth noting that the reply to the second objection in particular does seem to assert such a guarantee of assistance. We will return to this in the conclusion.)

Aquinas presents a total of three arguments that canonized saints are all in heaven: two as arguments *sed contra*, and one in his response. The first of these arguments *sed contra* is straightforward, strong, and frequently cited:[37] "There can be no damnable error in the Church; but there would be a damnable error if one who was a sinner were venerated as a saint, for then some, knowing his sin or heresy, could be led into error, if this should happen. Therefore the Church cannot err in such matters."[38] The force of the argument is drawn from the

---

35 Aquinas, *Quodlibet* IX, q. 8, arg. 2, "Praeterea. Quicunque in iudicando innititur medio fallibili, potest errare; sed ecclesia in canonizando sanctos innititur testimonio humano, cum inquirat per testes de uita et miraculis; ergo, cum testimonium hominum sit fallibile, uidetur quod ecclesia in canonizando sanctos possit errare [Further, anyone who begins to judge with a fallible means of proof can err in judging; but the Church in canonizing the saints begins with human testimony, since it inquires into the life and miracles through witnesses; therefore since the testimony of man is fallible, it seems that the Church can err in canonizing saints]."

36 Aquinas, *Quodlibet* IX, q. 8, ad 1 ("Ad primum ergo dicendum quod pontifex, cuius est canonizare sanctos, potest certificari de statu alicuius per inquisitionem uite et attestationem miraculorum, et praecipue per instinctum Spiritus sancti, qui *omnia scrutatur, etiam profunda Dei*") and ad 2: "Ad secundum dicendum quod divina prouidentia praeseruat ecclesiam ne in talibus per fallibile testimonium hominum fallatur [divine providence preserves the Church lest she be deceived by the fallible testimony of men]."

37 E.g., Lambertini gives it as his first argument in favor of the infallibility of canonizations, *De beatificatione et canonizatione*, bk. I, ch. 43, no. 9 (p. 198). Interestingly he joins it with Cano's argument that it does not matter whether one worship a devil or a condemned soul; by joining them he seems to conflate two distinct sorts of moral error.

38 Aquinas, *Quodlibet* IX, q. 8, sc 1: "Set contra. In ecclesia non potest esse error dampnabilis; set hic esset error dampnabilis, si ueneraretur tamquam

fact that saints are held up as models of Christian virtue, and thus the canonization of a saint can be interpreted as a sort of moral teaching. This argument echoes Bonaventure's argument concerning the *legenda*'s being reliable moral guides.

The thrust of both Bonaventure's argument and Aquinas's first *sed contra* is evidently not—as some commentators[39] would have it be—that the saints are infallibly in heaven, but that their lives, such as they are known to us, are examples of Christian virtue and worthy of emulation. This is perfectly explicit in Bonaventure. In Aquinas, note that the impossible situation only follows if the sinner's sin is known. The Church does not lead anyone into damnable error if the canonized simply is not in heaven. The impossibility follows only if the person is not in heaven because of some *known* fault.

Moving to the second argument *sed contra*, we find a considerably weaker argument and it seems to have achieved a well-deserved obscurity in the tradition (although I would note that Aquinas does not necessarily approve of an argument *sed contra*). It starts from Augustine's point that, if we admit any lie in Scripture, our faith—which depends on Scripture—will be shaken.[40] It then concludes that: "Just as we are bound to believe that which is in sacred Scripture, so too that which is determined by the whole Church in common.... Therefore it is not possible that the common judgment of the whole Church should be in error, and so [we reach] the same [conclusion] as the preceding [argument]."[41] This argument proceeds by drawing a false equivalence between the magisterium's infallibility and Scripture's inerrancy. Augustine holds that we must not admit any error of any sort in Scripture because he holds that Scripture is truly inspired by

---

sanctus qui fuit peccator, quia aliqui scientes peccata eius uel heresim, si ita contigerit, possent ad errorem perduci; ergo ecclesia in talibus errare non potest."
39 Prudlo, *Certain Sainthood*, 124–25.
40 *Epistle* 28, ch. 3, nos. 3–4.
41 Aquinas, *Quodlibet* IX, q. 8, sc 2: "Praeterea. Augustinus dicit in epistola ad Ieronimum quod si in scriptura canonica aliquod mendacium admittatur, nutabit fides nostra, que ex scriptura canonica dependet; set, sicut tenemur credere id quod est in sacra scriptura, ita id quod communiter per ecclesiam determinatur, unde hereticus iudicatur qui sentit contra determinationem conciliorum; ergo commune iudicium ecclesiae erroneum esse non potest. Et sic idem quod prius."

God, such that God is truly its Author, and that therefore everything it asserts is truly asserted by God, who can neither deceive nor be deceived.[42] Magisterial teaching has never been understood as *inspired* in the manner Augustine holds Scripture to be. The only guarantee of infallibility that the Church has ever claimed the magisterium to have is when it teaches specifically on faith and morals.

If the argument followed, it would prove that the magisterium is guaranteed never to err in any way, regardless of subject matter. But with this discrepancy between the infallibility of the magisterium and the inspiration of Scripture noted, to proceed with the argument would beg the question, for an error in the Church's teaching justifies questioning the authority of the Church and the faith that the Church teaches *only if* the teaching concerns faith and morals (that is, if it is an error concerning the things that the Church is guaranteed to teach infallibly). But whether canonizations are among those things is precisely what is being disputed.[43] I consider this argument dispensed with and will not return to it.

We can then turn to the body. Most of Aquinas's response is spent discussing how God providentially provides for the Church, directing her though the Holy Spirit, lest she err in teaching things that are

---

42 Cf. Augustine, *In genesi ad litteram* 2.9.20: "Breviter dicendum est de figura coeli hoc scisse auctores nostros quod veritas habet; sed Spiritum Dei, qui per ipsos loquebatur, noluisse ista docere homines nulli saluti profutura [It must be stated very briefly that our authors knew the shape of the sky whatever may be the truth of the matter. But the Spirit of God who was speaking through them did not wish to teach people about such things which would contribute nothing to their salvation]" (Augustine, *On Genesis*, trans. Edmund Hill, O. P., ed. John E. Rotelle [Hyde Park, NY: New City Press, 2002]).

43 This point was made by Muratori: "Ceterum si in his contingeret error . . . nihil probri in Ecclesiam aut in Romanum Pontificem recideret, cum sacrorum Pastorum coelestis praerogativa sita sit in immunitate non ab omnibus erroribus, sed ab erroribus in doctrina Christi, et in factis per Apostolorum calamum aut vocem traditis. Ecclesiam in aliis falli posse jam vidimus sine dedecore suo, sine fidei detrimento [If some error arose in these things . . . nothing shameful would redound to the Church or to the Roman Pontiff, for the prerogative of the holy, heavenly Pastors lies not in immunity from all errors, but from errors in the teaching of Christ, and in the facts handed down through the voice or pen of the apostles. We have seen already that the Church can fail in other things without disgrace and without detriment to the faith]" (*De ingeniorum moderatione*, bk. I, ch. 17 [p. 77]; see Schenk, *Die Unfehlbarkeit*, 60).

"necessary for salvation." He distinguishes three classes of things that the Church judges. The first are those we just mentioned that concern what is necessary for salvation, and he says of these that "it is certain that it is impossible for the judgment of the universal Church to err in things which pertain to the faith."[44] The second class he mentions concerns particular matters of fact: "But in other matters — those which pertain to particular facts, as when the Church deals with possessions, or criminal cases, or others things of this sort — it is possible that the judgment of the Church err on account of false witnesses."[45] He then asserts that canonizations belong to a third class that falls between these other two. And he then immediately and somewhat puzzlingly proceeds, "yet because the honor we show the saints is a certain profession of faith, i.e., the faith by which we believe in the glory of the saints, it is a thing to be piously believed [*pie credendum est*] that the judgment of the Church could not err even in these matters."[46]

There are two things that need to be cleared up: The first is what sort of faith is indicated when he claims that honoring the saints is a "certain profession of faith"? The second is what is the force of the conclusion he draws from this fact, that is, what he means by *pie credendum est*. To the first issue, there are two ways of interpreting the veneration of saints as a "certain profession of faith." The first possible interpretation is that in honoring, for example, Augustine, I profess my faith that Augustine is in heaven; that is, the "certain profession of faith" refers to the faith in the glory of the specific individual in question.[47] But this is trivial — obviously honoring Augustine as a saint shows that I believe he is a saint. It also renders

---

44 Aquinas, *Quodlibet* IX, q. 8, corp.: "Certum est quod iudicium ecclesiae uniuersalis errare in hiis que ad fidem pertinent, impossibile est."

45 Aquinas, *Quodlibet* IX, q. 8, corp.: "In aliis uero sentenciis, que ad particularia facta pertinent, ut cum agitur de possessionibus uel de criminibus uel de huiusmodi, possibile est iudicium ecclesie errare propter falsos testes."

46 Aquinas, *Quodlibet* IX, q. 8, corp.: "Canonizatio uero sanctorum medium est inter hec duo; quia tamen honor quem sanctis exhibemus quedam professio fidei est, qua sanctorum gloriam credimus, pie credendum est, quod nec etiam in hiis iudicium ecclesiae errare possit."

47 This is how Prudlo reads the argument: "The faithful make a quasi-profession of faith in the glory of *the* saint" (*Certain Sainthood*, 128; emphasis mine). Although in the translation given in the appendix, he preserves the ambiguous plural.

the conclusion either rank question-begging or a patent *non sequitur.* How does the fact that I believe that Augustine is a saint pertain to *that* faith that carries a divine guarantee? When I cross the road, I make a certain profession of faith that Houston drivers will yield to pedestrians, but there is — alas — no divine guarantee that *that* faith is well placed, nor would there be such a guarantee even if the Church attempted to define it. Does, then, the specific faith whereby I believe that Augustine is a saint — and which I obviously profess in honoring him — have a guarantee of infallibility when the Church declares it? But that is of course precisely the matter in question. Moreover, if my faith that the individual saint is in heaven is the same faith which the Church is guaranteed to teach infallibly, then one would naturally need to place the canonization of the saints in the first class of judgments; that is, it would be of the faith, and thus a thing which the Church simply cannot err in teaching. But Aquinas is explicit that canonizations are not in that class of judgment.[48]

Hence we must consider the other way the phrase can be taken, that is, to refer to the fact that in honoring Augustine I profess my

---

48 St. Antoninus (d. 1459) draws attention to this point. After first examining Joannes Neopolitanus's treatment of this text of Aquinas — in the course of which John places canonizations among those things in which the Church cannot err, since "praeponuntur per canonizationem sancti ut exemplar fidei et sanctae vitae et ab omnibus adorandi, et in necessaribus sui invocandi [In canonization, the saints are proposed as an example of faith, and of holy life, as ones to be worshiped by all, and as ones to be invoked in their necessities]" — Antoninus continues here: "Sed Thomas in quodlib. ponit canonizationem sanctorum in tertio genere eorum, quae fiunt per Papam, de quibus dicit, quod etsi, Papa possit errare; pie tamen credendum est, quod Deus non permitteret ecclesiam in huiusmodi errare: et forte ratio est, quia et talis determinatio pertinet ad ecclesiam universalem; sit tamen per attestationes hominum quae fallere possunt [But in the quodlibet, Aquinas places the canonization of saints in a third category of things done by the pope, of which acts he says that, although the pope could err, it is still to be piously believed that God would not allow the Church to err in this way. The reason is that, while such a determination [of sanctity] pertains to the universal Church, it nonetheless comes about through the testimonies of men, which can mislead]" (*Summa theologica moralis* III, tit. 12, ch. 8 [Verona: Ex Typographia Seminarii, Apud Augustinum Carattonium, 1740], cols. 541–42). Again, Prudlo is simply wrong when he writes that "St. Antoninus ... [cites] John's quodlibet as evidence of infallibility in canonizations, and ... [claims] that John accurately relays Thomas's teaching" (*Certain Sainthood*, 173).

faith in the glory of the saints *generically*, that is, my faith that God glorifies those who love and serve him as he commands in the Gospel. Thus interpreted, the argument has force, for it successfully ties the canonization of a saint to something that the Church is known to be guaranteed to teach without error, for these divine promises are matters of revelation and faith, and they are necessary for salvation, and they thus fall under a guarantee of infallibility. This interpretation also shows how canonizations are midway between matters of particular fact and matters of faith. The matter of faith (concerning which the Church cannot err) is the general set of truths revealed about salvation, which makes belief in the glory of the saints intelligible, while the particular historical fact (of which the Church can err) is the particular facts of this person's life and eternal state.

But so interpreted, the reply proves little more than the first *sed contra* did. With "faith in the glory of the saints" so understood, the argument proves that it would be a denial of the very faith that the Church is guaranteed to teach faithfully for the Church to honor as a saint one whose life is known not to fulfill the demands of the Gospel, for *that* would be tantamount to denying the faith which was revealed in the Gospel, and which the Church is guaranteed to guard infallibly. If the Church were to propose as a saint someone whose life was known to include grave moral failures, it would thereby implicitly either falsify or distort the promises and demands of the Gospel. But if this is the faith the text is speaking of, the conclusion can claim no more than that the Church could not propose as a saint one whose life is *known* to have fallen short of sanctity. After all, in what sense could it amount to a denial of this faith in the demands and promises of Christ for the Church to honor one who ostensibly lived the Gospel calling, yet who secretly failed?

Consider the Salmanticenses' likening the assent owed to the canonization of a saint to that owed to a consecrated host.[49] I demonstrate

---

49   Collegii Salmanticensis, *Cursus theologicus*, vol. 7 (Lugduni: Sumptibus Joannis Antonii Huguetaan, et Sociorum, 1679), tract. 17 *(De fide)* disp. I, dub. 4, sect. 7, no. 149: "Ecclesia in canonizatione Sanctorum non proponit illorum beatitudinem ut credendam per fidem divinam, sed illorum personas ut colendas. Ut autem duliae cultum Sanctis tribuamus, opus non est, quod per fidem supernaturalem credamus illos dignos esse tali honore; sufficit enim inferior assensus,

in my act of adoration two sets of belief. One set pertains to the promise of Christ that he is truly and substantially present under the species of bread after the priest duly consecrates the host. The second is that this here and now before my eyes is a duly consecrated host. The first of these is the one I am bound to believe by faith, and which the Church is divinely guaranteed to teach faithfully, as it is the thing that God revealed. And my faith in that remains pure and untouched if I err in my second judgment, and either the man at the altar is not actually a priest, or the "host" is a rice cake, or the formula he used is invalid, or he was saying a dry Mass.

The second thing that must be cleared up is the strength of the conclusion. From his argument, Aquinas concludes not that "the Church cannot err" in these matters — which would directly answer the question under consideration — but that "it is a thing that is to be piously believed [*pie credendum est*] that the Church could not err." The two are of course not the same. We may wonder why one would assert that one should believe something, without also asserting that it is actually true, but it stands, first, that Aquinas does make a point of adding the qualification to his conclusion, and second, that the qualification effectively carves out the possibility that the Church might in fact err. We may at this point ask whether there was some reason he thought it necessary to qualify the conclusion this way.

And there was. The "should be piously believed" is not just an odd circumlocution serving to soften the conclusion for some unspecified purpose, but it is at the heart of the response itself. "Possible" and "impossible" are exhaustive and mutually exclusive. The third, middle category of judgment (to which Aquinas assigns canonizations) is distinguished from the first precisely in this: that it is not "*certain* that it is

---

ut ex adoratione, quam exhibemus erga hostiam probabiliter consecratam, aperte liquet [In the canonization of the saints, the Church does not propose their beatitude as a thing to be believed with divine faith but their persons as things to be honored. In order for us to give the honor of *dulia* to the saints, it is not necessary that we believe through supernatural faith that they are worthy of such honor; a lesser assent suffices, as is made obvious from the example of the adoration which we give to a host that is probably consecrated]" (p. 50). Lambertini treats this point in *De beatificatione et canonizatione*, bk. I, ch. 43, no. 23 (p. 210). Muratori offers the same example and analysis, *De Ingeniorum Moderatione*, bk. I, ch. 17 (p. 77).

impossible" but it is "*to be piously believed* that it would not be possible."
A thing that "one should piously believe would not be possible" is midway between a thing that is "certainly impossible" and a thing that is
unqualifiedly "possible." The "should piously believe" is thus integral
to the very structure of the article and should not be lightly dismissed.

A further consideration bears mention. Given the historical controversy from which this question was born, Aquinas had a vested
interest in giving the most forceful defense he could of the authority
of canonizations. Consequently, if Aquinas leaves open the possibility
of error in canonization — even if tacitly — we should think this was
deliberate. Had such a possibility not been left deliberately, given the
larger context of the question and its ramifications for the mendicant
dispute, we would expect Aquinas to have firmly and unambiguously
denied it. But he did leave the possibility open.

In short, in light of the arguments he adduces, I am reading Aquinas
to hold (albeit tacitly) that the Church might in fact err, but to hold
explicitly that (even if she did err) we ought not believe she has erred.
Now someone might well object that his concluding expression that
"it is to be piously believed that the Church cannot err" means not, as
I interpret it, that the Church *might* err though we ought not *believe*
she has, but instead means that it is a likely opinion that the Church
is simply inerrant in such decisions, such that it is less than pious to
admit even in the abstract the possibility that the Church could err
or has erred. I think the strongest response to this objection can be
drawn from Aquinas's historical context, to which we must now return.

THE LEGAL TRADITION

While Aquinas is generally acknowledged to have been the first
theologian to consider the issue directly, he was not the first scholar
to consider directly whether a canonization might be in error; by
the time Aquinas wrote this question, the issue had already been
discussed by the canon lawyers — and an early consensus (a consensus
which — according to Eric Kemp — would last for centuries[50]) had
begun to be forged.

---

50 Kemp, *Canonization and Authority*, 157: "The first person to be conscious
of any conflict between the canonists and the theologians on this matter seems
to have been the [seventeenth-century] Spanish Jesuit, Juan Azor."

The first canon lawyer to address the issue was Innocent IV (d. 1254). In commenting on the recently published Decretals of Gregory IX, he takes up the question of the pope's exclusive right to canonize saints. After defending this exclusive right, he directly considers the question of the possibility of a pope's erring in such a canonization. His treatment is short but significant. He writes, "even if the Church should have erred — which is not a thing that should be believed [*quod non est credendum*] — then God would accept prayers offered in good faith through such [a non-saint]." He continues by giving a reason for this argument: "We do not deny that it is licit for anyone to extend prayers to any deceased person — whom one believes a good man — in order that he might intercede for him before God: we deny only that he can make a solemn office or solemn prayers for him."[51]

Two things are significant in this brief passage, a passage Aquinas likely read.[52] The first is that Innocent explicitly makes the same distinction I argued was found in Aquinas, and he does so using the same vocabulary and grammatical structure Aquinas used. The Church might err, but we should not believe it has. Second, he gives an argument why it would not matter if the Church did err: God accepts prayers offered in good faith. Invincible ignorance does not diminish the efficacy of the prayer, nor does such error bring about some grave and irreparable harm, a belief seen in the fact that the Church does not forbid us to pray (albeit privately) to people who are not canonized, but whom the one praying sincerely believes to have been holy. Said otherwise, if praying in good faith to one who is not in heaven were to bring about some serious harm, and if God were not able to make up for our mistake, then it would be morally wrong to pray to

---

51 Innocent IV, *Apparatus in quinque libros decretalium*, bk. III, rub. 45, ch. 1, in "Audivimus": "Item non negamus, quin cuilibet liceat alicui defuncto, quem credebat bonum virum, porrigere preces, ut pro eo intercedat ad Deum: quia Deus fidem eorum attendit, negamus tantum pro eis licet facere officium solemne, vel preces solemnes." Slightly before this in ch. 1, he says: "Item dicimus, quod etiam si ecclesia erraret, quod non est credendum, tamen preces per talem bona fide porrectas Deus acceptaret" ("We say: even if the Church erred — which is not a thing to be believed — nonetheless God would accept prayers offered in good faith through [the intercession of] such [a false-saint]").

52 While such citations are rare, Aquinas cites this commentary already in his *In III Sent.*, d. 5, q. 3, a. 3, arg. 4.

one who is not certainly in heaven. But no one holds that it is wrong. Therefore there is no serious harm done, and God can supply for the errors in our prayers. One must not overlook the significance of this last point. Innocent is anticipating Cano's argument that it makes no difference whether we venerate a devil or a lost soul, not only rejecting it but offering a compelling, if brief, counterargument.

A second figure in this decretalist tradition who needs to be noted is Henry of Segusio, known as Hostiensis (d. 1271). In his commentary on the Decretals of Gregory IX,[53] he considers this question in the same context, and his conclusion follows Innocent IV quite closely: "If the Church erred in this canonization, which though it is not to be believed [*non est credendum*], still could happen" — here he directs the reader to his commentary on a canon concerning the possibility of error in excommunications — "nonetheless," he continues, "God accepts prayers extended in good faith in the honor of such an individual, for all things are made clean in the faith of Christ, and be it that the truth of the canonization is wanting, still his faith is not wanting."[54]

---

53 Would Aquinas have read this work or at least have been exposed to its arguments as he conducted *Quodlibet* IX? Kenneth Pennington records that Hostiensis lectured on the Decretals at Paris in the 1230s and further suggests that he wrote a first, now-lost, edition of his commentary on the Decretals at that time ("An Earlier Recension of Hostiensis's Lectura on the Decretals," *Bulletin of Medieval Canon Law* 17 [1987]: 77–90, at 81). He further dates the Oxford recension (the second of three if indeed he wrote one while at Paris) to the years 1254–1265. We know further that the 1275 taxation list from the University booksellers includes an entry for an *Apparatus Hostiensis*; see H. Denifle (*Chartularium Universitatis Parisiensis*, ed. A. Chatelain, vol. 1 [Paris: Ex typis fratrum Delalain, 1899], 648). Hence it is altogether possible that Aquinas would have had access to some form of this commentary (either the Paris version — whether a published text or a *reportatio* of the lectures — or the Oxford text). This conclusion is also endorsed by Torrell, who considers it certain that Aquinas read Hostiensis (*Thomas Aquinas*, 1:134n60): "Henry of Suso, Hostiensis . . . whom Thomas surely read . . ."

54 Hostiensis, *Lectura sive Apparatus Domini Hostiensis Super Quinque Decretalium Libros Commentaria*, bk. III, tit. 45 (*De reliquiis*), 1 (*Audivimus*): "Quid si Ecclesia in hac canonizatione erret, quod non est credendum, licet accidere possit, ut patet in eo, quod legitur et notatur infra De sententia excommunicationis, A nobis, [citation]. Dicas quod nihilominus preces in honorem talis bona fide porrectas Deus acceptat, [citation]. Omnia enim in fide Christi purgantur [citation]. Et esto, quod veritas canonizationis deficiat, non tamen deficit fides ipsius, sicut [citations regarding baptism]. Illud etiam non negamus quin cuilibet in secreto liceat aliqui defuncto quem credit sanctam preces porrigere, ut pro

Both of these decretalists are defending precisely the odd conclusion Aquinas appears to draw in his conclusion: that the Church might err, but we should not *believe* that the Church *has* erred. Moreover we find them using the same language that Aquinas employs to draw this distinction. And Hostiensis, not unlike Aquinas, draws on the fallibility of the Church in rendering judicial sentences to support the thesis.

A second thing that is quite significant is that both of these lawyers anticipate and directly address Cano's argument that it makes no difference whether you pray to a devil or a condemned man — an argument we already saw that Bellarmine weakened considerably when he noted that the false worship would be merely material. For both Innocent and Hostiensis, it perfectly well does make a difference whether you pray to a devil or a condemned man, assuming you pray to the condemned man in good faith. And both of them actually provide a strong argument for why it does matter.

The echo of the decretalists in Aquinas is striking. And I find it difficult to believe that someone could read these passages side by side and conclude, as Donald Prudlo does, that Aquinas is clearly rejecting the decretalists' "tidy canonical solution."[55] Had Aquinas meant to reject the then-current theory — that canonizations could be in error, though we should not think they were — we would expect him to distinguish himself clearly from that theory, rather than speak in a manner that could be naturally interpreted as being of a piece with the current consensus.

Very briefly, I would like to bolster this contention that Aquinas is in fact adopting the decretalists' position by looking at his subsequent commentators. In the course of correcting John of Naples's misinterpretation of Aquinas, St. Antoninus explicitly attributes to Aquinas the belief that the pope might be able to err in such acts as canonizations: "Thomas places the canonization of the saints in a third category of things done by the pope, of which things he says, that although the pope could err [*etsi Papa possit errare*], still it is piously to be believed that God would not permit His Church

---

ipso ad dominum intercedat: quia et Deus fidem eius attendit. Non tamen licet pro tali officium sollemne facere, vel preces sollemne publice emittere" ([Joannes Schottus, 1512], vol. 2, fol. 185).

55 Prudlo, *Certain Sainthood*, 129 and 76.

to err in this way."[56] Antoninus here makes explicit the possibility that Aquinas tacitly left standing. No matter how one reads this line, Antoninus is taking Aquinas to be bracketing the question of whether the pope can err, and only addressing what we should believe. In so doing, Antoninus places Aquinas in the decretalist tradition.

In the next century, we find Thomas de Vio Cajetan (d. 1534) also reading Aquinas thus, though he is even more explicit and forceful. In the course of defending indulgences, he draws a parallel between the granting of an indulgence and the canonization of a saint.[57] What he says about the fallibility of canonizations is perfectly clear. First, he notes that for the Church to err in canonization would not amount to a lie or a false teaching, since he says, "for what does not pertain to the faith is not understood to be affirmed or proclaimed except with a grain of salt."[58] That is, in canonizations there are two facts at play; one is essential, *de fide*, and the other is not, and only the former is to be taken to be asserted without qualification. This is a development of the point that I consider Aquinas to be making: canonizations are midway between matters of faith and particular matters of fact, in the sense that the judgment that this person is in heaven is a conclusion based on both the promise and demands of the Gospel and the particular fact that this

---

56   Latin produced above, see note 48.

57   Thomas de Vio Cajetan, *De indulgentiis in decem capita divisus*, ch. 8, in *Opuscula Omnia Reveren. D. D. Thomae de Vio* (Antwerp: Apud Viduam et haeredes Ioannis Stelsii, 1567), vol. 1, tract. 15, 96. An extended quotation from this passage is produced in Lambertini, *De beatificatione et canonizatione*, bk. I, ch. 43 (p. 196). Lambertini is explicit that Cajetan is adopting the decretalists' position.

58   Cajetan, *De indulgentiis in decem capita divisus*, ch. 8: "Ita quod dato, quod iste canonizatus non esset sanctus, sed damnatus, ecclesiae doctrina aut predicatio non esset mendax aut falsa: quia hic non pertinentia ad fidem non intelliguntur affirmari, et praedicari nisi cum grano salis, hoc est stantibus communiter praesumptis. Praesumit enim ecclesia canonizationem rite factam, et similiter indulgentiam rite datam: et sic praedicat indulgentias valere quantum sonant" ("taking it as granted [for the sake of argument] that this canonized saint is not holy, but damned, the doctrine and pronouncement of the Church would not be false or a lie: for what does not pertain to the faith is not understood to be affirmed and proclaimed except with a grain of salt, that is, with the things commonly presumed in place. For the Church presumes that the canonization has been duly carried out, and likewise that the indulgence has been duly granted: and therefore that the indulgence really is as good as it sounds"); also cited in Lambertini, *De beatificatione et canonizatione*, 196.

person fulfilled the demands and merited the promise. The Church is only guaranteed not to err concerning the first of these two, because the purpose of the Church's authority is only to teach the first — the second is purely ancillary to the end of the Church's teaching office. In putting it thus, Cajetan touches with a needle the error in Aquinas's second argument *sed contra*. Cajetan continues, asserting without qualification that "a human error can intervene in the canonization of some saint (as S. Thomas says),"[59] and lest there be any ambiguity, he claims that, "if someone believes that the Roman Pontiff cannot err in these particular acts . . . he also believes the pontiff is not human."[60]

What of the possibility of our detecting errors in such judgments? He ruled this out at the beginning of the passage: "By law the presumption is in favor of the judge, unless there is a manifest error."[61] But he later warns that one should not try to determine in which cases there is such an error "unless one wishes to be wrong."[62] Cajetan, like the decretalists, is perfectly clear that the Church *could* err in canonization.[63] Yet he also holds that we should not think the Church has erred in any particular case — the presumption is always given to

---

59 Cajetan, *De indulgentiis in decem capita divisus*, ch. 8: "Sed sicut potest intervenire error humanus in canonizatione alicuius Sancti (ut san. Tho. dicit) ita potest intervenire error humanus in collatione indulgentiae."

60 Cajetan, *De indulgentiis in decem capita divisus*, ch. 8: "Si quis autem putet Rom. pontif. non posse errare in istis particularibus actionibus (quales sunt dispensationes bonorum, tam temporalium quam spiritualium ecclesiae) putet quoque ipsum non esse hominem." While this line is explicitly referring to the granting of indulgences, the point of the whole passage is that indulgences and canonizations are alike in being open to error.

61 Cajetan, *De indulgentiis in decem capita divisus*, ch. 8: "Praesumitur enim de iure pro iudice semper, nisi manifeste appareat error, et supponens ex causa legitima datam tantam indulgentiam, veritatem praedicat: sicut absque falsitate praedicat talem sanctum, supponens illum [esse?] canonizatum."

62 Cajetan, *De indulgentiis in decem capita divisus*, ch. 8: "ideo noli velle iudicare, an ista vel illa causa posita in indulgentia sit sufficiens, si non vis errare." Again, while the line is explicitly speaking of indulgences, none the less the force of the passage is precisely likening them to canonizations in this respect.

63 Lambertini forthrightly acknowledges that Cajetan is adopting their position (*De beatificatione et canonizatione*, 196). Hence Prudlo is simply wrong to assert that no one after the fourteenth century held the decretalists' position (*Certain Sainthood*, 177). Further, as noted earlier, this decretalist position also seems to have survived into the seventeenth century among the lawyers.

the judge unless an error is manifest, and we are not in a position to judge the Church. But notice not just that he adopts the decretalists' position, but that he attributes it to Aquinas. While Cajetan certainly is not an infallible interpreter of Aquinas, neither is he a stranger to Aquinas's thought. If he thought Aquinas held the decretalists' position, it should, I suggest, give pause to anyone who insists that Aquinas is manifestly rejecting it.

After a consideration of historical context combined with careful analysis of their actual texts (setting aside anachronistic categories and assumptions), it is, I would argue, no great stretch to place Innocent IV, Hostiensis, Bonaventure, Aquinas, Antoninus, and Cajetan on the same line, defending essentially the same attitude toward the authority of canonizations. It may, then, have been only through a series of errors that Aquinas came to be regarded as the *dux omnium qui pugnant pro summi Pontifici infallibilitate*. But as fascinating as the possibility may be that Aquinas was adopting the decretalists' position, ultimately what matters is not what Aquinas believed, but what his oft-cited arguments actually prove. And on that question I am quite confident: they prove something less than simple infallibility.

CONCLUSIONS

Before we conclude, we must ask: Why the incongruous discrepancy between fact and belief proposed by the decretalists, Cajetan, and, I would argue also, both Bonaventure and Aquinas? If the Church might well err, why should we not sometimes believe she has? Two things need to be noted.

First, briefly consider the four remaining arguments for the infallibility of canonizations that have not been dispensed with. The first is that the veneration of the saints is a certain profession of faith. We noted already that the faith the Church is guarded from error in teaching is the faith that God rewards with eternal glory those who respond appropriately to the Gospel. While that faith would be implicitly denied if the Church proposed as a saint one whose life was known not to have conformed to the Gospel's call to holiness, it is not compromised if, through invincible ignorance, the Church makes an error of fact in determining who so responded, just as my faith in the real presence of Christ in the Eucharist is not compromised if I make a factual error about whether the host before me now has been duly consecrated, although it would be compromised if I offered *latria* to a host I knew not to be consecrated.

Second, if we consider Aquinas's argument from the first *sed contra*, namely, that if the Church could err in canonization she might lead people into moral error by proposing a sinner as a saint, it should be noted, again, that scandal is given, and moral confusion arises, only if the sin is known. The argument, by its own force, cannot preclude the possibility either of a hidden sin or that the person is not in heaven because he never existed, as is clear in the text itself. The same is also true of Bonaventure's defense of the *legenda* as worthy moral examples.

Third, if we consider Cano's argument from the practice of the Church, namely, that if we could doubt the status of the saint, we could reject the universal practice of the Church in venerating the saints, or if we consider Bellarmine's more subtle version of the argument that we could find ourselves in a crisis of conscience (bound by the Church's authority to honor one as a saint whom we believe positively unworthy of such veneration), then we may note that the impossibilities follow only if we have a sound reason to doubt the Church's judgment. Indeed Bellarmine's conclusion is explicitly *not* that the saint is in fact in heaven, but that one is *not permitted to doubt* that the saint should be venerated — which is nothing else than the view of the decretalists and is exactly what I am suggesting was Aquinas's view.

Finally, if we consider Cano's argument that it makes no difference whether one venerate a demon or a condemned soul, this argument was anticipated and refuted by the decretalists: it makes no difference if the veneration of a condemned man was offered knowingly. Venerating a condemned soul out of invincible ignorance is no formal sin, and it causes no irreparable harm.

Each of these is a strong argument and each proceeds as a *reductio ad absurdum*. Yet the absurdities they leverage are all avoided if the Church can never propose as a saint one who lived and died in a way that was patently not an appropriate response to the Gospel's call to holiness. *That* is the conclusion supported by the arguments. None of these absurdities follows if the one who is canonized is excluded from glory because of some hidden, secret fault, nor do they follow if the person in question is purely legendary.

The second thing that must be noted to explain the disparity between fact and belief is that, if the above arguments successfully prove that the Church could not propose as a saint a person whose life patently did not merit heaven, then it follows that the faithful will never have an objectively sound reason to call a canonization into question; as Cajetan pointed out, the competent authority to judge receives the benefit of the doubt, unless an error is manifest (a point wholly in line with Bonaventure's argument that we accuse the Church of playing the fool if we deny that miracles are trustworthy indications of holiness). But the one thing that the arguments we have considered validly concluded was precisely that there could never be a manifest error in canonizations. Hence, it will necessarily be rash, temerarious, and presumptuous for a member of the Church to deny the sanctity of a canonized saint. As Cajetan noted, one should not try to find an error in such judgment, unless one wishes to be wrong.

These last two points may also shed light on Aquinas's treatment of the subject, and in particular his reply to the second objection. If Aquinas is defending the decretalists' consensus, then his assertion of providential assistance should be read (in light of the argument in the corpus) as a qualified assistance that prevents the Church from falling into a particular sort of error, namely, the error of proposing as a saint one whose life is marred by grave and known moral fault, thereby falsifying the Gospel and leading the faithful into error in matters necessary for salvation. So read, his unique contribution to this tradition would be, for the first time, offering an explanation for why (as the decretalists held) the faithful are never to reject a saint, even though the canonization could have been wrong. That was, we might note, all that the mendicants needed to prove to defend their orders.

Hence I propose two things. First, the Church does possess a real sort of divinely guaranteed infallibility in canonizations; this is not however the infallibility theologians since Lambertini typically assign canonizations. According to the conclusion I believe we can reach with certitude, the faithful can be sure that the Church will never impose on the whole

Church the *cultus* of one whose life is manifestly not in conformity with the call of the Gospel — said otherwise, it is guaranteed that the saints led lives worthy of veneration and imitation insofar as we know them.[64] Consequently, the Church cannot err in canonization insofar as the Church, in proposing a saint as a model of Christian virtue, thereby indirectly teaches concerning morals, which the Church is guaranteed to teach infallibly. But this infallibility, of itself, does not guarantee that each canonized saint is ultimately in heaven, or actually died in a state of grace, or even that he existed. It guarantees only that the person's life as it is known is worthy of emulation and glory, leaving intact the fact that our knowledge of such things is necessarily limited and only probable. The Church's determinations of such matters, which are not of themselves *de fide* or *de necessariis ad salutem*, are to be taken *cum grano salis*, while only those implicit assertions that touch on what is necessary for salvation are guaranteed to be inerrant. Canonizations, so understood, are like liturgical norms which, though not infallible, are nonetheless guaranteed not to contradict the Faith. The likeness to liturgical norms is fitting given that a canonization is in fact a form of liturgical norm determining whom the Church venerates.[65]

Second and consequently, although one may — I think — hold that the Church *could* err in canonizing, one may not hold that the Church *has* erred in any given canonization without thereby incurring the censure of temerity. One will never have an objectively sound reason to deny the sanctity of any particular saint.

My claim, then, is that the arguments from the theological tradition used to defend the absolute infallibility of canonizations are insufficient

---

64 It is worth noting the congruity between this conclusion and the reserved claim of the *Catechism of the Catholic Church*, §828: "By canonizing some of the faithful, i.e., by solemnly proclaiming that they practiced heroic virtue and lived in fidelity to God's grace, the Church recognizes the power of the Spirit of holiness within her and sustains the hope of believers by proposing the saints to them as models and intercessors."

65 Indeed, Muratori understood canonizations as disciplinary rather than doctrinal acts: "Disciplinae leges eorum cultum ita indicere possunt, et ad universam Ecclesiam extendere, ut non solum pium ac laudabile sit, hujusmodi Sanctos invocare, et sibi adsciscere patronos apud Deum, sed etiam impietatem sapiat eorum cultum improbare, atque contemnere" (*De ingeniorum moderatione*, bk. I, ch. 17 [p. 76]).

to establish such a guarantee.⁶⁶ In short, I hold that it is no more than a mistaken, if pious, opinion that canonizations are infallible declarations that the saint is in heaven, and therefore, that to insist that they are infallible is to open the faith to ridicule and to erect a very real and unnecessary barrier to true Christian unity. But of course, I submit to the Church's determination of the matter if and when it is given.⁶⁷

---

66 Indeed I am not sure that many of the historical authors advancing them understood themselves to be defending infallibility in the modern theological sense of the term. I cannot read Bellarmine's arguments, with as many unambiguous qualifications as he provides, and conclude that he means to ascribe to canonizations the sort of infallibility that was defined at Vatican I. Aside from what has already been treated, note the fourth argument that Bellarmine provides: If we do not doubt the existence of Pompey and Caesar (though attested to only by fallible historians) why would we not believe in the sanctify of the saints when it is attested through miracles? Although "miracula magna, et diligenter examinata, faciunt rem evidenter credibilem [great and diligently examined miracles make a thing evidently credible]" (*De sanctorum beatitudine*, ch. 9), such evident credibility obviously does not amount to a divinely revealed guarantee of magisterial infallibility, and Bellarmine certainly realized this. One might do well here to note the case of Augustinus Triumphus, who explicitly defends the inerrancy of the Church in canonization, and who was (until Lambertini) commonly cited in defense of the infallibility of canonizations. While he said the pope "non errat," he first qualified, "secundum praesentem justitiam," speaking of which human justice he says "potest falli et fallere," which amounts to saying the pope cannot lie (though he can err) — or as Lambertini summarizes, the pope may "materialiter mentiatur" (see Augustinus Triumphus, *De potestate ecclesiae*, q. 14, a. 4, as well as Lambertini, *De beatificatione et canonizatione*, bk. I, ch. 43, no. 3 [pp. 196–97]). Even as recently as 1907, Beccari, in the *Catholic Encyclopedia*, puzzlingly writes: "Theologians generally agree as to the fact of papal infallibility in this matter of canonization, but disagree as to the quality of certitude due to a papal decree in such matter. . . . [The majority hold] such a pronouncement to be theologically certain, not being of Divine Faith as its purport has not been immediately revealed, nor of ecclesiastical Faith as having thus far not been defined by the Church" (2:367). How can a papal decree be infallible while falling under neither divine nor ecclesiastical faith? What sense is there in calling an infallible decree merely *certa?* While I confess I may be missing some subtlety, it seems to me that either there is at least an implicit divine guarantee that formal canonizations be true (in which case the individual's sanctity and beatitude will be *de fide ecclesiastica*) or there is no such guarantee (and in that case there is no theological basis for claiming that the teaching is simply infallible).

67 It may be worth here noting that in their "Doctrinal Commentary on the Concluding Formula of the *Professio fidei*" (issued concurrently with John Paul II's *Ad Tuendam Fidem*), Joseph Ratzinger and Tarcisio Bertone include the canonizations of saints as an example of a truth "connected to revelation

In discussions of God's guarantees to the Church, the onus falls to those defending some guarantee to show either that it is explicit in revelation or that it is necessary for the Church to carry out her divine mission. To the first, Christ made no explicit promise that the Church can discern without error who is in heaven. To the second, the purpose of the visible Church is to make saints of the living, not of the dead.[68]

---

by historical necessity" and therefore "to be held definitively" (no. 13). Dulles notes (*Magisterium*, 91, esp. note 12) that presumably the authors did not mean to settle current controversies in proposing this as an example, and he quotes Ratzinger's later clarification: "The listing of some doctrinal examples as examples does not grant them any other weight than what they had before" (from Ratzinger, "Stellungnahme," *Stimmen der Zeit* 217 [1999]: 168–71). See also Dulles, *Magisterium*, 86n7, where Dulles discusses the authority of this commentary, noting that "it does not emanate from the Congregation as such" and yet it was "composed by the Congregation as a whole and approved by the cardinals in assembly and also by the pope."

68   Which raises a line of argument we do not have space to follow, namely, the historical incongruities. If (as, e.g., Suárez claims) the canonization of saints is "re maxime necessaria Ecclesiae," how did the Church manage to struggle on for the first millenium with no formally canonized saints? As Muratori argued: "Quomodo vero dicamus necessarium hominibus, fidei et Ecclesiae esse cultum novi alicuius sancti, fidemque de illius beatitate coelesti? *Utile* est, non necessarium ista habere, ista scire. Innumerae aliae veritates sunt, quas novisse in utilitatem Christianorum cederet, et illas tamen certo decernere numquam sibi tribuit aut tribuere potest Ecclesia" ("But how do we say that the cult of some new saint and the faith in his heavenly beatitude are necessary for men, for the faith, and for the Church? To have such things — to know such things — is *useful*, not necessary. There are innumerable other truths that it would be useful for Christians to know, and yet the Church never grants to herself nor could she grant to herself [the task and ability] to discern them with certainty") (*De ingeniorum moderatione*, bk. I, ch. 17 [p. 77]). See also Schenk, *Die Unfehlbarkeit*, 60–61. On the other hand, if the very universality of the cult in the Church is what forms the basis of the guarantee (as the argument from the Church's practice seems to suppose), would not those saints honored in the Church's calendar without formal canonization be just as certainly saints? And yet we have numerous cases of universally venerated saints being removed from the calendar because of every sort of historical uncertainty (e.g., St. Sabina or the very Alexius whose example was cited and defended by Bonaventure; see in particular *Calendarium Romanum: Ex Decreto Sacrosancti Oecumenici Concilii Vaticani II Instauratum Auctoritate Pauli PP. VI Promulgatum* [Rome: Typis Polyglottis Vaticanis, 1969], 68–70) or of widely venerated saints whose cult was suppressed because of new historical knowledge of the individual (Barlaam and Josaphat) or a reevaluation of the previously established facts (St. Philomena). I would like to thank Eric J. DeMeuse, for his numerous helpful comments on this paper, and William H. Marshner.

5
Infallibility and Canonizations: A Disputation[†]

THOMAS CREAN, O.P.

I. PRELIMINARIES

The question of whether canonizations are infallible can have several meanings. It could mean: "Is it certain that the canonized person is saved, i.e., that he is not in hell?" It could mean: "Is it certain that the canonized person is now in heaven?" Again, it could mean: "Is it certain that the canonized person is in heaven and is worthy of veneration on account of the eminent holiness of his or her life on earth?" The third formulation, which is substantially that of the *Catechism of the Catholic Church*,[1] doubtless corresponds best to what Catholics understand a canonized saint to be. Hence, in his monumental work *On the Beatification and Canonization of the Servants of God*, Prospero Lambertini, for many years Promoter of the Faith ("devil's advocate"), and later to reign as Pope Benedict XIV, offers this definition:

> In a canonization, the supreme pontiffs do nothing other than to declare that certain servants of God who are resplendent by reason of their virtues, their remarkable death, and their extraordinary miracles, and who thus are triumphant in heaven, must be venerated by the Church.[2]

---

1 *Catechism of the Catholic Church*, 828.
2 *De servorum Dei beatificatione et beatorum canonizatione* (Padua, 1743), Bk. I, ch. 12.8: "In Canonizatione, Summos Pontifices nihil aliud agere dicimus, quam declarare hos et illos Dei Servos virtutibus, insigni morte, eximiisque miraculis praefulgentes et sic in Caelo triumphantes esse in Ecclesia colendos."

† The author thanks Dr. Alan Fimister, Dr. John Joy and Fr. Reginald-Marie Rivoire FSVF for their comments on an earlier draft of this chapter, and Timothy Wilson for his help in locating some of the books discussed in it. This work appears here for the first time.

Elsewhere, the same author explains that infants who have been baptized but who died before the age of reason are not apt for canonization even though they are in glory and enjoy the beatific vision, because they did not possess heroic virtue while on earth.[3] He also notes that the veneration to be given to canonized saints consists in seven things: their names are placed in the roll of the saints;[4] they are invoked in public prayers; altars and churches may be erected in their honor; Mass may be said in their honor; they are assigned a feast day in the calendar; they may be displayed with a halo in public images; and their relics may be publicly honored.[5]

Not all authors explicitly include heroic virtue in their definition of canonization. St. Robert Bellarmine writes:

> A canonization is nothing other than the public testimony of the Church to the true holiness and glory of some person who is now deceased; and at the same time, it is a judgment and decision by which those honors are decreed for him which are due to those who are reigning with God in bliss.[6]

St. Thomas Aquinas likewise speaks simply of the saints as those in glory, without considering the question of heroic virtue.[7] We may of course suppose that had the question been put to them, these authors would have agreed that infants dying before the age of reason were not apt for canonization, as this has never been the Church's practice. In what follows, I shall however follow the example of St. Thomas and understand canonization as the official, papal declaration that the

---

3 Ibid., ch. 14.3. Sinibaldo dei Fieschi (= Innocent IV) had made the same point in his commentary on the decretals, *Apparatus in quinque libros decretalium* (Frankfurt, 1570), Bk. III, tit. 43, ch. 1.3.

4 Since, as he goes on to explain, the "roll (*catalogus*) of the saints" is not a material book but simply the totality of those who have been publicly proclaimed to the Christian people as saints and worthy of veneration, this hardly differs from the canonization itself.

5 *De servorum Dei*, Bk. 1, ch. 38.1.

6 *Disputationes de controversiis christianae fidei* (Milan, 1858) [hereafter, *De Controversiis*], "On the Church triumphant," Bk. 1, ch. 7: "Canonizatio nihil est aliud, quam publicum Ecclesiae testimonium de vera sanctitate, et gloria alicuius hominis iam defuncti: et simul est iudicium ac sententia, qua decernuntur ei honores illi, qui debentur iis, qui cum Deo feliciter regnant."

7 *Quaestiones quodlibetales*, IX.8.

soul of the canonized person is now in heavenly glory.[8] I shall call "inerrantism" the opinion that canonization so defined will always be true; the opposite position I shall call "errantism."

2. HISTORICAL SURVEY

Since canonizations in the modern sense did not exist in the patristic period, we naturally do not find a discussion of our question in the Fathers of the Church. Nevertheless, later authors sometimes adduce two patristic quotations as tending to support inerrantism. St. Augustine is quoted for his statement in a letter to one Januarius that it would be "the height of arrogant madness" to discuss whether or not we should comply with something done by the whole Church in the celebration of the Mass of Maundy Thursday.[9] From this, some authors draw the principle that something done by the whole Church in the celebration of the liturgy, for example the honoring of a particular saint, cannot be in error. Again, authors cite St. Gregory the Great's letter of 591, "Consideranti mihi," sent to the Eastern patriarchs. Speaking of the first five ecumenical councils, and of the persons anathematized by them, the pope declared:

> All those persons whom these venerable councils reject, I reject; those whom they venerate, I embrace; for, since these things have been established by universal acceptance, the person who presumes to loose what they have bound, or to bind what they have loosed, destroys not them but himself.[10]

Although the subject of the letter was doctrinal rectitude rather than sanctity, certain authors argue by analogy that no one venerated by the universal Church can be unworthy of veneration.[11]

We may also mention a passage from St. Bernard, also sometimes quoted by inerrantists. In a letter sent to the canons of Lyons, the Mellifluous Doctor wrote: "For my part, I confidently hold on to what I have received from the Church, and I pass it

---

8 Other authors in this book will take issue with this minimalist definition of what canonization means. — *Ed.*

9 *Letter* 54.6.

10 Quoted in DH 472.

11 For example, Suárez, *De Fide* (from *Opus de triplici virtute theologica: fide, spe, et charitate*, Lyon, 1621), disp. 5, sect. 8.8.

on."[12] The context of his words was the need to preserve the feast-days of the Blessed Virgin which are customary in the Church, and not to introduce new ones by private authority without the approbation of the church of Rome. From this, one might deduce that it will be at least unlawful to put in doubt the holiness of a person whose feast is generally celebrated in the Church.

It is apparently only in the thirteenth century that the question began to be raised of the fallibility or infallibility of canonizations. This was no doubt a consequence of the fact that the Church's law began at this time to reserve canonizations to the Holy See.[13] The first author known to have addressed the question is Sinibaldo dei Fieschi, later to reign as Pope Innocent IV. He states somewhat ambiguously that "even if the Church should err, which is not to be believed, God would nevertheless accept prayers made in good faith through such a one," that is, through a canonized person who is not in heaven.[14] It is not clear whether the parenthetic clause means that one should believe that such a false canonization will not occur, or that one should not believe that it will occur (i.e., that one should suspend one's judgment about the possibility of such a thing), or that one should not believe in a given case that it has occurred.

The canonist Henry of Segusio (d. 1271), also called Hostiensis, whilst otherwise using the same words as Sinibaldo in his commentary on the same part of the *Decretals*, adds after "which is not to be believed" the clause *licet accidere possit*, "although it can happen."[15] An anonymous glossator commenting on another text in the *Decretals* expresses the same opinion as Henry.[16] A somewhat later canonist, Felino Sandeo (= Felinus, 1444–1503), likewise thought it easier to

---

12   *Letter* 174.2: "Ego quae accepi ab Ecclesia, securus teneo, et trado."
13   In 1234, St. Raymond of Peñafort inserted into the *Decretals* the decree "Audivimus" written by Pope Alexander III to the King of Sweden in 1171–72, saying that no one ought to be venerated as a saint without the consent of the Roman Church; see D. Prudlo, *Certain Sainthood: Canonization and the Origins of Papal Infallibility in the Mediaeval Church* (Ithaca and London: Cornell University Press, 2015), 71–72.
14   *Apparatus*, Bk. 3, tit. 45, ch. 1.4 (457).
15   *In tertium decretalium librum commentaria* (Venice, 1581), *Audivimus*, 10 (172).
16   *Liber sextus decretalium* (Rome, 1582), *De Reliquis*, tit. XXII (582).

support the opinion that an error in canonization was possible.[17] All
these authors are mentioned by Lambertini as the principal authorities
for errantism among canon lawyers.[18]

St. Thomas Aquinas was apparently the first theologian to consider
our question explicitly. As we shall see, he concludes that it is to be
devoutly believed [*pie credendum est*] that the Church's judgment does
not err in canonizing the saints. He is thus described by Lambertini as
the "leader," *dux*, of inerrantism.[19] Among later theologians, the only
major figure to espouse the contrary opinion appears to be Cajetan,
who in his work *De indulgentiis* states in passing that a pope could err
in canonizing, as he could err in assigning an indulgence for an insufficient cause. He notes, however, speaking explicitly about indulgences
but by implication also about canonizations, that the presumption is
always in favor of the one in authority, unless the error be obvious.[20]

The shock of the Reformation appears to have purged even this
minority errantist opinion from Catholic theology. Writing a lifetime after Cajetan, St. Robert Bellarmine could affirm that there are
only two views on the question: that of the heretics, who say that a
pope can err in canonizing saints, and that of the Catholics, who say
that he cannot.[21] This contrasts strikingly with his discussion of, for
example, the possibility of a heretical pope, and of the best manner

---

17 *Commentaria in decretalium libros V* (Basle, 1567), t. II, *De testibus et
attestationibus*, ch. 52.2–3 (825).

18 *De servorum Dei*, Bk. 1, ch. 43.3.

19 *De servorum Dei*, Bk. 1, ch. 43.4: "Dux omnium est Sanctus Thomas." This
standard interpretation of St. Thomas has recently been challenged by William
Matthew Diem, "The Infallibility of Canonizations: A Revisionist History of the
Arguments," *Nova et Vetera*, English Edition, 17.3 (2019): 653–82. [Reproduced
herein as chapter 4; references will henceforth be made to page numbers in the
present volume.—*Ed.*]

20 *Opuscula* (Lyons, 1575), t. I, treatise 15, *De indulgentiis*, ch. 8 (96). One might
also mention here the name of Augustine of Ancona (= Augustinus Triumphus,
d. 1328), who held that a pope would never err in canonizations in regard to
the available evidence, but might err absolutely speaking; *Summa de potestate
ecclesiastica* (Rome, 1584), q. 14, a. 4 (97–98).

21 *De Controversiis*, "On the Church triumphant," Bk. 1, ch. 9: "Certum esse
Ecclesiam non errare in Sanctorum canonizatione, ita ut sine ulla dubitatione
sancti ab Ecclesia canonizati venerandi sint." Although he speaks of the "Church,"
rather than "the pope," this is not significant, since in the rest of the chapter he
makes it clear that he is speaking of a saint canonized by the pope.

of responding to such an emergency, where Bellarmine distinguishes five different opinions held by Catholic authors. By the eighteenth century, Lambertini could write:

> This judgment, of the infallibility of the supreme pontiff in canonizing, according to the teaching of St. Thomas, is defended by all theologians, both by the disciples of St. Thomas, and by those of Scotus; and those others who are called "Moderns" (*neoterici*) unanimously agree with them.[22]

Among the moderns, Lambertini mentions Bellarmine, Suárez, and Gabriel Vasquez. He is aware of the mildly errantist position of the earlier canonists, but cites none later than Felino Sandeo, mentioned above, while citing many on the other side. This suggests that he is not aware of errantism as a continuing opinion among canon lawyers.[23] This consensus continued into the twentieth century, with the standard manuals and encyclopedias stating either straightforwardly that canonizations are infallible, or, more cautiously, that it is the common opinion that they are. The non-magisterial "Commentary on the Concluding Formula of the *Professio Fidei*" published by the CDF in 1998 is a late echo of this consensus.

Of importance also is the fact that prominent authors in the post-Reformation period state not only that canonizations are infallible, but also that those who deny the infallibility of canonizations, whether in general or in particular, are not simply in error, but are guilty of an offense, and thus worthy of censure. We have seen that Bellarmine treats errantism as a mark of heresy; the Dominican theologian Melchior Cano (d. 1560) describes it as rash, imprudent, and irreligious,[24] while Suárez calls it impious and rash.[25] Lambertini, likewise, treats it as not only false but unlawful, and dedicates a

---

22 *De servorum Dei*, Bk. 1, ch. 43.5 (258).
23 On the other hand, he is aware of the writings of the historian Ludovico Muratori (=Lamindus Pritanius, 1672–1750). Muratori denied that Catholics were obliged to accept inerrantism, but added that "this rite [canonization] is now so accurately and carefully carried out by the Apostolic See that one should have a devout belief [*pie credendum sit*] that there has been no room for error in this matter, nor will there be"; *De ingeniorum moderation in religionis negotio* (Frankfurt, 1716), Bk. 1, ch. 17 (152).
24 *De locis theologicis*, Bk. 5, ch. 5.5.
25 *De Fide*, disp. 5, sect. 8.8.

chapter of his treatise to considering whether it is to be censured as heretical or with some lesser note. In the end, he leaves the question undecided, but concludes that a man who affirms that the pope has erred in this or that canonization is

> even if not a heretic, nevertheless rash, a bringer of scandal to the whole Church, injurious to the saints, favoring heretics who deny the authority of Church to canonize, savoring of heresy insofar as he opens a way to unbelievers to mock the Faith, an assertor of erroneous propositions and liable to severe penalties.[26]

Among more modern authorities, while some, by teaching the inerrantist position as simply "the common opinion," apparently treat the errantist one as lawful, others follow by implication the severity of Lambertini. Thus T. Ortolan, writing in the *Dictionnaire de théologie catholique*, asserts that it is "implicitly of divine faith" that the pope is infallible in canonizing in general, and of ecclesiastical faith that he is infallible in having canonized this or that person.[27]

The weight of theological opinion thus naturally inclines us toward accepting inerrantism; but do the official statements of the Church herself oblige us to do so? The popes and ecumenical councils have not directly enjoined the inerrantist position in the abstract in their magisterial or legal acts. On the other hand, they have by no means always left Catholics free to accept canonizations or not, as they saw fit. John XV's canonization in 993 of St. Ulric is sometimes reckoned the first solemn canonization by a pope, and the bull of canonization declares anathema anyone who refuses it.[28] In 1173, Alexander III became the first pope personally to address a bull of canonization to the whole Church. Canonizing Thomas Becket, he addressed all Catholic prelates in these terms: "We warn you and the whole Church, that by the authority that we discharge, we strictly command that you solemnly celebrate the feast of the said glorious Martyr annually on the anniversary of his death."[29] The formula

26 *De servorum Dei*, Bk. 1, ch. 43.28.
27 In the article, "Canonisations dans l'Eglise romaine," IV.2.
28 Quoted by Lambertini, *De servorum Dei*, Bk. 1, ch. 45.27 (277).
29 See Prudlo, *Certain Sainthood*, 37–38. The author notes: "It is from this date that papal bulls presume that the honor paid to their new saints would be

itself of canonization was "formalized, elevated, and standardized" during the thirteenth century.[30] Since then it has concluded with some such words as "decernimus et definimus N ... sanctorum cata-logo ascribendum" ("we decree and define that X is to be enrolled in the list of the saints"), and generally with a command that he or she be venerated by the Christian people. The word *definimus* implies, at least, a judgment not admitting of appeal; as for the command, this imposes a positive obligation at least on those bound to perform liturgical actions according to a calendar into which the saint is placed, while it apparently imposes at least a negative obligation on the whole people not to deny that the one canonized is in glory.[31]

In the light of all this, we may now consider what has been, or could be, said on either side of the question.

3. ARGUMENTS FOR INERRANTISM

St. Thomas defends inerrantism in the *Quodlibetal Questions*, IX, q. 8. He offers two reasons in the *sed contra* and one more in the body of the text. The first is that there cannot be any "damnable error" in the Church, as would happen if a heretic or sinner were mistakenly proposed to the faithful as a model to imitate. The second is that we are bound to believe (*credere*) "the common judgment [*determinationem*] of the Church" — which is why, he notes, those who contradict a judgment of the Councils are reckoned heretics.

The reason given in the body of the question, and hence, it would seem, the most important one, is that "the honor which we show to the saints is a kind of profession of the Faith by which we believe in the glory of the saints."[32] What does this mean? Just as the Church's symbols of belief, such as the Nicene Creed or the Creed of Pius IV,

universal. Though this veneration sometimes did not materialize, papal canonization was assumed to create a universal cult *ipso facto*."

30 Ibid., 130–32.

31 The Council of Constance in 1415, however, taught the existence of a stronger obligation in regard to three saints: in condemning a list of the errors of Wycliffe judged "contrary to the Christian religion and the Catholic faith," the council included his suggestion that SS. Augustine, Benedict, and Bernard might be in hell; session 8, error 44.

32 "Honor quem sanctis exhibemus, quaedam professio fidei est, qua sanctorum gloriam credimus."

cannot be in error, since they are official, irrecusable means by which she expresses (some of) that which she believes by the virtue of faith, so the official *cultus* of the canonized saints cannot be in error, since it is also an official means by which she expresses something of what she believes, namely that God glorifies His friends after death. "Piety," or, as we might say, the Christian people's knowledge and experience of God's love for them, will lead them to believe [*pie credendum est*] that He will not permit an error in something so closely related to and supportive of the Faith itself.

Note that what this argument concludes is not just that, as an abstract principle, it is not wrong to venerate saints, but that it is not wrong to venerate *these* saints, whom the Church officially venerates: for it is not (only) by maintaining an abstract principle, but by performing particular acts of veneration, such as kissing certain relics or attending certain Masses, that the Christian people profess their faith in the dogma of the glory of the saints. In other words, the *cultus* of (say) St. Augustine is normative for Christian belief, as the Nicene Creed is normative, though the latter norm covers a wider field of doctrine.[33] The canonization and subsequent *cultus* of a saint are a way in which a revealed truth is taught and professed throughout the Church, and so piety will incline us to believe that God will not permit them to err, lest the credibility of this truth be dangerously undermined.[34]

St. Robert Bellarmine offers five arguments for inerrantism.[35] The

---

33   Hence, I do not agree with W. Diem's interpretation of Aquinas's argument: on his account, St. Thomas must be saying that by venerating a saint we are saying, in effect, "*if* St. X lived the kind of life which he is reputed to have lived, he will be in heaven, since the gospel teaches that such a life leads to glory"; see above, pp. 65–66. A *professio fidei* is an absolute, not a conditional, affirmation.

34   Thus, I disagree with W. Diem's interpretation of *pie credendum est*. He writes, "I am reading Aquinas to hold (albeit tacitly) that the Church might in fact err, but to hold explicitly that (even if she did err) we ought not believe she has erred": see above, p. 68. In the *ad* 2 of this question, Aquinas states straightforwardly: "Divine providence preserves the Church so that in these things [*sc.* canonizations], she is not deceived by the fallible testimony of men," while in the *ad* 1, he writes: "The pope can be made certain of the state of someone through the enquiry into his life and the witness of miracles, and most of all through an instinct of the Holy Ghost, who *searches all things, even the depths of God.*"

35   Bellarmine, *Controversiae*, "On the Church triumphant," Bk. 1, ch. 9.

first is that we must *venerate* the saints, and so, since we mustn't act contrary to conscience, we must hold that the person so honored is indeed in heaven. The reasons adduced for our duty to venerate the saints are the passages from St. Augustine and St. Bernard mentioned above, and the fact that we are bound to obey the pope when he institutes a new feast day. This argument of Bellarmine's appears in effect to be the same as St. Thomas's second argument, that from the determination of the universal Church.

Bellarmine's next argument is *ex incommodis*, that is, from the unfitting consequences entailed by errantism. He mentions three. Those wrongly canonized would be deprived of the suffrages of the Church on earth. We ourselves would be deprived of much necessary help, calling in error on those who could not help us. Still worse, the Church militant might call down a curse on herself, praying for the same reward as a damned soul. This would be absurd. In part, this argument is an argument from the Church's holiness, as Suárez explicitly says.[36]

The third argument is that canonizations are confirmed by miracles, and thus by God.

The fourth is the rigor of the process leading to canonization, involving as it does much prayer and fasting and close study of the evidence. "It cannot be believed," writes the saint, "that God should not be present to His Church when she is so disposed and suppliant."

Fifthly, inerrantism is confirmed *a posteriori*: "In other matters, in which popes can err, sometimes mistakes are indeed found to have occurred; but in this, no error has ever been discovered."

A final argument for inerrantism may be drawn from the words in which the popes have spoken about their own canonizations. The formula of canonization itself, as we have seen, includes the word *definimus*. Moreover, certain pontiffs have referred to their canonizations as infallible acts. Lambertini gives the example of Pope Sixtus V, who is reported to have said in the consistory before the canonization of St. Didacus that it is to be believed not only piously but "necessarily and with most certain faith" that a pope cannot err in canonizing.[37]

---

36 *De Fide*, disp. 5, sect. 8.8.
37 *De Servorum Dei*, Bk. 1, ch. 43.2, quoting from Galesinius's *Acta*.

As more recent examples, we may cite Popes Pius XI and Pius XII. The latter, speaking in an official letter about his own recent canonization of three saints, stated: "We . . . seated on the throne, discharging the inerrant Magisterium of Peter, solemnly have pronounced: *Ad honorem* etc."[38] To the argument that these popes could simply have misdescribed their own action, an inerrantist could reply that the power to teach infallibly implies also the power to declare when one has taught infallibly, since otherwise believers will be thrown back on their private judgment, and the objective possibility of professing the true faith will be taken away from the earth.[39]

While other inerrantist authors appeal to the assistance given to the Church, or the pope, by the Holy Spirit, this is an explanation of how the infallibility of the judgment made in canonization is ensured rather than a reason for believing in the infallibility of *this* kind of judgment and not in the infallibility of some other papal judgments. We appear, then, to have eight arguments for inerrantism, even if they may not all be perfectly distinct from each other. For convenience they may be summarized as the arguments from (i) the absence of "damnable error" in the Church; (ii) the need to accept the Church's common judgments; (iii) the truth of the Church's professions of faith; (iv) the losses that errantism would, if true, entail for the faithful on earth and in purgatory; (v) miracles; (vi) the meticulous process of canonization, considered as ensuring sufficient divine aid; (vii) the absence of counterexamples; (viii) the testimony of the popes. Before examining these arguments, we shall first give arguments on the other side.

4. ARGUMENTS FOR ERRANTISM

St. Thomas proposed to himself what are perhaps the two most obvious arguments for errantism, namely a man's inability to know with certainty even his own inner state, let alone that of another, and the fallibility of the human witnesses by whose testimony a saint is canonized.[40]

---

38 Pius XII, *Acta Apostolicae Sedis* [*AAS*] 41 (1949), 137; see also Pius XI, *AAS* 25 (1933), 425–26; *AAS* 26 (1934), 539ff.; and Pius XII, *AAS* 33 (1941), 105.
39 See Franzelin, *De divina traditione*, thesis 12, principle 5.
40 *Quodlibetal Questions*, IX, q. 8, obj. 1 and 2.

Another argument may be drawn from the scope of ecclesial, or papal, infallibility. The gift of infallibility is granted by God to the Church for the sake of preserving the deposit of faith. It therefore extends to two different kinds of object: principally to those truths which are divinely revealed, and secondarily to those without which the deposit of faith cannot be securely preserved and expounded.[41] An example of a primary object of infallibility is that marriage between the baptized is a grace-giving sacrament; an example of a secondary object is that the Council of Trent was a legitimate ecumenical council. By contrast, it is clearly not part of the deposit of faith, given once for all to the apostles, that St. Bernard of Clairvaux, for example, is in heaven; nor does it seem that the deposit of faith could not have been securely expounded in AD 1174 if Pope Alexander III had not then canonized him. Hence it does not seem that his canonization was preserved from error on account of the Church's charism of infallibility.

On the other hand, if one were to claim that St. Bernard's heavenly status is a conclusion that must be held with certainty as following from the general principle that "the Church has the power to declare infallibly that someone is in heaven," combined with the historic fact of his canonization, one could object that this general principle cannot in fact be taught by the Church, since it seems to be itself neither contained in divine revelation, nor necessary for expounding revelation.

Again, it is objected that saints who were previously universally or widely venerated have been removed from the calendar, or had their cults suppressed, as new facts of history became available, or came to be differently assessed; or that unworthy candidates have in fact been canonized.[42]

A fifth objection is sometimes drawn from the prayers traditionally made during the ceremony of canonization, where the guidance of

---

41   Cf. *Relatio* given by Bishop Vincent Gasser to the First Vatican Council (Mansi 52:1226); Second Vatican Council, *Lumen Gentium* 25, with the commentary of the Theological Commission (AS III/1, 251); Congregation for the Doctrine of the Faith, *Mysterium Ecclesiae* (1973); Congregation for the Doctrine of the Faith, *Donum Veritatis* (1990).

42   For the last claim, see J. Lamont, "The Infallibility of Canonizations and the Morals of the Faithful," chapter 9 in this volume. For the other claims, see W. Diem, "The Infallibility of Canonizations," above, p. 79, n. 68.

the Holy Spirit is implored lest the Church err: it seems unnecessary to do this, if canonizations are divinely guaranteed.

A sixth objection may be made that the word "canonization" is said equivocally of modern and earlier canonizations, the criteria for what counts as sanctity having changed. For example, Lambertini, in speaking of the canonization of popes, quotes with approval the dictum of St. Robert Bellarmine that a pope's principal task is the appointment of good bishops, whom he must if necessary compel to fulfill their duties; Lambertini adds that canonized popes must be zealous for the maintenance of ecclesiastical discipline.[43] By contrast, Cardinal Angelo Amato, prefect of the Congregation for the Causes of Saints, stated just before the beatification of Pope John Paul II that he was not being beatified because of his impact on the Church.[44] But if the very meaning of canonization has changed, then inerrantist arguments made by earlier authors are now doubtful.

A final objection is drawn from the analogy between a canonization and the confection of a sacrament.[45] Just as Christ has given the Church the power to confect a sacrament, for example the Holy Eucharist, and hence we must hold by faith that any host consecrated by a true priest with the right intention is the Body of Christ, even though we are not obliged to believe of a particular host displayed for adoration that it is the Body of Christ, since, for all we know, the priest might have had a defect of intention in consecration — so also,

---

43 *De servorum Dei*, Bk. III, ch. 32.3ff. Having defined the pope as supreme pastor of Christians, the bishop of Rome, the Metropolitan of the Roman province, the primate of Italy and the patriarch of the West, he concludes that those investigating a papal candidate for beatification must consider, before other things, whether and how well he fulfilled the primary responsibilities of these offices. [See the Appendix below for the pertinent texts in Latin and in English. — *Ed.*]

44 See "John Paul II the Christian being beatified," *CathNews New Zealand*, April 22, 2011, https://cathnews.co.nz/2011/04/22/john-paul-ii-the-christian-being-beatified/. Cardinal Amato was addressing a conference at the Pontifical University of the Holy Cross in Rome. His remarks may have been made in part in response to a "Statement of Reservations" about the impending beatification published the previous month by a large number of clergy, scholars, and other Catholics. See https://www.remnantnewspaper.com/2011-0331-statement-of-reservations-beatification.htm.

45 The analogy, found in the Salamanticenses, is used by W. Diem in arguing for the fallibility of canonizations; see "The Infallibility of Canonizations," above, pp. 66–67, 74–75.

it is urged, Christ might have given the Church the power to declare that a soul is in heaven, and yet our assent to the heavenly status of a given canonized soul might fall short of certainty, from our ignorance of whether the process of canonization was duly performed.

Thus we have seven errantist arguments, drawn from (i) the impossibility of knowing anyone's inner state; (ii) the fallibility of witnesses; (iii) the limited scope of ecclesial infallibility; (iv) the existence of counterexamples; (v) the prayers made at the ceremony; (vi) an alleged change in the meaning of canonization; (vii) the analogy with sacramental ministers confecting invalidly.[46]

5. INERRANTIST ARGUMENTS ASSESSED

I shall begin by considering the eight inerrantist arguments. Of these, I shall consider first the final five arguments, which, though important, do not proceed from the very nature of canonization itself. I shall then return to the first three, which go to the heart of the question.

Argument (iv) by itself is not conclusive. It is possible that God might allow an error to occur even if we or the souls in purgatory were thereby deprived of suffrages: this could be a just punishment. Yet the argument has force on the hypothesis that the process of canonization is an honest attempt to discover the truth for the glory of God, since it would seem strange for God to turn such an endeavor into an occasion of punishing His people.

Argument (v), from miracles, is capable of producing moral certainty, again on the assumption that the evidence is meticulously and fearlessly examined. This certainty, deriving from human testimony, would then rest on reason rather than on faith or on an instinct of faith.

Argument (vi) expressly relies on the meticulous carefulness of the process, this time considered as infallibly calling forth divine assistance, and assuming again such meticulous care, we may judge it as at least highly probable.

---

46 I pass over merely extraneous and contingent arguments drawn from circumstances which might invalidate not just canonizations but acts of governance in general, for example if a pope were merely feigning to canonize, or if he had lost the possibility of exercising jurisdiction by reason of heresy. These are conceivable cases, but ones which it would belong to a later pope to rule on with authority.

Argument (vii), from the factual absence throughout history of erroneous canonizations, might seem impossible to assess, since — except on the assumption of inerrantism, which is what is in question — we cannot infallibly judge the final state of anyone dying after apostolic times. But presumably Bellarmine's point is that no canonized person has ever been discovered later to have been secretly vicious, or even perhaps simply less than heroically virtuous. This, if true, is also a weighty argument, though we have seen that the fourth errantist argument urged that some persons with serious *known* faults have now been canonized.

Argument (viii) was drawn from the statements of some popes about their own canonizations. Lambertini, however, did not find it decisive in regard to the statement of Sixtus V, who seemed to him to have spoken "as a private teacher."[47] This phrase might seem strange, since the speech of Sixtus, if correctly reported, was an official papal act, as were the acts of Pius XI and Pius XII mentioned above: yet it is true that they do not explicitly declare that the faithful are bound under pain of separation from the Church to accept the canonizations in question. Hence, while we should accept the argument that the papal power to teach infallibly must include the power to declare infallibly that one has done so, it *could* be held that the intention of binding the Church is not so clearly manifested by these papal statements that they certainly fulfill the criteria of infallible declarations.[48] In this case, the errantist would presumably have to argue that the *definimus* used in the formula of canonization simply refers to putting an end to a disputed question in a manner that admits of no appeal.

Turning now to arguments (i)–(iii), we see that they are closely related, appealing as they do to the Church's indefectibility in truth and grace, and there is surely something correct about them. For if someone were to say, for example: "Maybe St. Bernard was secretly

---

47 *De Servorum Dei*, Bk. 1, ch. 43.2.

48 We may however note the statement of Joseph Fenton: "A document is not disqualified from consideration as something in which the Roman Pontiff speaks with the fullness of his apostolic authority merely by reason of the fact that it mentions no penalties or sanctions to be imposed against those who refuse to accept its teaching"; see "The Doctrinal Authority of Papal Encyclicals," in *American Ecclesiastical Review* 121 (1949): 136–50.

an atheist and is damned," the instinct of a Catholic would be to consider the suggestion blasphemous, and to say something like: "Of course St. Bernard is in heaven; he's been canonized; everyone's always venerated him as a saint; he's had a feast day for ever so long; he's a doctor of the Church," etc. We should spontaneously appeal, that is, to the fact of his universal *cultus*, resting on the act of canonization, and extended across time and space.

But *why* do the holiness and truthfulness of the Church ensure that the judgment made in a canonization is true? Here we can recall that St. Thomas places canonizations between two other kinds of judgments, namely those which pertain to the Faith, in which the supreme organs of the Church cannot err, and those which pertain to matters of individual (earthly) fact, such as possessions or criminal cases, in which they can err, for example by reason of false testimony. [49] It is incompatible with the Church's holiness and truthfulness that an ecumenical council define that Christ had no human will or define that all Catholics must avoid the sacrament of confession, while it is compatible with the holiness or truthfulness of the Church that such a council might erroneously decide, say, that Bishop X had occupied a see unlawfully, or that monastery Y had the right to a certain portion of land. The relevant difference between the two classes of judgment is that the former must be correct in order that the true religion be preserved and the way to salvation remain open, whereas the latter, even if erroneous, do not tend to the abolition of the true religion or to the damnation of souls.

The canonization of a saint, as traditionally understood, though it resembles the latter class of judgments in dealing with a matter of fact not contained in public revelation, resembles the former in that *it obliges Catholics to profess and practice the divinely revealed religion in a particular way.* Such judgments, if erroneous, would corrupt religion, not indeed in its principles, but in its exercise. But for the supreme authority of the Church, acting officially, to oblige Catholics to corrupt the true religion would appear contrary to her indefectibility.

It is true that the feast of St. Bernard, to continue with the same example, is not, and as far as I know, has never been, a feast of

---

49 *Quodlibetal Questions*, IX, q. 8.

obligation. Other things being equal, Catholics remain blameless if they go through life without praying to him, venerating his relics, or going to a Mass or other liturgical act celebrated in his honor. Yet for hundreds of years all the dioceses of the Latin Church have been obliged to honor him as a saint of God. An instinct of faith—St. Thomas's *pia credulitas*—revolts at the idea that he might be in hell for a secret sin.[50]

This appeal to universal veneration and to the holiness of the Church suggests that the certainty which we have that a given saint is in heaven may best be understood by reference to the guarantee traditionally understood to belong to universal disciplinary laws. It is in fact in this way that Melchior Cano begins his discussion of the certainty of canonization. This Dominican theologian first notes that the Church's teaching on moral or practical matters necessary for salvation is guaranteed in the same way as her teaching on the speculative truths of faith. He gives the example of the teaching of the council of Constance, confirmed by Pope Martin V, that it is heretical to claim that it is necessary for salvation to receive Holy Communion under both species.

Cano concludes, further, that "the Church cannot command anything contrary to the gospel or natural law when she legislates for the whole people in a serious matter which tends greatly to the shaping of Christian behavior."[51] He applies the principle, among other things, to canonizations:

---

50 W. Diem's position seems to allow such a possibility, though obviously I do not attribute it to him. He writes: "The Church cannot err in canonization insofar as the Church, in proposing a saint as a model of Christian virtue, thereby indirectly teaches concerning morals, which the Church is guaranteed to teach infallibly. But this infallibility, of itself, does not guarantee that each canonized saint is ultimately in heaven, or actually died in a state of grace, or even that he existed. It guarantees only that the person's life as it is known is worthy of emulation and glory, leaving intact the fact that our knowledge of such things is necessarily limited and only probable": see above, p. 77. In effect, this is a revival of the position of Augustinus Triumphus; see above, note 20.

51 *De locis theologicis*, ed. J. B. Plans (Biblioteca de Autores Cristianos: Madrid, 2006), Bk. 5, ch. 5, q. 3 (205): "Ecclesiam, cum in re gravi quidem et quae ad Christianos mores formandos apprime conducat, leges toti populo dicit, non posse iubere quicquam, quod aut evangelio aut rationi naturae contrarium sit."

To know whom one must religiously venerate is of great importance for the common behavior of the Church. Hence, if the Church were to err in these things, she would fail seriously in moral matters. Just as the Church would shamefully err, were she to promulgate a law of abstinence contrary to reason or the gospel, so therefore would she shamefully err in the teaching of morals if she promulgated a law to venerate a saint who is no saint, and she would be at war with reason and the gospel.[52]

It might of course be argued that no harm would come to the Christian people if they were bidden to take as a saint someone with apparent virtues and merely secret crimes; yet to *venerate* such a person would be contrary to reason and to the gospel, and since such veneration, as Bellarmine points out, would deprive them of the help which they desire (the venerated one not being in fact able to intercede for them), a law commanding them to do this would indeed prove harmful in the shaping of Christian behavior.

Cano's judgment about universal laws of the Church seems to have been solemnly confirmed by Pope Pius VI in the bull *Auctorem Fidei*, which condemned the Jansenist claim that "the Church could have established discipline which is not only useless and burdensome for Christian liberty to endure, but which is even dangerous and harmful and leading to superstition." This proposition is described in the bull as "false, rash, scandalous, dangerous, offensive to pious ears, injurious to the Church and to the Spirit of God by whom it is guided, at least erroneous."[53] From this I conclude that the Church will not positively oblige all her children to venerate as a saint someone who is not in heaven: to do so would be, as St. Thomas indicates, a "damnable error," a corruption of the profession of faith, and, absurdly, a "common determination" of the Church about the exercise of religion from which her children would do well to dissent.

---

52 Ibid., 207: "Multum refert ad communes ecclesiae mores scire quos debeas religiose colere. Quare, si in illis erraret ecclesia, in moribus quoque graviter falleretur. Atque si ecclesia abstinentiae legem rogaret, quae vel rationi vel Evangelio adversa esset, turpiter ab illa profecto erraretur: turpiter ergo etiam errabit in doctrina morum, si legem ferat de colendo divo, quem colere, si divus non est, et cum ratione et cum Evangelio pugnat."
53 DH 1578.

Indeed, the teaching of *Auctorem Fidei* goes beyond that of Cano, in that it does not explicitly limit itself to "universal laws"; it may naturally be taken to apply to any laws by which the supreme authority of the Church requires a certain religious practice, even if they do not bind all of her members. This is of importance for our question, since many canonized saints are not found on the calendars of the Eastern Catholic churches. However, whether or not we deduce from the teaching of Pius VI that *any* person whose celebration is declared obligatory in *any* part of the Church must be in heaven, we should note that the indefectibility of the local Roman church is itself also a part of tradition. Pope Sixtus IV condemned the opinion of Peter of Osma that "the church of the city of Rome can fall into error" as containing manifest heresy.[54] It seems therefore reasonable to conclude that any indefectibility enjoyed by universal disciplinary laws would apply also to the laws of the local church of Rome, and hence that popes will not declare obligatory even in their own diocese alone the celebration of any saint who is not in heaven.

What if the celebration of some saint is declared merely lawful, but not obligatory? If a pope declares that Masses or other offices may, but need not be, celebrated in honor of a saint, he is no longer establishing the canons of the Christian religion, and so one may wonder whether the divine assistance promised to him when he establishes such canons is still guaranteed. In this respect, we may note that none of the saints canonized since the introduction of the *Novus Ordo* Mass has been made compulsory either for the whole Latin church or for the church of Rome, on account of the fact that the celebration of the so-called *Vetus Ordo* or *usus antiquior* of the Roman rite has always been lawful.[55] Nevertheless, since the formula of canonization

---

54   In the bull *Licet Ea*, of August 9, 1479, given by Denzinger-Banwart 730. For a further discussion of the infallibility of the local church of Rome, see Joseph Fenton, "The Local Church of Rome," *American Ecclesiastical Review* (June 1950): 454–64.

55   Pope Benedict XVI, *Con Grande Fiducia* (Letter to the bishops accompanying *Summorum pontificum*), July 7, 2007. [In other words, since priests of the Latin rite may freely offer Mass using either the traditional or the modern missal, and many priests use only the former, the more recent saints that have been added solely to the new calendar cannot be considered a liturgical veneration obligatory for all. In chapter 10 below, Fr. Hunwicke considers how

for these saints has retained the command that they be venerated, a command addressed in an undifferentiated way to the whole Church, it appears, in order that this command not lack all force, that the faithful are positively obliged to believe that the souls thus canonized are in heaven, such belief being already a certain kind of veneration of them. If this is so, the inerrantist argument drawn from universal disciplinary laws, which may better be called the argument from the indefectibility of the Church in truth and holiness, would apply also to these canonizations.

6. ERRANTIST ARGUMENTS ASSESSED

St. Thomas answered the first two errantist arguments by appealing to the divine help which the Church receives. The pope can be assured of the state of the saint by the assistance of miracles and human witnesses, "and above all by an instinct of the Holy Spirit, *who searches all things, even the depths of God*,"[56] while divine providence prevents false witnesses from perverting his judgment.[57]

We may note here that several popes have themselves expressed a conviction that canonization is in this sense a superhuman task which relies on more than human means. Innocent III, in the bull of canonization of St. Wulstan, remarks that "a judgment of this kind is divine, rather than a judgment of man."[58] Lambertini, recalling how processes of canonization had often unfolded contrary to human expectation, with evidence sometimes being unearthed that resolved apparently insuperable objections, and other causes being equally unexpectedly impeded, declares: "We ourselves, who performed the

---

the praxis of the Eastern Catholic churches weakens still further the force of universal public veneration. —*Ed.*]

56 *Quaestiones quodlibetales*, IX, q. 8, ad 1: "Pontifex, cuius est canonizare sanctos, potest certificari de statu alicuius per inquisitionem uite et attestationem miraculorum, et praecipue per instinctum Spiritus sancti, qui *omnia scrutatur, etiam profunda Dei.*"

57 Ibid., ad 2.

58 "Cum divinum sit iudicium huiusmodi quam hominum. . . . " Pope Celestine III had used a similar phrase in canonizing St. Ubald, and Pope Julius II would use the same words in instructing the archbishop of Canterbury to investigate the cause of King Henry VI of England. Both are quoted in Lambertini, *De servorum Dei*, Bk. 1, ch. 15.2, 3, 9.

task of Promoter of the Faith for so many years, saw as it were with our own eyes the divine Spirit assisting the Roman pontiff."[59]

The third errantist argument was that canonizations fall outside the proper scope of ecclesial, and therefore papal, infallibility, since they are judgments about matters neither contained in divine revelation nor necessary for its exposition. The inerrantist may reply to this in two ways. First, while admitting that the sanctity of a given post-apostolic person is not contained in public revelation, he could claim, contrary to the objector, that the general principle that "anyone canonized by the Church is in heaven" is so contained, perhaps appealing to Christ's promise to the apostles that the Holy Spirit would guide them into all truth. Alternatively, he might agree that the heavenly status of, say, St. Bernard, is not directly either a primary or secondary object of infallibility, but argue from the Church's indefectibility, and in harmony with *Auctorem Fidei*, that the Church would not have been permitted by God to have required St. Bernard's veneration had he not been among the blessed. From there he could conclude that the Church could *now* define infallibly that St. Bernard is in heaven, since the fact of this universal obligatory veneration causes his presence in heaven to be *now* a secondary object of the faith, inasmuch as the revealed truth of the Church's holiness could not be adequately defended if it were treated as doubtful whether someone so venerated by her was really among the blessed.

The fourth argument, from counterexamples, would be convincing if it were possible to show that someone formally canonized by a pope had never existed, but this has not been done. As for the claim that people have been canonized who did not manifest heroic virtue, even if this be granted, it would not follow that the person so canonized is not now in heaven.

The fifth argument, from the incongruity of offering prayers for a correct canonization if the process is divinely guaranteed, was considered by Lambertini. He argues that such prayers are also made

---

59 "Nos ipsi, qui tot annorum spatio munus Fidei Promotoris sustinuimus, nostris, ut ita dicimus, oculis vidimus Divinum eundem Spiritum Romano Pontifici assistentem in definiendis Canonizationis causis"; *De servorum Dei*, ch. 44.4.

by those who attend ecumenical councils, despite the infallibility which Catholics attribute to the definitions and anathemas of such bodies, quoting a prayer in the *Ordo* for the celebration of councils which includes the words: "Let not ignorance draw us to the wrong side."[60] Yet even if someone were to say that this prayer is not offered so that a conciliar definition may be true, but so that it may be opportune, a second response of Lambertini would still hold good, namely that it is not absurd to pray for what we know with certainty will take place, since Christ prayed before His passion that He might be glorified.[61]

The sixth objection was that the word "canonization" is said equivocally of modern and earlier canonizations, the criteria of sanctity having been changed. I reply that the act of canonization itself is still today, as in past years, at a minimum the assertion that a certain servant of God is in heavenly glory. It is this act which, as creating a positive obligation for the whole Church, or for the church of Rome, to venerate him or her as a saint, seems to be protected by the Church's indefectibility. If the process leading to the act of canonization was deficient, for example, because objections to the heroic virtue of the candidate were not duly considered, then a grave fault is thereby committed but the validity of the canonization is not undermined, just as, *mutatis mutandis*, the sacramental validity of the Mass is not undermined if a priest approaches the altar in an irreverent spirit.[62] If it is established that a canonization process has not taken such objections into account, and if the canonization has not created any *positive* obligation on any Catholic, but merely a negative one, as when his celebration has been made merely optional, then it does not seem that the faithful can be blamed if they avoid

---

60 Ibid., ch. 44.21: "In sinistrium nos ignorantia non trahat." He notes that Cardinal de Monte used these words while presiding over the Council of Trent.

61 Ibid., ch. 44.20: "Nec enim inconveniens putari debet, ut a Deo petamus id, quod certo certius scimus, ipsum facturum esse; cum exemplum extet Christi Domini, qui Ioann. 17 se clarificari petiit."

62 Lambertini warned that if the judgment of canonization were given without due care having been taken with the process, "the heretics would cry out, and rightly, that we were acting badly" ["quod quidem iudicium si ab illis fierent sine praeviis diligentiis, clamarent Haeretici et merito, male agi"]; *De servorum Dei*, Bk. 1, ch. 12.8.

the use of the title "saint" in regard to such a one, provided that they do not positively assert that the individual canonized is not in heaven.

Finally, the analogy with the possibility of an invalidly consecrated host is unconvincing, since the faithful are commanded to believe not that some given host was validly consecrated but rather the general proposition that validly consecrated hosts are the body of Christ.

A NOTE ON "PIOUS BELIEF"

We have seen that St. Thomas concludes that it is to be "piously believed" that the saints canonized by the Church are in glory. Prospero Lambertini explains this phrase, distinguishing three grades of "pious belief" (*fides pia*). The lowest grade is when something is believed, in harmony with religion, which however may also be not believed, without any damage to religion: for example that St. Prosper of Aquitaine was a bishop. The second grade is when something is believed which it would be culpable arrogance to deny, for example that the Blessed Virgin was presented in the Temple. The Church does not qualify statements of this kind, says Lambertini, as indubitable truths, but nevertheless she forbids that they be contradicted, at least publicly. The highest grade of pious belief is found when the Church declares that something must be held very certainly (*certo certius tenenda*), including things which "are determined and promulgated by a definitive judgment of the supreme pontiff for the right governance of the whole Church," among which things, he adds, are canonizations of saints.[63] He also states that St. Thomas had in mind this third level of "pious belief" in the *Quodlibetal Questions*.

---

63 *De servorum Dei*, Bk. 1, ch. 43.13.

6

A Response to Fr. Crean

WILLIAM MATTHEW DIEM

FR. CREAN HAS OFFERED US AN HISTORICAL
survey of the question of the authority of canonizations, which is
remarkable for its evident efforts to assess the tradition fairly and
clearly. Despite his obvious efforts to offer a fair assessment of each
side's arguments, I find his treatment of the inerrantist position
rather softer than it might have been and his representation of the
errantist position incomplete in crucial respects. In particular, he
accepts the common inerrantist reading of Aquinas's *Quodlibet* IX,
8, with little scrutiny. This is particularly relevant because, although
Crean acknowledges with fairness that many of the arguments for
inerrantism are inconclusive and can be answered, he judges the
three arguments offered by Aquinas—one in each of the two *sed
contra*s and one in the body of the article—sound and compelling.[1]
I propose therefore to evaluate his treatment of these inerrantist
arguments and to note certain shortcomings in his presentation
of errantism.

THE SECOND *SED CONTRA*: THE COMMON DETERMINATION
OF THE CHURCH
   To begin, let us consider Crean's second argument for inerrantism,
which is Aquinas's second argument *sed contra* in *Quodlibet* IX, 8.

> Augustine says in a letter to Jerome, if any lie were allowed
> in the canonical Scriptures, our faith, which depends on
> canonical Scripture, would waver. But just as we are bound
> to believe that which is in sacred Scripture, so too [we are
> bound to believe] that which is determined by the whole
> Church in common; which is why they are judged heretics

---

1   Crean, 94–100. Since my essay and Fr. Crean's are published in this book,
citations to either text will use the page number (and, if revelant, footnote
number) as found herein.

who think contrary to the determination of the councils. Therefore it is not possible that the common judgment of the whole Church should be in error....[2]

Crean summarizes this argument briefly: "we are bound to believe (*credere*) 'the common judgment (*determinationem*) of the Church'—which is why, [Aquinas] notes, those who contradict a judgment of the Councils are reckoned heretics."[3] But as I had already pointed out, we are bound to *assent* to the common judgment of the Church[4] *only in matters that pertain to faith and morals*—those matters Aquinas later calls "necessary for salvation," which, he says, the Church is certain to teach inerrantly. The argument, thus, amounts to question-begging: is the eternal beatitude of particular post-apostolic individuals a matter of the faith, or not? Is it a question of things necessary for salvation, or not? If it is not, then an error in the Church's judgment in such matters need not touch either the faith or the Church's credibility as teacher of the faith.[5] The argument, thus, presumes precisely the conclusion it needs to prove.

Moreover, as I have noted before[6] and will highlight again below, that which the argument presumes actually conflicts with Aquinas's argument in the corpus. There, he explicitly places the canonizations of saints in a category distinct from matters necessary for salvation, matters which belong to the faith, and matter concerning which "it is certain that it is impossible for the judgment of the universal Church to err." Thus, insofar as the argument suggests that canonizations are equivalent to those teachings that are necessary for

---

2   *Quodlibet* IX, 8, sc 2: "Augustinus dicit in epistola ad Hieronymum, si in Scriptura canonica aliquod mendacium admittatur, nutabit fides nostra, quae ex Scriptura canonica dependet. Sed sicut tenemur credere illud quod est in sacra Scriptura, ita illud quod est communiter per Ecclesiam determinatum: unde haereticus iudicatur qui sentit contra determinationem Conciliorum. Ergo commune iudicium Ecclesiae erroneum esse non potest; et sic idem quod prius."
3   Crean, 88.
4   Which, one must note, is not the same as being bound to comply externally with universal practices or laws.
5   A point Muratori made clearly: see Diem, 63n43. See also quotation produced below.
6   See Diem, 65n48.

salvation, that pertain to the faith, and that we must accept on pain of heresy, it directly conflicts even with the plain text of Aquinas's own answer. And if canonizations are not *de fide*, then there is no reason that our faith must waver (*"nutabit fides nostra"*) if we entertain the possibility that they might be in error.

Crean bolsters this argument by identifying it with another, namely, Bellarmine's argument that "we must venerate the saints, and so, since we mustn't act contrary to conscience, we must hold that the person so honored is indeed in heaven."[7] The force of the argument (as Bellarmine presents it) is that the Church would potentially place us in a crisis of conscience if we could licitly deny that a saint is in heaven while at the same time the Church binds us in conscience to venerate him. But as I already pointed out,[8] the only conclusion Bellarmine draws from this is that *"we cannot doubt whether he is to be venerated who is canonized by the Church."* He does not conclude that canonizations are simply inerrant. The impossibility follows only if we may licitly hold that a particular canonization was in fact wrong and that therefore the one we are bound by the Church to honor as a saint is in fact unworthy of such honor.

In short, this first argument (or set of arguments) fails to establish a simple inerrancy of papal canonizations. The argument from the second *sed contra* simply fails, while the argument from Bellarmine does not actually claim to establish that every canonized saint is in fact in heaven, and thus, taken on its own terms, is compatible with the errantist position.[9]

CORPUS: *QUAEDAM PROFESSIO FIDEI*

Let us turn next to a second argument, which Crean also takes from the corpus of Aquinas's article. Crean quotes it thus: "the honor

---

7 Crean, 90. Though I would note that the two arguments seem to me entirely distinct: one deals with the assent that we owe to the Church's common judgments on faith and morals; the other treats our conformity with the Church's universal discipline.

8 Diem, 55.

9 It must be borne in mind that the historical errantists have always admitted that — at least under ordinary circumstances — one ought not to deny particular formal canonizations.

which we show to the saints is a kind of profession of the faith by which we believe in the glory of the saints," and then explains:

> Just as the Church's symbols of belief, such as the Nicene Creed…, cannot be in error, since they are official, irrecusable means by which she expresses (some of) that which she believes by the virtue of faith, so the official *cultus* of the canonized saints cannot be in error, since it is also an official means by which she expresses something of what she believes, namely that God glorifies His friends after death.[10]

He then proceeds to insist that "the *cultus* of (say) St. Augustine is normative for Christian belief, as the Nicene Creed is normative."[11] He goes so far as to liken the kissing of certain relics to the recitation of the Creed, in their both being normative expressions of Christian belief. And he argues that, since these acts of veneration are professions of faith, they must be performed absolutely and not conditionally or tinged with any shadow of doubt, for "a *professio fidei* is an absolute, not a conditional, affirmation."[12]

I reply as follows: Despite certain similarities between venerating a saint and reciting the Creed, there are also many obvious differences between them. The Nicene Creed clearly, unambiguously, and directly articulates the articles of the Christian faith. Honoring a saint does not. That is precisely why Aquinas calls honoring a saint only "*quaedam* professio fidei." It is, as Crean translates this expression, only "a kind of profession of the faith."[13] The differences between a formal recitation of the Creed and kissing a saint's relic are too manifold and manifest to require exhaustive enumeration here. Suffice it to note that one who recites the Creed with a mental reservation sins against faith, while one who rejects some article of the Creed and who therefore refuses to recite it at all is a heretic. In contrast, one who doubts that some relic is authentic does not sin against the faith, and one who refuses to venerate a particular relic (say, the veil of Veronica) because of such doubt or even denial is not a heretic.

---

10 Crean, 88–89.
11 Crean, 89.
12 Crean, 89n33.
13 Crean, 88.

What is both more interesting and far more important for the argument than enumerating the many dissimilarities between reciting the Creed and venerating some saint is articulating precisely how they are alike. In what particular respect does kissing the relic of a saint constitute a "certain profession of faith"? That is the question that must be answered before we can say that canonization or veneration of a saint is equivalent to promulgating or reciting a creed in any particular respect (for example, in being protected from error by a divine guarantee or in being a condition of remaining in the Church). What then is the faith that we profess in honoring a saint? Is that faith the very faith that the Church cannot err in teaching? And how is that faith professed in venerating the saints? Crean answers correctly when he says that, in the veneration of the saints, the Church expresses her belief "that God glorifies His friends after death." That is indeed a matter of the faith that the Church is guaranteed to teach infallibly—and to that matter of faith we give a certain witness in venerating the saints. So far so good.

But to close the argument, Crean asserts that an error in canonization would cause "the credibility of this ['revealed'] truth [presumably, 'that God glorifies His friends after death'] to be dangerously undermined."[14] I must query: why should that revealed truth be dangerously undermined if it were allowed that some canonization might err in identifying who was a true friend of God? That is the question Crean must answer to make this argument prove inerrantism. On the one hand, my faith in revelation is in no sense logically contingent on my belief that particular post-apostolic individuals are not in heaven;[15] on the other hand, the heavenly beatitude of no specific, post-apostolic individual follows as a necessary consequence from the truth of revelation. Rather, the truth that some post-apostolic

---

14 Crean, 89.

15 This is *not* to say that the visible earthly lives of the saints, displaying as they so often do manifest and heroic virtue, may not serve as an important motive of credibility—here consider especially the powerful witness of the martyrs. The two are different claims: The manifest heroic virtue of their lives serves as a motive of credibility *precisely because it is manifest and visible to us prior to our response of faith*; their eternal beatitude, however, is neither manifest nor visible to us.

individual is in heaven depends on both the revealed truth that God rewards His friends *and equally* on non-revealed contingent historical facts. That we might conceivably err in judging these particular historical facts does not have any logical consequence for the revealed truth. The proposition that God glorifies His friends after death remains unshaken and unassailable, because it is a universal that will always be true: any true friend of God will deserve to be glorified.

Illustrating this point was the purpose of the example of offering, out of invincible ignorance, *latria* to an invalidly consecrated host. The faith compels me to believe that Christ is present in every validly consecrated host, but the faith does not extend to my determination of which particular hosts have been validly consecrated. Therefore a faultless error in determining which particular hosts have been validly consecrated does not compromise my faith. Crean seems to have missed the significance of this example, taking it not as an example — a parallel case illustrating the force of an argument — but as an independent argument in its own right and indeed an argument that (as he reads it) presupposes precisely what it is offered to deny (that the Church is guaranteed to proclaim saints infallibly).[16] Little wonder that Crean finds the argument uncompelling;[17] it was never meant as an independent argument and, as he interpreted it, the example makes no sense, as it presumes the position it was provided to refute.

We will return to this last point in a moment, but before we move on from Crean's treatment of the corpus of Aquinas, a final point must be made. "'Piety'...will lead [the faithful]," Crean says, "to believe (*pie credendum est*) that He will not permit an error in something so closely related to and supportive of the faith itself."[18] It may be pious to believe that God guards the Church in canonizations; I don't dispute that. But Crean offers this observation to substantiate the stronger and unqualified claim that "the official *cultus* of the canonized saints cannot be in error." Here I object. What our piety might lead us to accept is not necessarily guaranteed to be true. The job of theology is not simply to repeat pious thoughts and speculations

16 Crean, 93–94.
17 Crean, 103.
18 Crean, 89.

as though they are certain. There are many opinions I am inclined to accept as true based only on my belief in God's goodness and omnipotence, but I have no business proposing them as sound and certain conclusions of theology, let alone as matters of revealed faith.

For example, I should have liked to believe that, although a pope does not perform an infallible act when he promulgates a catechism for the whole Church, still God, in His loving providence, would not allow a pope to promulgate to the whole Church a catechism that either errs or speaks with such ambiguity that it could be naturally read to teach error concerning not just morals, but a matter of life and death. Yet we now have a catechism promulgated by a pope that appears, on a natural reading, to be in direct disagreement about the moral permissibility of capital punishment, not only as a prudential consideration but apparently at the level of moral principle. Add to this that a catechism promulgated by a pope can certainly be called, in at least *some* sense, a normative expression of the Catholic faith — certainly it is more normative than kissing any particular relic; it is clearly both an "official means by which [the Church] expresses something of what she believes" and "a way in which a revealed truth is taught and professed throughout the Church." Yet here we find ourselves: confronted with one of these official means of teaching the faith, apparently in error on a rather important moral issue.

The lesson is this: It is a grave danger to divine science to conflate a pious thought, based on what *we* think in *our* prudential judgment a good God would do for us, with a rigorous scientific conclusion firmly rooted in God's promises made in public revelation. As a further example: my knowledge of God's love and omnipotence shown forth in the Gospel might well have led me to accept universalism as true, were it not for God's having revealed otherwise.

MATERIAL ERROR AND THE FIRST *SED CONTRA*

An absolutely crucial point in the errantists' arguments is and has been from the beginning the distinction between formal and material error. It was this distinction that the example of the invalidly consecrated host was offered to illustrate.[19] Consider Hostiensis's

---

19 This use of the example as illustrating the distinction between material

explaination of why nothing impossible would follow if a formal canonization were in error: "God accepts prayers extended in good faith in the honor of such an individual [viz., one wrongly canonized], for all things are made clean in the faith of Christ, and if it be that the truth of the canonization is wanting, still the faith [of the one mistakenly venerating the false saint] is not wanting."[20] Likewise Muratori, having just noted, by way of example, that the faith does not extend to whether an individual host held up by the priest for adoration is actually the Body of Christ, writes:

> Thus errors and other difficulties may have and can still arise from these things. But they are not such as can defile the true religion or cause its failure or blemish it. They are, to use a scholastic term, material errors, which must be avoided as far as possible but are no danger to souls and cause no disrepute for the true Church. But when we pray to or venerate one we think is in heaven, our prayers and devotion are directed always to God, prayer and devotion to Whom cannot cause faith to go astray.[21]

Despite the centrality of this point to the errantists' case, it is a distinction that Crean essentially writes out of the history of the dispute: the expression "material error" is nowhere found in Crean's text. Nevertheless, he seems to touch the idea when he poses the following hypothetical argument from an errantist: "It might of course be argued that no harm would come to the Christian people if they were bidden to take as a saint someone with apparent virtues and

---

and formal error as applied to veneration of saints is perfectly clear in Muratori, *De ingeniorum moderatione in religionis negotio*, Bk. I, ch. 17 (Venice: Johannis Baptistae Pasquali, 1752), p. 77; see quotation below.

20 Quoted in Diem, 70n54.

21 "Errores igitur, et incommoda ex his potuerunt, et possunt adhuc accidere. At non ea sunt, ut eorum caussa foedari, aut deficere Religio vera, aut rugas inde contrahere possit. Isti sunt, ut Scholarum vocabulo utar, errores materiales, cavendi quantum fieri potest, sed nullum animabus periculum, nullam verae Ecclesiae infamiam creantes. Orationes autem nostrae, cultusque noster, vel quum rogamus, atque veneramur quempiam quem caelitem putamus, semper ad Deum feruntur, in quo rogando, atque colendo fieri non potest ut fides aberret." Muratori, *De ingeniorum*, p. 77. For assistance with the translation of this passage, I am indebted to Fr. Dylan Schrader.

merely secret crimes."[22] Yet, having raised an issue so central to the errantist's position, he continues the sentence brushing the point aside and simply asserting the contrary:

> yet to venerate such a person would be contrary to reason and to the gospel, and since such veneration, as Bellarmine points out, would deprive them of the help which they desire (the venerated one not being in fact able to intercede for them), a law commanding them to do this would indeed prove harmful in the shaping of Christian behavior.

This response ignores the crucial issue just raised: *in what respect* can such a mistake be accurately described as "contrary to reason and to the gospel"? How would it be contrary to either reason or the Gospel to venerate one whom we believe to have lived and died faithful to the Gospel and who we believe now rejoices with God in heaven? How precisely would I violate reason in honoring as a saint one whom I reasonably believe is in heaven? How would I violate the Gospel in praying to one whose life, as far as I can know it, was an exemplary response to the Gospel? As to the charge that it would be harmful: would God deprive me of the grace I ask, because I requested the intercession of one who I could not know was unable to intercede for me? Are we to think that God is such a malevolent literalist that He would reward us with damnation if we asked Him to reward us as He rewarded one whom we mistakenly believe He has saved? Moreover, if it is as Crean says, would I, then, violate reason and the Gospel by asking the intercession of some mere Servant of God, not yet canonized? Would I have brought grave spiritual harm on myself if it turned out that, though declared a Servant of God, this soul was not actually in heaven? Or do I violate reason and the Gospel when I venerate one of the many saints (say Augustine) honored by the Church, although they were never formally canonized by a pope? And does the Church, in tolerating and even promoting their cults, bring harm on the faithful?

On such questions rests practically the whole of the dispute, and yet here, the only time Crean touches the notion of material error, it is brushed aside with question-begging.

---

22 Crean, 98.

In the passage just quoted, Crean mentions, as confirmation of his position, an argument from Bellarmine that he had previously presented — the argument "*ex incommodis*," summarized earlier as follows:

> Those wrongly canonized would [if an error could arise in formal canonization] be deprived of the suffrages of the Church on earth. We ourselves would be deprived of much necessary help, calling in error on those who could not help us. Still worse, the Church militant might call down a curse on herself, praying for the same reward as a damned soul. This would be absurd.[23]

Yet notice the rather more cautious manner in which Bellarmine actually ends the argument: "Although the Church would not ask the malediction except materially, nonetheless it seems absurd." In other words, Bellarmine frankly and forthrightly admits that the error would be merely material, and realizing this, he is compelled to qualify the conclusion correspondingly. Crean has omitted Bellarmine's significant concession that such error is merely material, and — thus freed of minding this subtle but crucial nuance — he has unwarrantedly strengthened the conclusion from the cautious and qualified "still this seems absurd" to the categorical and absolute "this would be absurd."

At this point Crean introduces the authority of *Auctorem Fidei* as confirmation, to show that the Church cannot introduce a "discipline which is not only useless and burdensome for Christian liberty to endure, but which is even dangerous and harmful and leading to superstition." But once the distinction between formal and material error is noted, this canon is rendered completely irrelevant to the question,[24] for, as the errantists have insisted from the start, a false canonization, made in good faith, *would not actually be harmful to anyone*. Praying to one whose presence in heaven has not been

---

23 Crean, 90.

24 To say nothing of the fact that even an erroneous canonization can hardly be said to establish a "burdensome" discipline. A canonization binds the faithful to do nothing that could be reasonably described as "burdensome." Saints are, today, canonized all the time with absolutely no impact on the lives of most of the faithful.

infallibly established cannot be described as "dangerous and harmful and leading to superstition," even if it turns out that it was materially erroneous. As Sinibaldo dei Fieschi (later Innocent IV) had already pointed out when this question first arose, "even if the Church should err [in canonization]..., God would nevertheless accept prayers made in good faith through such a [false saint]."[25] God will not fail to hear our prayers when we, in good faith, implore the intercession of one whom we believe loved God heroically, even if that one is, as it happens, not actually able to intercede for us. Nor will God rain down damnation on us when we ask to be rewarded as were those whom we erroneously but sincerely believe to have lived as His friends, whom we believe to have cooperated with His grace while one earth, and whom we thus also mistakenly believe to rejoice with Him now in heavenly glory. This, plainly, is why the Church allows us to pray to those who have not been formally canonized.

Labeling it harmful, dangerous, and superstitious to pray to one whose heavenly beatitude has not been ascertained with infallible certitude leads to absurdities. The first is the fact that the Church not only tolerates but recognizes the cult of many saints who were never formally canonized — practically all the saints of the Patristic era. Indeed there were *no* canonized saints until the Middle Ages, but the Church has nevertheless continuously honored post-apostolic individuals as saints, installing their relics in altars and celebrating their feasts in her liturgies. Who would dare say that the universal custom of the Church for the first millennium of her existence — namely, the custom of formally and liturgically honoring uncanonized local saints — was a harmful and superstitious practice?[26] The second absurdity to follow is that the canonization of a saint requires prior miracles worked through the individual's intercession; but such miracles can occur only if people are already

---

25 *Apparatus in quinque libros decretalium*, Bk. III, rub. 45, ch. 1, in "Audivimus," produced in Diem, 69n51.

26 Of course, it *was* superstitious and harmful in some particular cases, which is why the popes came eventually to reserve the authority of canonization to themselves. Such abuses, however, were local abuses, perpetrated by particular bishops, not a necessary feature of the universal practice of the Church during those centuries.

asking that individual's intercession prior to his canonization. Are we to believe that the entire cult of the saints as a whole, including the very process of formal canonization, presupposes superstitious, dangerous, and, at least potentially, harmful devotional practice?

Now, I certainly agree with Crean that canonizations constitute disciplinary laws and so fall under the Church's indefectibility. Indeed, I made those points myself.[27] But I deny that a good-faith error in determining who is a saint must establish a dangerous and harmful discipline leading to superstition. I equally deny that an erroneous act of canonization would "oblige Catholics to corrupt the true religion."[28] Such crucial elements of the inerrantist argument have not been substantiated. And therefore I deny that *Auctorem Fidei* says anything that could settle the precise question now in dispute.

Furthermore, this crucial distinction between material and formal error is implied even in Aquinas's first *sed contra*, the remaining inerrantist argument that Crean thinks sound. Crean summarizes this argument thus: "There cannot be any 'damnable error' in the Church, as would happen if a heretic or sinner were mistakenly proposed to the faithful as a model to imitate."[29] Yet in presenting and deploying the argument, Crean passes in silence over Aquinas's explanation of *why* and *in what respect* such an error would constitute a "*damnable* error." Here is the argument as formulated by Aquinas:

> There can be no damnable error in the Church; but there would be a damnable error if one who was a sinner were venerated as a saint, for then some, knowing his sin or heresy, could be led into error, if this should happen. Therefore the Church cannot err in such matters.[30]

The error is only made damnable — that is, apt to lead someone away from salvation — if it leads someone into moral error by causing him to believe that the false saint's sin is not a sin. *That* is the

---

27 Diem, 77.
28 Crean, 96.
29 Crean, 88.
30 "Sed hic esset error damnabilis, si veneraretur tamquam sanctus qui fuit peccator, quia aliqui scientes peccata eius, crederent hoc esse falsum; et si ita contigerit, possent ad errorem perduci."

impossibility, and, as is both obvious in itself and perfectly clear in the text, that impossibility only arises if there are *"aliquis scientes peccata eius"* — some *who know the sins* of the one infelicitously canonized, and who might thus be led to think the Church has, in canonizing the sinner, condoned that sinful behavior.[31] Thus the argument does not touch the possibility of a truly secret fault, nor can it rule out the canonization of a purely legendary figure. It rules out as damnable error only the canonization of someone *known* to be a sinner. But that sort of impossible error in canonization would not be a merely material error but a formal error on the Church's part. Such *formal* error is what is ruled out not only by Aquinas but by *Auctorem Fidei*.

CREAN'S REPLIES TO ERRANTIST ARGUMENTS

We have treated the three arguments for inerrantism that Crean judges strong. What, then, of his replies to the arguments on behalf of errantism — specifically, those Crean enumerates as the first and third errantist arguments: that we cannot know the state of another's soul just as we cannot know the state of our own soul, and that canonization of post-apostolic individuals exceeds the scope of infallibility which is given for the guarding of the deposit of faith?

His reply to the first of these is simply to say that Aquinas addressed them in his own replies:

> St. Thomas answered the first two errantist arguments by appealing to the divine help which the Church receives. The pope can be assured of the state of the saint by the assistance of miracles and human witnesses, "and above all by an instinct of the Holy Spirit, who searches all things, even the depths of God," while divine providence prevents false witnesses from perverting his judgment.[32]

But if one considers the actual replies Aquinas offers, they fall well short of genuine rebuttals, and (presuming that they mean what Crean takes them to mean) amount to no more than bare counter-assertions. A simple denial is not a refutation. No one denies that

31 One could go a step further and point out that they would think the Church condones the sin only if they not only know of the sin themselves but believe that the Church also knows of the sin.

32 Crean, 100.

God can preserve the Church from error in canonization; the issue is whether it is certain that He always does. Even if Aquinas does here assert (either clearly or opaquely) what Crean thinks he asserts, it doesn't actually matter what Aquinas *asserts*. Aquinas is a theologian, a doctor of the Church; he is neither a Father of the Church nor a pope. His authority to settle difficult questions rests ultimately on the arguments he provides, not on the bare fact that he teaches some thesis. Extrinsic probability is a poor (if frequently very useful) proxy for intrinsic probability. As a whole litany of authorities (including Aquinas) testifies, argument from authority is the weakest form of argument. In other words, what matters is not what Aquinas believed or what Aquinas asserted but the *reasons* Aquinas had for holding that position.[33] And in the article, Aquinas offers no argument as immediate justification for his apparent assertion either that the pope is able to judge infallibly the eternal state of the departed through the *"instinctum spiritus sancti"* or that *"divina providentia praeservat Ecclesiam ne in talibus per fallibile testimonium hominum fallatur."*

But here arises a still more fundamental point. Even if Aquinas's opinion were decisive by virtue of his authority alone, his position on this question is not at all clear, and what precisely he means to assert is open to serious and legitimate doubt. Although Crean subscribes without question to the common opinion that "St. Thomas defends inerrantism in the *Quodlibetal Questions*, IX, q. 8"[34] and although he also mentions Cajetan's errantism,[35] he neglects to mention that Cajetan *explicitly attributes his errantist position to Aquinas*. Cajetan was a more than competent speaker of Latin. If then Aquinas unambiguously holds what Crean thinks he unambiguously holds, how did a figure of Cajetan's erudition, intelligence, and linguistic competence manage to read him as saying the opposite of what Crean asserts

---

33 And the same is doubly true of Crean's closing section in which he cites Lambertini's interpretation of the meaning with which Aquinas uses the expression *"pie credendum est"*; Crean, 103. Lambertini's interpretation of Aquinas has only as much weight as the arguments he marshals to support that interpretation, of which Crean provides exactly none; and even if his interpretation of Aquinas is shown to be correct, what Aquinas believed is still only as good as the arguments Aquinas, in turn, marshaled for that conclusion.

34 Crean, 88.

35 Crean, 85.

Aquinas holds? It seems to me the most plausible, indeed inevitable, conclusion is that whatever Aquinas holds, his position is not so clear as Crean (among many other inerrantists) supposes it to be.

On this note, I cannot but make some mention of Crean's passing treatment of Muratori.[36] In a footnote, Crean mentions that

> Muratori denied that Catholics were obliged to accept inerrantism, but added that "this rite [canonization] is now so accurately and carefully carried out by the Apostolic See that one should have a devout belief [*pie credendum sit*] that there has been no room for error in this matter, nor will there be."[37]

Indeed Muratori did deny the obligation. This simply proves that the "*pie credendum est*" formula and the text of Aquinas's *Quodlibet* IX, 8 wherein he defends that formula can be read in an errantist sense (as Cajetan read it before him), for Muratori — who is undoubtedly an errantist — proceeds in the very next line to quote from Aquinas's text and, following Aquinas's own distinction in the text, to distinguish what is *necessarily* to be believed from what is only *piously* to be believed: "It is therefore to be believed not necessarily, but still piously, as St. Thomas says, that the Church could not err even in these judgments."[38]

Finally, what of Crean's reply to the third errantist argument — that canonization exceeds the scope of infallibility? He suggests two possible replies. One possibility would be to "argue from the Church's indefectibility, and in harmony with *Auctorem Fidei*, that the Church would not have been permitted by God to have required St. Bernard's

---

36 Muratori is known today principally as the archivist who discovered the Muratorian Fragment, yet he was an accomplished and respected scholar in his day, and his arguments concerning the limits of infallibility exerted a marked influence on, at least, German theologians. See Ulrich Lehner, "Introduction," in Beda Mayr and Ulrich Lehner, *Beda Mayr, Vertheidigung der katholischen Religion (1789)* (Leiden: Brill, 2009), ix–lxxvi, at lvii–lix. I think it not altogether impertinent to note that Muratori maintained a correspondence with Benedict XIV himself, who consulted with him on matters of import. Moreover, when, in the course of a heated and long-running public theological debate, Muratori was denounced for heresy, it was Benedict XIV who vindicated his orthodoxy.

37 Crean, 86n23.

38 "[N]on necessario igitur, sed tamen *pie credendum est,* ut inquit sanctus Thomas, *Quodlibet* Lib. 9, art. 16, *quod nec etiam in iis judicium Ecclesiae errare possit.*"

veneration had he not been among the blessed." This first step in the argument was addressed above, and if the answer I made to it there deserves to stand—if, that is, a merely material error in naming a saint would not violate the Church's indefectibility or impose a dangerous and harmful discipline—then there is no need to examine this possible reply any further, since it rests on that previously refuted argument.

The other reply Crean suggests is that one defending the infallibility of canonizations could claim, contrary to the objector, that the general principle that "anyone canonized by the Church is in heaven" *is* contained [in public revelation]—perhaps appealing to Christ's promise to the apostles that the Holy Spirit would guide them into all truth.

This reply does not take the objection seriously. Yes, one could simply contradict the objector. One could simply assert that the beatitude of post-apostolic saints does fall under the Church's charism of infallibility. Such a response would not be an argument but a bald assertion that ignores the objection, which was based on the universal teaching of theologians that the Church's infallibility extends only as far as is necessary to guard and teach the deposit of faith. To answer the objection, one would need to show either that that universal teaching of theologians is false or that canonizations are necessary for the Church to guard and teach the deposit of faith. As I wrote previously, "In discussions of God's guarantees to the Church, the onus falls to those defending some guarantee to show either that it is explicit in revelation or that it is necessary for the Church to carry out her divine mission." That burden remains unlifted.

7

Canonization and Infallibility†

MSGR. BRUNERO GHERARDINI

FOR SOME TIME NOW, THERE HAS BEEN A CON-
versation about this again: doubtless an interesting subject. Yet, until
recently, nothing led one to believe that the position which seemed
definitive according to the man who became Benedict XIV[1] would
be once more up for discussion. To tell the truth, recent debates and
articles have proposed little that's new: they have only recalled our
attention to the relationship between papal infallibility and canonization.
The doubtful or even negative position was not new; the affirmative
position was not new. On both sides the reasoning of the past was
repeated and no contribution was made to a more profound knowledge
of the problem or to the establishment of a critical foundation of a
proposed solution—with, perhaps, the lone exception of Daniel Ols.[2]

Since the "demon" of curiosity and second thoughts also crossed
my path, I put together here the essential points in a sort of provocation. I told myself: who knows whether someone might help
me to understand it all better! It seems superfluous to state that my
rethinking of the question springs from the concrete situation of
a "truth" that has not been dogmatically defined, with the consequent margin of freedom — a freedom limited, of course, by some

---

1 See Prospero Lambertini, *De Servorum Dei beatificatione et de Beatorum canonizatione*, Prato 1839–42: I, n. 28, 336B: "Si non haereticum, temerarium tamen,
scandalum toti Ecclesiae afferentem, in Sanctos iniuriosum, faventem haereti-
cis negantibus auctoritatem Ecclesiae in Canonizatione Sanctorum, sapientem
haeresim, utpote viam sternentem infidelibus ad irridendum Fideles, assertorem
erroneae propositionis et gravissimis poenis obnoxium dicemus esse qui auderet
asserere, Pontificem in hac aut illa Canonizatione errasse . . . et de fide non esse,
Papam esse infallibilem in Canonizatione Sanctorum . . . "

2 See D. Ols, "Fondamenti teologici del culto dei Santi," in AA. VV. dello
"Studium Congreg. de Causis Sanct.," pars theologica, Rome, 2002, pp. 1–54.

† First published in *Divinitas* 46.2 (2003): 196–221; republished in *Chiesa Viva* in
2003, issues 354–356 (October–December). Translated by Jonathan Arrington.

"theological notes," but nevertheless not suffocated by them. It is to be understood that my "provocation" remains within these limits.

I. THE COMMON TEACHING

Neither Denzinger,[3] nor the 1983 *Code of Canon Law*,[4] nor even the *Catechism of the Catholic Church*[5] expounds the status of canonizations, which is an evident sign that it lies outside the ambit of what the Church declares and promulgates *definitorio modo* (in a definitive manner). Thus, the common teaching on canonization must be sought elsewhere — to be precise, in Church teaching that is not *ex cathedra*, that is, in the bulls of canonization, in other ecclesiastical but not dogmatic interventions, and in theological debate.

1.1. Their analysis allows us to define canonization thus: *an act by which the sovereign pontiff, by an unappealable judgment and a definitive decision, formally and solemnly inscribes a servant of God (previously beatified) in the list (or canon) of saints.* Such a definition is ordinarily completed by the specification that the pope intends to declare thereby the presence of the canonized saint in the bosom of the Father, i.e., in heavenly glory, as well as the saint's exemplary holiness as a model for the whole Church and the duty to honor the saint everywhere with the *cultus* due to the saints.

In order to determine its nature more accurately, it should also be borne in mind that canonization is specified either as formal or equipollent: it is formally specified when all the procedures are carried out according to the norms; it is equivalent to a canonization (equipollent) when someone is called a saint in force of the saint's veneration from time immemorial (*ab immemorabili*).[6]

---

3 DS 675 constitutes a minor exception, in regard to the canonization of Ulderic, Bishop of Augsburg, at the Lateran Synod on January 31, 993; DS 2726–2727bis only deals with the approval of writings of those being raised to the altars.

4 A single reference is in c. 1403/1: "Causae canonizationis Servorum Dei reguntur peculiari lege pontificia."

5 Here too there is only one reference, n. 828, indicating for what end the Church canonizes some of her best children.

6 See T. Ortolan, "Canonisation dans l'Eglise romaine," in *DThC* II, Paris, 1932, cc. 1636–39.

Therefore, generally and formally speaking, a blessed is canonized: the distinguishing mark between beatification and canonization is recognizable in the fact that one prepares for the other and that the latter — from a formal standpoint — is not independent of the former. Yet, while canonization extends devotion to the new saint to the entire Church, beatification merely permits it in a locale — a diocese, a province, a nation, a religious order or congregation. It appears, in fact, from the formulas habitually used[7] that, in canonizing a blessed, the pope's intention is to extend the saint's *cultus* to a universal level. The pragmatic verbs are unequivocal in this regard: *statuere, decernere, mandare, constituere, velle,* clearly distinguishable from those used in simple beatifications: *indulgere, licentiam concedere.* One also cannot ignore, as a confirmation of the formal difference between canonization and beatification, that within the bulls of canonization one reads expressions of a will that is not only preceptive, but also threatening: *Si quis... temerario ausu contrarie tentaverit, sciat se... anathematis vinculo innodatum.*[8]

1.2. It is not only from the extension of the *cultus* to the entire Church, with the consequent involvement of all the faithful, but also from the declaration of the exemplary life of the newly canonized and from the implicit assurance that the saint is enjoying heavenly glory, that the common teaching has deduced an infallibility in the act of canonizing a saint.

It should be immediately noted that advocates of said infallibility use, I would say, inductive reasoning of the *reductio ad absurdum* type: "It would be intolerable if the pope, in such a declaration that implicates the entire Church, were not infallible."[9] He is therefore infallible

---

7   Here are some: "Inter sanctos et electos ab Ecclesia universali honorari praecipimus"; "Apostolicae Sedis auctoritate catalogo sanctorum scribi mandavimus"; " ... anniversarium ipsius (sancti) sollemniter celebrari constituimus"; "statuentes ab Ecclesia universali illius memoriam quolibet anno pia devotione recoli debere."
8   In this regard, see Ortolan, "Canonisation," c. 1634–35; F. Veraja, *La beatificazione: storia, problemi, prospettive,* Rome, 1983; G. Stano, "Il rito della beatificazione da Alessandro VII ai nostri giorni," in AA. VV., *Miscellanea in occasione del IV Centenario della Congregazione per le Cause dei Santi (1588–1988),* Città del Vaticano, 1988, pp. 367–422.
9   See G. Löw, "Canonizzazione," in *EC* III, Rome, p. 604; Federico Dell'Addolorata, "Infallibilità," ibid., VI, pp. 1920–24; Ortolan, "Canonisation," c. 1640.

because it would be intolerable if he were not! Obviously, there is no shortage of theological reasoning that would replace "intolerable" with "impossible": the promised divine assistance to the Church's magisterium, hence the guidance of the Holy Spirit, would connect canonizations with the truths of faith and morals, that is, with the specific object of papal infallibility.[10] Regarding such a connection, however, there are a few reasons to undertake more discussion.

All this opens a range of historical and theological reflections on the thesis under consideration; in particular, on the true notion of the ecclesiastical magisterium and of papal infallibility, as well as the ecclesiological implications of the substantial distinction between beatification and canonization. Precisely these sorts of clarifications are either lacking or lacking in specific relevance, both in the authors who are favorable to the common opinion and in those who are against it. The monotonous repetition of reasons insufficiently thought-through, but also reasons linked with concrete facts (for example, St. John Nepomucene and St. Maria Goretti in the past, others in the present) that might appear to call into question if not outright exclude the infallibility of canonization, will give neither the affirmative nor the negative positions wings to fly very high.

2. THE MAGISTERIUM OF THE CHURCH

"It is the power conferred by Christ on His Church, strengthened by the charism of infallibility, by virtue of which the teaching Church is made the sole depository and authentic interpreter of Divine Revelation, to be proposed authoritatively to men as the object of faith so as to attain eternal life."[11] Do not ask me for a theological demonstration of this definition; this is not the place to do it.

I am not sure to what extent this would be the correct application of the undeniable general principle from St. Thomas, *Quodl.*, IX, 16: "Si vero consideretur divina providentia quae Ecclesiam suam Spiritu Sancto dirigit ut non erret... certum est quod judicium Ecclesiae universalis errare in his quae ad fidem pertinent, impossibile est" (a passage to which we will return).

10   See A. P. Frutaz, "Auctoritate Beatorum Petri et Pauli—Saggio sulle formule di canonizzazione," in *Antonianum* 42 (1947): 1–22. On the question in general, instructive are the pages of M. Schenk, *Die Unfehlbarkeit des Papstes in der Heiligsprechung*, Fribourg, 1965.

11   See P. Parente, A. Piolanti, S. Garofalo, *Dizionario di Teologia Dogmatica,*

Still, it is well known to anyone well-versed in theology that such a magisterium rests on unequivocal assertions in the New Testament (Mt 16:16–20, 28:18), according to which we see that Christ made it the living instrument for the propagation and defense of His message, concentrating it above all in Peter (Mt 16:18–20; Lk 22:32; Jn 21:15–18). In him He obviously foresaw the unbroken chain of legitimate successors, thus characterizing the magisterium itself with the notes of universality, perpetuity, and infallibility (Mt 16:18–20; 18:18–20).

The Church's Tradition, explicitly or otherwise, has always seen in Peter and in his legitimate successors, as well as in the College of Apostles and the bishops who succeed them in governing the Church in communion with the pope — and never against, or without, or above him — the title-holders of this magisterium or teaching office, which by that fact is placed before the conscience of each believer and of the whole Church as the *regula fidei proxima* (proximate rule of faith). Indeed, Vatican I, followed by Vatican II, seemed to identify primacy and magisterium — even if formally one belongs more to the sphere of inter-ecclesial relations and the other to the sphere of Faith:

> That apostolic primacy which the Roman Pontiff possesses as successor of Peter, the prince of the apostles, includes also the supreme power of teaching. This Holy See has always maintained this, the constant custom of the Church demonstrates it, and the ecumenical councils, particularly those in which East and West met in the union of faith and charity, have declared it.[12]

The internal logic of the Faith, firmly resting on the rock of Divine Revelation, can therefore look to the ecclesiastical magisterium as the perennial and infallible charism of Christian Truth.

Rome, 1943, p. 154.

12 "Ipso autem Apostolico primatu, quem Romanus Pontifex tamquam Petri principis Apostolorum successor in universam Ecclesiam obtinet, supremam quoque magisterii potestatem comprehendi, haec Sancta Sedes semper tenuit, perpetuus Ecclesiae usus comprobat, ipsaque oecumenica Concilia ea imprimis in quibus Oriens cum Occidente in fidei caritatisque unionem conveniebat, declaraverunt." See Conc. Vat. I, Sess. IV, Constit. Dogm. *Pastor Aeternus*, cap. IV, DS 3065. See, in this regard, together with all the manuals of "Roman Theology," the two classics: J. V. Bainvel, *De Magisterio et Traditione*, Paris, 1905; L. Billot, *De Ecclesia Christi*, Rome, 1927. For Vatican II, see especially *LG* 22b and 25a–c.

2.1. The magisterium does not express itself univocally. It is not by chance that we speak — not always, unfortunately, correctly — of the "solemn," "extraordinary," and "ordinary and authentic" magisterium.

The magisterium's solemnity is in regard to its form. It reaches its height of solemnity when an ecumenical council is convened. The pope, too, can solemnly reprove an error and proclaim a doctrine or canonization; but although there is no council unless convened ("*per se vel per alios*") and confirmed by the pope, the solemnity of the papal act does not reach that of a council. This is given by the authoritative synergy of the bishops who, in communion with the Pope, are themselves the "subject of supreme and full power in the universal Church" (*LG* 22b), which they authentically represent and for which they collegially work. The fullness of magisterial power, in fact, resides not only in the Pope, but also in the *corpus episcoporum* in communion with him. Therefore, the solemnity of the magisterial act is realized personally in the pope and collegially in the ecumenical council; in both cases it is the Church's response to exceptional circumstances.

The extraordinary or ordinary character of the ecclesiastical magisterium depends on the manner in which it is conveyed, as well as on the circumstances in which and for which it is conveyed; it does not depend on its efficacy and extension. There is an ordinary magisterium of the Pope and an ordinary magisterium of the bishops, both individually and collegially considered, as successors of the Apostles and qualified witnesses of the faith. The extraordinary magisterium is expressed in the forms of the ecumenical council and of the *locutio ex cathedra* (i.e., a dogmatic pronouncement from the chair), but the ordinary magisterium is by far the most frequent throughout history, with modes of intervention that are neither *ex cathedra* nor conciliar. The pope exercises this ordinary magisterium through a range of interventions without a solemn or extraordinary form, in response to important but not extraordinary circumstances; the same is exercised by the bishops, in communion of faith and teaching with the pope, in the Episcopal Conferences, in their own dioceses, by written and oral teaching, with diocesan synods, with the composition and approval of catechisms, with the prudent cultivation of liturgical life. However, in the case of bishops, none of them can claim infallibility:

their infallibility is solely collegial, in the context, for example, of an ecumenical council.

It is customary also to speak of an "authentic" magisterium, recognizable in papal or episcopal interventions of which one wishes to attest either the undeniable pertinence and legitimacy, or its doctrinal and disciplinary validity. Vatican II's *Lumen Gentium* speaks of it three times: in 25a, in regard to bishops, who are called "authentic *doctores*, that is, teachers endowed with the authority of Christ"; again 25a, with reference to the pope, to commend "religious submission of will and intellect . . . in a special way to the authentic magisterium of the Roman Pontiff, even when he is not speaking *ex cathedra*"; and finally in 51a, to affirm that "the authentic *cultus* of the saints consists not so much in the multiplying of external acts, but rather in the greater intensity of our love."

Whence we can deduce the following: the Church's magisterium

i. is authentic by virtue of the one who pronounces it or the truth that is pronounced;

ii. is always authentic in each of its forms: solemn, extraordinary, and ordinary;

iii. can also be authentic outside of these forms, in less specific papal or episcopal interventions, as long as they are connected with Divine Revelation and the doctrine of the faith.

3. THE MAGISTERIUM'S INFALLIBILITY

I am not referring directly to the authentic magisterium which, as I have indicated above, may or may not be covered by the charism of infallibility. I am asking whether, why, and under what conditions the magisterium — solemn, extraordinary, or ordinary — is infallible. Given the aforementioned promise of divine assistance, the infallibility of magisterial interventions, within the limits of the promise, is among the prerogatives of the magisterium itself.

3.1. Divine assistance is the inescapable premise of any talk of the Church's and the pope's infallibility. It is the profound reason for the irreformable nature of every authentic magisterial intervention in matters of faith and morals (*in rebus fidei et morum*) — the profound reason too, therefore, for papal infallibility: with such assistance, God commits Himself, so to speak, in a papal declaration as a guarantee of its immutable truth. For this reason, "the definitions of the Roman Pontiff are irreformable of themselves, and not by the consensus of the Church."[13]

That the Lord has truly committed Himself to this finds testimony in his own words: by his prayer for the indefectibility of Peter and of his mission as universal teacher (Lk 22:32); by the assurance of his being with the Church until the end of the world (Mt 28:20); by the sending of the Spirit of Truth to the Church of yesterday, today, and tomorrow, so that he may lead her into all truth (Jn 16:13) and safeguard her from all error. It is a matter of divine assistance, which, according to the New Testament passages in support, cannot be classified solely as merely negative (*mere negativa*). It is regrettable that this limitation is still insisted upon by some, perhaps in order to avoid the danger of confusion between the assistance of the Holy Ghost and a private illumination or revelation.

Without a doubt, the infallibility of the pope must not be connected with some personal illumination from on high, nor with an equally personal revelation; but rather "for the upbuilding of the faith" (*ad aedificationem fidei*, Eph 4:29). In point of fact, if the "function" of the Spirit of the Father and of the Son is to lead the faith of the Church and of the Christian conscience itself into the "possession of all truth," then to limit this to some pure and simple preservation from error — that is the notion that we called *mere negativa* — is a mortifying debasement of it and deprives the magisterium of its propositional capacity.[14]

3.2. The previous coupling of papal infallibility and the infallibility of the Church is correct. It is right, because it conforms to Tradition and is confirmed by Vatican I: "We define that the Roman Pontiff possesses that infallibility which the divine Redeemer willed his Church

---

13 "Romani Pontificis definitiones ex sese, non autem ex consensu Ecclesiae, irreformabiles sunt." See Conc. Vatic. I, Sess. IV, Constit. Dogm. *Pastor Aeternus*, cap. IV, DS 3074.

14 That is, its authority to declare true propositions that accurately convey the teaching of Divine Revelation and must be believed. — *Ed.*

to enjoy in defining doctrine concerning faith or morals."[15] There are not two infallibilities in play that are added together or cancel each other out, but rather one and the same charism, which has its legitimate title-holders in the Church, in the pope, and in the bishops considered collegially and in communion with the pope. This charism is expressed in a positive form, before and perhaps more than in a negative form. It is at work when the magisterium, in proclaiming Christian truth or in settling eventual controversies, remains faithful to the *depositum fidei* (1 Tim 6:20; 2 Tim 1:4) or discovers in this deposit new or hitherto unexplored implications. It is also at work, in a way active and passive, in the so-called *sensus fidelium*, by which the entire People of God enjoys an infallibility that is not only reflexive but also propositional, both because of the presence within and among them of the teaching Church, and because of the Christian and prophetic witness of the laity.[16]

The mention of the *mere negativa*, moreover, underlines a function of infallibility that—so far from being a private prerogative, owing to an exceptional intelligence or to an extraordinary illumination from above—depends rather on the aforementioned divine assistance, to which it owes both the negative aspect (it preserves the Church from error) and the positive one (it leads her into all truth).

3.3. The pope, too, has been considered the holder of this infallibility, in both its negative and positive aspects, since the beginning of the Christian era. "Considered" is not the same as "defined," although in the final analysis it is the thing that counts, not how it is proposed.

St. Clement authoritatively inserted himself into questions of faith that arose in Corinth; St. Ignatius is seized with admiration for the Church in Rome; St. Irenaeus seeks communion with it; St. Cyprian recognizes in it the root of unity; St. Ambrose is the first to use Matthew 16:18 as the basis for discerning the true Church; and St.

---

15 "Definimus Romanum Pontificem ... ea infallibilitate pollere, qua divinus Redemptor Ecclesiam suam ... instructam esse voluit." Conc. Vatic. I, Sess. IV, Constit. Dogm. *Pastor Aeternus*, cap. IV.

16 If so desired, one may also distinguish between essential or absolute infallibility and participatory or relative infallibility: the first belongs to God *"qui nec falli nec fallere potest"*; the second is the charism granted by God to His Church.

Augustine does not hesitate to declare that, in the Roman Church, "the supremacy of an apostolic chair has always flourished,"[17] for the reason that the Lord Jesus "placed the teaching of truth in the chair of unity."[18]

It is part of this historical-traditional testimony that the popes, after Clement of Rome, always exercised, throughout the centuries, a universal and ungainsayable magisterial power. The grand era of Scholasticism, with Thomas, Bonaventure, and John Duns Scotus, added nothing new to the nearly universally-held doctrine of papal infallibility, except a greater theological foundation. Vatican I, finally, made it a dogma of faith, without thereby deifying a man or annulling in him the Church's prerogatives and, still less, her essence.

3.4. It seems most fitting at this point to turn our attentive consideration to the very words of the dogma:

> We define that the Roman Pontiff, when he speaks *ex cathedra*, that is, when, in the exercise of his office as shepherd and teacher of all Christians, in virtue of his supreme apostolic authority, he defines a doctrine concerning faith or morals to be held by the whole Church, he possesses, by the divine assistance promised to him in blessed Peter, that infallibility which the divine Redeemer willed his Church to enjoy in defining doctrine concerning faith or morals. Therefore, such definitions of the Roman Pontiff are of themselves, and not by the consent of the Church, irreformable.[19]

Words weighed with extreme rigor. Not only do they not deify a human being, but, in the very act of recognizing in him a charism no one else possesses, they set clear limits and rigid conditions to the exercise of it. The pope, in fact, "is not absolutely infallible simply by

---

17 See *Ep.* 43, 3/7 (*PL* 33, 163): "semper apostolicae cathedrae viguit principatus."
18 See *Ep.* 105, 5/16 (PL 33, 403): "in cathedra unitatis doctrinam posuit veritatis."
19 "Definimus Romanum pontificem, cum ex cathedra loquitur, id est, cum omnium Christianorum pastoris et doctoris munere fungens pro sua suprema Apostolica auctoritate doctrinam de fide vel moribus ab universa Ecclesia tenendam definit, per assistentiam divinam ipsi in beato Petro promissam, ea infallibilitate pollere, qua divinus Redemptor Ecclesiam suam in definienda doctrina de fide vel moribus instructam esse voluit; ideoque huiusmodi Romani pontificis definitiones ex sese, non autem ex consensu Ecclesiae, irreformabiles esse."

the fact that he is pope (*simpliciter ex auctoritate papatus*)."[20] Perhaps the time has come to repeat frankly and firmly what has already been reiterated in the recent and distant past about the need to free the papacy from a kind of "papolatry" that certainly does not contribute to the honor of the pope and of the Church.

Not all papal declarations are infallible, not all of them being on the same dogmatic level. Most of the speeches and papal documents, in fact, even when they touch upon something doctrinal, contain common teachings, pastoral guidelines, exhortations, and advice, which in regard to form and content are far from a dogmatic definition. Nor is there such a definition unless the conditions set forth by Vatican I are met. For that, it is necessary for the pope to speak:

- "*ex cathedra*"[21]: the expression takes its meaning from the exemplary and moderating function which, from the beginning, made the Bishop of Rome the teacher of the universal Church and made Rome itself the *locus magisterii*. In use since the second century as a symbol of a bishop's magisterial function, the *cathedra* (see, seat, chair) later became the symbol of the pope's magisterial function.[22] To speak *ex cathedra* means, therefore, to speak with the authority and responsibility of the one who enjoys supreme, ordinary, immediate, and full jurisdiction over the entire Church and over each of her faithful, including the pastors, in matters of faith and morals, but not without disciplinary repercussions and effects.
- "*omnium Christianorum pastoris et doctoris munere fungens*": this phrase makes explicit the content of *ex cathedra*. New Testament biblical sources and documents of Tradition

---

20 See *Acta et Decreta sacrorum Conciliorum recentiorum* in the *Collectio Lacensis*, Freiburg im Br., VIII, 248–56.

21 The formula comes from Melchior Cano (d. 1560), but the reference to the *cathedra* is frequent in the Fathers and obviously in authors who follow Cano as well: "Auctoritas infallibilis et summa cathedrae S. Petri" (D'Aguirre, d. 1699); "Cathedrae Apostolicae oecumenicae auctoritas" (anonymous, d. 1689). See E. Dublanchy, "Infaillibilité du Pape," *DThC* VII, Paris, 1972, c. 1689; see also M. Maccarrone, "La 'cathedra sancti Petri' nel Medioevo da simbolo a reliquia," in *Rivista di storia della Chiesa in Italia* XXXIX (1985): 349–447.

22 See M. Maccarrone, "'Cathedra Petri' und die Entwicklung der Idee des päpstlichen Primats vom 2. bis 4. Jahrhund.," in *Saeculum* 13 (1962): 278–92.

converge in the definition of Vatican I to affirm that the infallibility of the papal magisterium arises only when the pope teaches the contents of Divine Revelation to everyone and makes that teaching obligatory on all.

- *"Pro suprema sua Apostolica auctoritate"*: this is the formal reason for his infallible and universal teaching. Such a reason is due to the pope's apostolic succession from Peter, who was the first — but not the only — bishop of Rome, and was pope in virtue of being the bishop of Rome. Therefore, all that Christ had given to Peter, by reason of the office and not of the person (*ratione officii, non personae*), belongs to each of his successors on the "Roman chair." This is why it is less correct to say "the pope's personal infallibility" than to say "papal infallibility." Yet, even if someone wants to insist, as some do, on "personal infallibility," one should always distinguish in the pope his "public person" (*persona publica*) from his "private person," recalling that his "public person" is determined by his office.
- *"Doctrinam de fide vel moribus"*: that is, it must be a matter of truths to be believed and determining Christian existence (morals), contained directly or indirectly in Divine Revelation. Any different object of papal teaching cannot claim to be covered by the charism of infallibility, which extends as far as Divine Revelation itself.
- *"Per assistentiam divinam"*: not just any intervention of the pope, not his simple warning, not just any teaching of his, is guaranteed by the assistance of the "Spirit of Truth" (Jn 14:17; 15:26), but only that which is in harmony with revealed truths and manifests what the Christian, as such, must believe and put into practice.[23]

It is only in full and absolute adherence to these conditions that the pope is guaranteed infallibility: he can therefore appeal to it when he intends to oblige (that is, bind) Christians in faith and morals. It should also be added that it must be clear from the entirety of the papal intervention and from the words expressing it that, adhering to the previously indicated conditions, the will of the pope is indeed to define a truth as

23 See Dublanchy, "Infaillibilité," 1699–1705.

something directly or indirectly revealed, or to settle a disputed question *de fide et moribus*; as a result, the whole Church must then conform its teaching and coordinate its practice with what has been defined.

3.5. It is evident here that we are dealing not with generic and ambiguous notions of infallibility but rather with a rigorously theological notion of it. And even within this circumscribed definition, infallibility can be understood only if one avoids the lexical ambiguity of, for example, a Karl Barth, who confuses infallibility with indefectibility. [24]

On the other hand, the concept is not clarified, from a theological point of view, by ignoring it, [25] by relegating it transversally to other contexts, [26] or by considering it under formally incomplete aspects. One might think of a negative notion like *Irrtumlosigkeit* [27] (inerrancy), which certainly isn't false as far as it goes; but one should learn to speak of the *positive* side of infallibility: its fundamental worth, the grace, the charism that, by the will of Christ, enriches the Church and the pope.

Indeed, the positive meaning is primary and should be emphasized as such. On the one hand, it gives the maximum guarantee of truth (*fide divina vel divino-ecclesiastica*), and on the other hand it safeguards the truth itself from every erroneous or heretical counterfeit. Infallibility is thus shown to be infinitely more than the absence of error and the impossibility of error; it is the presence of truth, it is the superior certainty of truth, intimately and indissolubly united with the Church's own being. An error on the part of the Church with regard to the truths to be believed or the morals to be lived would work against the Church herself, destroying her. [28]

In short, and for these reasons, theological infallibility has a conceptual framework strongly conditioned by Revelation and therefore has little in common with philosophical, scientific, and juridical infallibility.

---

24   See *Kirchliche Dogmatik*, IV/1, pp. 770–72.
25   See, e.g., H. Fries (ed.), *Handbuch theologischer Grundbegriffe*, Munich, 1963.
26   See ibid., I:180, 809, 854, 857; II:270, 274.
27   See ibid., I:718, 817, 857; II:518.
28   See Rahner and Vorgrimler, *Kleines theolog. Wörterbuch*, Freiburg im Br., 1961, cit. by M. Löhrer, "Portatori della Rivelazione," in *MS* 2, Brescia, 1973, p. 87.

4. INFALLIBILITY AND THE ORDINARY MAGISTERIUM

Before we ask ourselves whether the canonization of a blessed fully and absolutely respects the above-mentioned conditions and therefore enjoys infallibility, it is necessary to go back to the question of the ordinary magisterium of the pope and to verify whether or not it is infallible. One would be mistaken to judge that the adjective "ordinary" is synonymous with "less important or less valid." Its meaning is inferred from the papal office and its reference to what is certainly an authentic form of the exercise of that office, even when it is not solemn or extraordinary.

Now, not being obliged to always treat of matters *de fide et moribus*, nor only at extraordinary moments and for extraordinary reasons, nor to always treat of such things in the solemn form of the *locutio ex cathedra* — in point of fact, this rarely happens! — most of the time the pope treats of these things in the ordinary form, by having recourse particularly to encyclicals, bulls, constitutions, and so forth.

In the Church's more recent history, we know of some encyclicals that are certainly solemnly *ex cathedra* in form, from Pius IX's *Ineffabilis Deus*[29] to Pius XII's *Munificentissimus Deus*,[30] dedicated, respectively, to the dogma of the Immaculate Conception and to that of the Assumption; some[31] would include among these *Humanae Vitae* of Paul VI, on the transmission of human life.[32] Dublanchy,[33] a bit overzealous, recognizes the dogmatic character of some of Leo XIII's encyclicals by virtue of their doctrinal content: the doctrine on Christian marriage in *Arcanum* (February 10, 1880); on the divine origin of all power, including civil power, in *Diuturnum Illud* (June 20, 1881); on the sovereign and innate independence of the Church from the State in *Immortale Dei* (November 1, 1885); on the inspiration and inerrancy of Sacred Scripture in *Providentissimus Deus* (November 18, 1893); on the primacy of the Supreme Pontiff and on the nature of the Church in *Satis Cognitum* (June 29, 1896).

---

29 December 8, 1854: DS 2800–804.
30 November 1, 1950: DS 3900–904.
31 See E. Lio, *«Humanae vitae» e infallibilità*, Città del Vaticano, 1986.
32 July 25, 1968: *AAS* 60 (1968).
33 See "Infallibilité," 1705–6.

The fact is that the charism of infallibility can also be found in the pope's ordinary magisterium, even if it does not meet all the conditions of an *ex cathedra* definition. If the pope really wanted to proclaim a truth as a dogma of the faith, or to determine its exact meaning and connection with the Catholic Faith, the *locutio ex cathedra* would be the most suitable form for the purpose; in that case, the pope is also required to explicitly manifest his will and his awareness of speaking as "pastor and teacher of the entire Church" and of declaring his "definitory" intention. As we have said, he does not, however, always proclaim a truth *definitorio modo*, i.e., *ex cathedra*.

If a truth has already been defined or it is a matter of a truth deduced from revealed truths, or one strictly connected with revealed and defined truths; or if the manner of speaking in the papal discourse is, in its circumstances and content, of an ordinary character, then in such a case the pope's words do not go beyond the level of *definitive tenendum* (to be definitively held). In either case, however, the charism of papal infallibility is in action due to the presence of evidently dogmatic conditions. In the *definitorio modo*, it is so directly and immediately because all the conditions are met to which it is linked; in the *definitive tenendum*, it is so indirectly and almost reflexively. The key datum that emerges, at any rate, is that infallibility is present. How, in fact, can it be denied to a magisterium which, albeit in ordinary form, re-proposes the truths contained in the Creed and in the various professions of faith, in the Anti-Modernist Oath (in the first and second paragraphs), in the sacred liturgy (which is dogma prayed), and in the Church's sacramental life?

The question, then, against the background of the foregoing, is whether a canonization — be it formal or equipollent — falls within the dogmatic framework of papal infallibility and therefore enjoys this prerogative.

5. THE DOGMATIC FACT

Let it be noted: my heading says "fact" — not truth or doctrine. That it is defined as "dogmatic" does not in and of itself imply that we're dealing with a supernatural fact. The Incarnation of the Word, His Passion and redeeming death, His resurrection and ascension into heaven—to give just a few examples—are undoubtedly facts. But their occurrence on the supernatural plane excludes them from being qualified as dogmatic in the sense used by post-Tridentine theology: they are themselves true and proper dogmas, truths divinely revealed, inserted by the Church into her Creed.

According to theology after the Council of Trent, dogmatic facts belong to the concreteness of things, to their factual reality and natural knowability, while maintaining their relationship with the world of faith. By analogy, they can be connected with natural truths, i.e., those known by the sole powers of human reason, such as God's existence, the soul's spirituality and immortality, and the moral law: natural truths which then find confirmation in Christian Revelation and thus also become objects of supernatural knowledge. Indeed, even so-called dogmatic facts maintain a connection between their natural and supernatural realms. They are not just any facts; their very factuality pertains to revealed truths. They are therefore related to dogma; hence their qualification as dogmatic facts.

However, it must be acknowledged that, in theology, there is no univocal judgment on dogmatic facts. It can only be said that in theological authors there is preeminent reference to concrete situations or events—e.g., that St. Peter was present in Rome as the bishop there; the history of an ecumenical council, the collision of its internal currents and the debates over its doctrine—in which there is also clearly to be found a dogmatic significance by virtue of their logical and necessary connection with truths contained in Revelation and dogmatically defined.

The question over dogmatic facts erupted when, on May 31, 1653, Innocent X condemned five propositions extracted from Jansen's work *Augustinus*. By distinguishing between the doctrine of the five propositions and their inclusion in *Augustinus*, some objected to the infallibility of the condemnation by denying that the condemned teaching was actually found in the incriminated work. The controversy is well known and thus there is no reason to insist on it: I say only that both the Church's magisterium as well as theological reflection have demonstrated the groundlessness of that distinction. In particular, the great Bossuet, later followed by Fénelon, highlighted twenty-four cases in which the ecclesiastical magisterium had author-itatively and definitively made a pronouncement regarding *facts*, prior to or instead of doctrines.[34]

The subsequent development of theological reflection connected dogmatic facts with certain defined truths of faith, thanks to the presence in them of a bond, either intrinsic or extrinsic, between facts and truth. One would call "intrinsic" the bond that connects facts integrally with a dogma, e.g., original sin. One would call "extrinsic," on the other hand, the bond that connects facts and dogma but from outside the dogma itself, e.g., the defense of a defined truth, the legit-imacy of a papal election, the condemnation of a heterodox book or a heretical teaching.[35] These are always "contingent facts... having a necessary 'moral' connection with the Church's primary end, which is to preserve and explain the revealed deposit."[36]

Attention to such facts is justified, therefore, not by a purely his-torical interest in them, but because of their involvement with dogma. And since "among dogmatic facts canonization is universally num-bered,"[37] the consequence that it is infallible must be considered unexceptionable from the formal point of view.

But does the formal point of view suffice?

It was especially Fénelon[38] who asserted the infallibility of magis-terial judgments regarding dogmatic facts, but even he justified this with a *reductio ad absurdum*: if it were not infallible in such matters, the magisterium would deceive itself and, with it, the whole Church. And in this he continued, in substance, the constant teaching of the Church, at least from St. Bernard onwards — and particularly St. Thomas Aquinas, on whose words I will speak shortly. This teach-ing still insists today on the need to recognize in dogmatic facts their

---

34   In this regard, see E. Dublanchy, "Eglise," in *DThC* IV, Paris, 1939, esp. 2188–210.

35   See G. De Rosa, "Fatti dogmatici," in *EC* III, Rome, 1995, p. 1058.

36   See F. Veraja, *La canonizzazione equipollente e la questione dei miracoli nelle cause di canonizzazione*, Rome, 1975, p. 14.

37   Ibid.

38   See "Instruction pastorale," February 10, 1704, in *Oeuvres complètes* III, 579ff.; "Instruction pastorale," March 2, 1705, ibid., IV, 16ff.; "Deuxième lettre à l'évêque de Meaux," IV, 338; "Lettre sur l'infaillibilité de l'Eglise touchant les textes dogmatiques," V, 108ff., in Dublanchy, "Eglise," 2190–91.

intrinsic or extrinsic infallibility, so that the Church may be able to respond with certainty to her universal mission. An error in such a matter — and here the *reductio ad absurdum* reappears — would have deleterious repercussions on Christian life. The approval or disapproval of a religious order, congregation, or institute would have the same repercussions if the Pope could fall into error in such matters. Religious life, for example, would lose the certainty of being presented to the Christian conscience as an instrument of perfection.

The possibility of such an error, targeted by Melchior Cano,[39] was already decisively rejected in his time. Both in the field of the aforementioned approbations and condemnations and in that of canonizations (and therefore in relation to every dogmatic fact), the pope's ordinary magisterium was claimed to have that infallibility which is usually recognized in the exercise of the extraordinary and solemn magisterium, even in the absence of formal definitions. In establishing discipline for the universal Church as well as for the Diocese of Rome, and in teaching it as its pastor and doctor, the pope enjoys, in fact, the same infallibility with which Christ endowed his Church. Nevertheless, in order for him to be able to appeal to this infallibility, it is necessary that his interventions always be traceable, directly or not, to Christian Revelation.

But is a canonization so traceable? That is the issue.

6. THEOLOGICAL ELABORATION

The overwhelming majority of theologians responded in the affirmative: those who lean towards a negative response or even only a doubtful one are very few. The question, as I said at the beginning, is now back on the table.

6.1. The press agency of the Priestly Fraternity of St. Pius X[40] has called into question the infallibility of canonizations only for contingent reasons: the canonization of this or that candidate. Others, with reasons of undoubted theological weight and for underlying reasons, had already raised doubts. Among them, for example, is Francis A. Sullivan, for

---

39 See *De locis theologicis* V, 5 in *Opera omnia*, Venice, 1759, p. 140.
40 See *DICI* 50, March 22, 2002.

whom "it is not clear why a canonization ought to enjoy papal infallibility" or how it allows the "magisterium . . . to preserve and explain the deposit of Revelation."[41] On the level of historical verification and theological criticism, Fr. De Vooght also took a negative stance with a powerful essay in which he laments, among other things, that "the infallibility of the Church and the pope has not only not prevented but has even authorized and encouraged the Christian people for many centuries to venerate saints, of whom today we know that they never existed."[42]

At the same point in time, with an eye to concrete facts, P. Delooz reached similar conclusions.[43] De Vooght expresses them, however, with his unheard-of peremptory style: "Papal infallibility — it must be proclaimed very loudly for the honor of the Church — is the infallibility of a man who, also as a pope, can err and has frequently erred."[44]

More recently, Daniel Ols, a Dominican, has spoken on the subject. His conclusion is quite clear: "Since canonization is not necessary for the safeguarding and defense of the faith, it does not seem that it can be a subject of infallibility."[45] On the other hand, in recent times, some have spoken out again in favor of it: F. Ricossa[46] and E. Piacentini,[47] in line with the position of the aforementioned majority which, in the preconciliar and immediately postconciliar period, counted among its members E. J. Kieda,[48] E. Spedalieri,[49] and U. Betti,[50] besides those we've already named: Frutaz, Veraja, Löw, and

---

41   See *Il magistero della Chiesa cattolica*, Assisi, 1986, pp. 155–56.

42   See "Les dimensions réelles de l'infaillibilité papale," in E. Castelli (ed.), *L'Infaillibilité, son aspect philosophique et théologique* (Atti del Convegno del Centro Intern. di Studi umanistici e dell'Istituto di Studi filosofici, Rome, February 5–12, 1970), Paris, 1970, esp. 145–49.

43   See *Sociologie et canonisation*, Liège, 1969.

44   See "Les dimensions," 156.

45   See Ols, "Fondamenti teologici," 35.

46   See "L'infallibilità del Papa e la Canonizzazione dei Santi," in *Sodalitium* XVIII/54 (2002): 4–5.

47   See *Infallibile anche nelle cause di canonizzazione?*, Rome, 1994.

48   See "Infallibility of the Pope in his decrees of Canonization," in *The Jurist* 6 (1946), esp. 405–15.

49   See "De infallibilitate Ecclesiae in Sanctorum canonizationis causa," in *Antonianum* 22 (1947): 1–22.

50   See "Il magistero infallibile del Romano Pontefice," in *Divinitas* 5 (1961): 581–606.

so many more. It's an impressive group that supports the more traditional doctrine. For this school, there's no doubt that at least an indirect correlation exists between the infallibility of canonizations and Christian Revelation. What is not convincing, however, is the common blandness of the reasons marshaled, as well as the absence of a true, proper, and critically profound examination and the absence of personal elaborations of the doctrine — although the same thing can be said for those who oppose it.

6.2. As proof of the link between canonization and Revelation, it is customary to distinguish between the primary and secondary objects of infallibility. With the *per se* impossibility of including canonization among the primary objects of infallibility — since they are obviously not the direct and explicit content of Revelation — one would include it among the secondary objects of the so-called "connected truths," and a "theological conclusion"[51] would suffice to make such an inclusion legitimate. In this way canonization would then find itself covered by the charism of papal infallibility — in the same way as dogmatic facts and ecclesiastical legislation — because it is "connected" with Revelation by two truths of faith: worship or *cultus*, and the communion of saints. Thus linked to Revelation, it consequently assumes a universal force, which the Pope himself echoes during the rite: by canonizing a blessed, he proposes the saint's exemplarity to the whole Church and authorizes, if not outright demanding, veneration everywhere.

Such universality, which simultaneously extends a canonization to the entire Church in space and time, is one of the elements on which the defense of the infallibility of canonizations is ordinarily based. The pope, it is said, cannot make mistakes in that which concerns the Church of today and tomorrow, here and everywhere: he cannot lead her to the brink of the abyss, much less feed her with poison. If, therefore, he makes a gesture that involves the whole Church, the charism of his "personal" infallibility is triggered with it and in it. Moreover, together with this universality, other reasons too would militate in favor, as listed by Piacentini[52]:

---

51 On this point, see "Conclusione teologica," *EC* III, Rome, 1950, c. 184ff.
52 See "Infallibile," 39–47.

- an implicit requirement to venerate the saints, as in Tridentine legislation;
- a consequence of the formulas in use and the defining tenor of them;
- the need for universally valid models to imitate, venerate, and invoke;
- the direct appeal of the pope to his infallibility;
- the presence of a theological conclusion drawn from two premises, one of faith and the other of reason;
- the nature of canonizations as a dogmatic fact;
- right worship and the communion of saints as a dogmatic nexus of canonization and Divine Revelation.

6.3. It does not seem to me that such reasons should be rejected *en bloc* and *a priori*; I too perceive a certain value in them, albeit minimal and equivocal. Yet I also recognize the weight of contrary arguments, particularly those deriving from cases of non-existent saints or of saints who were not actually saints (holy). It seems to me to be useless and hardly honest to hide behind the cover of the declared enemies of Holy Church, from whose denigration, and only from that, would depend the historical non-existence of this or that saint, or his moral unworthiness. Such cases exist and the Church, the teacher of truth, has nothing to fear in recognizing and disavowing them. The most recent example, in confirmation of this point, was the postconciliar suppression of certain feasts of saints on whom historical research had not been able to shed light. I must therefore conclude that not all of these reasons present an identical incontrovertible force. What's more, even the weighter arguments offer some areas for discussion.

I welcome, then, this discussion — not only for the benefit of the *subiecta materia*, but also to guard against the monotony of the unconvinced and even less convincing repetitions.

7. OBJECTIONS AND RESERVATIONS

This paragraph's title does not allude to an anti-infallibilist position, to use a term frequently deployed in the diatribes on papal infallibility before and after Vatican I. It refers to only one aspect of this discussion — that relating to the infallibility of canonizations — and not in order to say no, *tout court*, to such infallibility, but rather to point out, according to my personal judgment, the questionability of the reasons that support it. I am well aware that I am placing myself among the minority[53] and I am not ignorant of that most grave judgment of the acknowledged master in this matter[54] against those who would dare to oppose this type — or, better said, *object* — of infallibility. Such a person could not escape the notes of "temerarious and scandalous," "injurious to the saints and favorable to heretics"; may God deliver me from such! Yet I think that the already mentioned margins of freedom allow me to say why the reasons from which such drastic consequences are drawn do not seem cogent to me.

I commence with the nature of canonization: everyone agrees that it is *non immediate de fide*. In order to qualify as such, it would have to coincide with what Vatican I calls a *locutio ex cathedra* and not circumvent any of its conditions. However, it is evident that canonization does not define any revealed truth; and as regards its "moral and necessary connection" with some such truths, by virtue of which (and therefore *mediate*) canonization would become, at least implicitly, *de fide*, I ask myself if the reasons inferred by St. Thomas are correctly interpreted and persuasive.

The Angelic Doctor says, and all monotonously repeat after him: "Because the honor we show the saints is a certain profession of faith, i.e., the faith by which we believe in the glory of the saints, it is a thing to be piously believed that the judgment of the Church could not err even in these matters."[55] Just before that he had stated:

> If Divine Providence were to be considered which directs His Church by the Holy Spirit so that she might not err . . . it is certain that for the judgment of the Church universal to

---

53 In favor of papal infallibility in the declaration of saints, there is the greater part of the great theologians, especially St. Thomas, *Quodl.* IX, 16; Melchior Cano, *De locis theologicis* V, 5, 5, 3; Suárez, *Defensio fidei adv. Anglic. sect. errores* in *Opera omnia*, Paris, 1856–78, XII:163 and XXIV:165; Lambertini, *De Servorum Dei beatificatione*, I:44,4 and II:229,2.

54 See Lambertini, I:45,28. Cf. Ols, "Fondamenti teologici," 49.

55 "Quia honor quem sanctis exhibemus, quaedam professio fidei est, qua sanctorum gloriam credimus, pie credendum est quod nec etiam in his iudicium ecclesiae errare possit."

err in these things which pertain to faith is impossible.... Whereas in other sentences, which pertain to *particular facts*, as when the Church deals with possessions or crimes or things of this sort, it is possible that the judgment of the Church should err on account of false witnesses.[56]

St. Thomas' shrewdness—and Fr. Ols points this out as well[57]—is such as to lead him to distinguish between certainty and certainty: dogmatic certainty, which is expressed in the area of faith; and non-dogmatic certainty, which is expressed in areas not directly connected with faith. The one peremptorily excludes the possibility of error (*certum est quod impossibile est*), while the other has room for it (*possibile est*). And the reason for this admission is not only human fallibility but also human malice (*propter falsos testes*; and he had already stated: *iudicium eorum qui praesunt Ecclesiae errare in quibuslibet, si personae eorum tantum respiciantur, possibile est*: for the judgment of those who are over the Church to err in whatever matters, if only their persons should be regarded, is possible). Despite the fact that the Angelic Doctor also includes canonization in the ambit of those things to which the promise of divine assistance extends (and for that reason he recognizes its infallibility), it must be highlighted that for him canonization is not part of *hiis quae ad fidem pertinent* and that, therefore, considered outside of that divine assistance—that is, in the judgment *eorum qui praesunt Ecclesiae*—it could also be subject to error. It's not by chance that I emphasized the words *particularia facta*: that was to indicate that even the so-called dogmatic fact to which canonization is usually assimilated, in that which concerns its singular concreteness and contingency, could be judged erroneously, with grave prejudice to its connection with dogma. If the Angelic Doctor saves canonization from error, it is not because he does not remember that *qui praesunt Ecclesiae errare possunt*; or because he

---

56 "Si consideretur divina providentia quae Ecclesiam suam Spiritu Sancto dirigit ut non erret, ... certum est quod iudicium Ecclesiae universalis errare in his quae ad fidem pertinent, impossibile est ... in aliis vero sententiis, quae ad *particularia facta* pertinent, ut cum agitur de possessionibus vel de criminibus vel de huiusmodi, possibile est iudicium ecclesiae errare propter falsos testes." See S. Thomas, *Quodl.* IX, 16 c. (Emphasis added.)
57 See "Fondamenti teologici," 45.

does not take into account the fact that canonization is extraneous to Revelation, convinced as he is that there is no infallible teaching of the Church except in matters of revealed truths and in things necessary for eternal salvation. He limits himself to saying that papal infallibility in canonizing someone is the object of "pious belief" (*pie creditur*), since canonization itself *quaedam professio fidei est... ad gloriam Sanctorum.*

There is nothing to object to regarding Thomas's link between canonization and the profession of faith in the glorification of the saints. Yet it is certainly not a link of such a sort that it transforms a papal judgment on the uncommon, indeed heroic, quality of a Christian witness into a divinely, albeit implicitly and indirectly, revealed truth. Lacking then the revealed object, it would hardly be respectful of dogma and of its exigencies to assimilate canonization to such an object

i. simply because the Pope "cannot err" without that act entailing very serious consequences for the whole Church;

ii. and simply because he observes, also while canonizing, a universal intentionality that guides his every *locutio ex cathedra*.

These two points, in any case, would have to be verified in light of the limits and conditions to which every dogmatic pronouncement is subject.

A second point concerns the eternal salvation of the one canonized. I offer as a premise that if the infallibility of canonization is not rigorously *de fide*, neither are the *declaratio* and the *praesumptio* of the status of *comprehensor* with regard to a canonized person. The problem, therefore, lies entirely in that expression "rigorously *de fide*." If it were really so, canonization would be grafted onto the whole (the "Symbol") of the truths to be believed. Since the evidence excludes such a graft, it insists rather on the *non immediate de fide*, that is, on a reflexive, indirect, implicit faith — except that, in its entirety, divine Revelation does not offer a single link between any of its truths and canonization; and then it is not seen how one would base on canonization the direct and necessary deduction of a theological conclusion that connects it to the faith, albeit *non immediate*.

The unique connection could be gathered from the texts (Mt 16:18–19, 18:18) that promise a divine endorsement of the pope's and the Church's work. The result would not be *de fide divina* but rather *de fide ecclesiastica*, based on a magisterial deduction and on an application of a divine promise for the magisterium's exercise. The certainty of divine endorsement is, here, beyond discussion; it has on its side the reality of the divine promise and the continuous "witness of the Church and of Her visible Head, to whom God promised infallibility."[58] But God promised it for a well-circumscribed exercise of magisterial power, as is clear from a sound exegesis of the texts cited above and from the very decree of Vatican I. This delimitation excludes the possibility that canonization and dogmatic definition are equivalent. And it also excludes the possibility that the immediate object of canonization comprises the eternal glory of the canonized in one and the same expression *de fide*.[59]

The decisive role of the pope's will in beatifying and canonizing someone is well known: it delimits beatification to particular churches or to well-defined portions of the People of God, and it confers on canonization a universal force, declaring it valid if not also obligatory for the whole Church. This is a role that no Catholic disputes: all recognize it as firmly linked to the power of the keys (*potestas clavium*). However, this does not mean that the charism of infallibility arises from it. This, as we have seen, is always legitimized by the *reductio ad absurdum*: "otherwise the Church would teach error; otherwise the Church would not be *Mater et magistra*; otherwise the faithful would be deceived."

Yet it seems to me that the charism of infallibility when linked to the *reductio ad absurdum* loses much of its value and remains difficult to understand. In fact, it does not explain how and why it is activated in the case of canonization and not in that of beatification. No one, let's be clear, intends to limit the freedom of the pope any

---

58 See Ortolan, "Canonisation," 1641.

59 The statements contrary to the common teaching, following Bellarmine, *De sanctorum beatitudine* II, col. 699 (1,7), and Lambertini, *De Servorum Dei*, I:39,5 (II,170), all rest on the already mentioned logical *reductio ad absurdum*. In any case, only the formal declaration of the pope who does the canonizing would be *de fide*—not the eternal glory of the one who is canonized; indeed this heavenly glory would be very difficult to deduce from a revealed truth, or as something simply subordinate to such a truth.

more than the sacred texts and dogma require; and no one, therefore, is able to prevent the pope, in the freedom of his primatial power, from extending the efficacy of one of his acts either to the universal Church or to a particular Church. But neither this freedom nor the extension of its exercise implies or requires as necessary the coverage of infallibility. On the contrary, it is an ecclesiological reason that excludes precisely this coverage. The Church, to be sure, is not a sum of particular churches:

> Jesus Christ did not, in point of fact, institute a Church to embrace several communities similar in nature, but in themselves distinct, and lacking those bonds which render the Church unique and indivisible after that manner in which in the symbol of our faith we profess: "I believe ... in one Church."[60]

This being the nature of the Church, *LG* 26a rightly draws the following conclusion: "This Church of Christ is truly present in all legitimate local congregations of the faithful."[61] This means that even the most remote Christian community, as long as it is legitimate, is the Church: in it is the Catholic Church. Therefore, every ecclesiastical decision *in rebus fidei et morum* addressed to "a legitimate particular congregation of the faithful" concerns that group insofar as it is "Church," because it *is* the Church. And this has, at least implicitly, a universal as well as a particular extension. It is from the universal Church, in fact, that the particular Church derives its legitimacy as Church. So, this unitary compactness or coherence of the Church means that every magisterial decision along universal lines touches all the individual churches; and *vice versa*, whatever is addressed to them is not extraneous to the universal Church. What sense, then,

---

60 "Ecclesiam suam Iesus Christus non talem finxit formavitque, quae communitates plures complecteretur genere similes, sed distinctas neque iis vinculis alligatas, quae Ecclesiam individuam atque unicam efficerent, eo plane modo quo 'Credo unam ... Ecclesiam' in Symbolo fidei profitemur." See Leo XIII, Encycl. *Satis cognitum*, June 29, 1896, DS 3303; cf. DS 3305: "At vero qui unicam condidit, is idem condidit unam: videlicet eiusmodi, ut quotquot in ipsa futuri essent, arctissimis vinculis sociati tenerentur ita prorsus, ut unam gentem, unum regnum, corpus unum efficerent."

61 "Haec Christi Ecclesia vere adest in omnibus legitimis fidelium congregationibus localibus."

does it make to distinguish canonization, said to be infallible because it is universal, from beatification, said to be not infallible because it is local? If the one is supported by the charism of infallibility, why shouldn't the other be? And if beatification is not infallible, why is or should canonization be?

In the history of the Church, even recently, there have been questionable saints who have been (and continue to be) subject to not exactly positive remarks. Others, as I have already pointed out, did not even exist. It is not my intention to descend into details, submitting one or the other to an investigation *super virtutibus* and for historical verification: I am not writing to polemicize. On the other hand, those who have done so have received unconvincing answers, especially when "constructed at the expense of history." No one is authorized — not even the pope or the Church — to place as a saint in the reality of history those who did not live as saints and even less those who did not live at all because they were never born. The critical question is therefore inescapable: Did the canonization of questionable or non-existent saints, or even the mere tolerance of their official cult, take place under the banner of infallibility?

The proclamation of a new Doctor of the Church can be considered closely related to the charism of infallibility — perhaps even more so than canonization itself.[62] Not long ago there was one that, previously, had been clearly rejected by another pope. It is true that the "no" was not the result of a formal act, but of an informal decision. It was, however, an authentic decision and one that could be

---

62 Gherardini seems to have in mind the fact that canonization, at least according to some theologians, means no more than that a soul is in heavenly glory and that the faithful must acknowledge this glorification; whereas the act of naming a certain theologian a Doctor implies that his teaching on faith and morals is a trustworthy guide for all Christians everywhere and of all times, which is arguably more immediately pertinent to and engages more fully the magisterium as a *teaching* authority. Against this proposal would stand the fact that the proclamation of a saint as a Doctor is done with far less solemnity than that which a canonization is done (the language alone makes that clear), nor does there appear to be a unanimous and authoritative definition of what exactly a Doctor is and exactly what are the obligations of the faithful towards the Church's Doctors, apart from acknowledging their orthodoxy with reverence. St. Thomas Aquinas would, however, be a unique case, as he has been not only singled out by dozens of popes as the prince of theologians, but even made the subject of canonical requirements. — *Ed.*

linked, by virtue of its object, to the ordinary magisterium. And here, once again, is the critical question: which of the two popes was infallible — the one who said no, or the one who said yes?

That being the case, questions, perplexities, and reservations coagulate, making the union of infallibility with canonization very difficult to maintain. Difficult, because the reasons for the yes vote, under the scrutiny of criticism, lose not a little of their force.

- The Tridentine approval of the cult of saints is historically undeniable, as well as theologically unexceptionable and dogmatically indisputable. That this approval reveals the *potestas sanctificandi* (power of sanctifying) can also be readily granted. But that the Council of Trent considered this *potestas* infallible is at least something to be demonstrated. Between the power to proclaim new saints and the infallibility of the proclamation there is such a diversity of formal aspects that the one thing is not, nor does it demand, the other. And those who would claim otherwise would behave in a logically and theologically incorrect way.

- As regards the communion of the saints, whoever knows its precise theological notion can only abstain from making it a foundation of papal infallibility to guarantee canonization: moreover, the terms "saints" in this formula ("communion of saints") does not allude either exclusively or even principally to the canonized.

- It does seem at first sight to be an indubitable fact that the formulas in use, and especially the reference that some popes make to their infallibility in the very act of canonizing, as well as the recourse of papal bulls of canonization to expressions typical of "definitory" language, would testify to a *praesumptio infallibilitatis*. Yet it is precisely this factual datum — in light of the questions and reservations I have expounded here — that gives this critical question an even stronger impact and a greater emphasis: How and why was this presumption possible? How and why is it still possible today? Upon what basis of indisputable theological validity?

- It is evident that today as well as yesterday, and tomorrow too, man has a vital need for Christian models to imitate. But there is an abyss of gratuitousness in going from this to qualifying as infallible the proposal of any single model.

It is true that canonization is comparable to a dogmatic fact. But it is precisely insofar as it is a dogmatic fact that it raises certain questions about its connection with Christian Revelation and with truths that the Church has defined as revealed. Indeed, it remains to be demonstrated whether, concretely, a dogmatic fact is linked to dogma thanks to an intrinsic bond or an extrinsic one. The bond is there by definition and cannot be denied; therefore, at least indirectly and implicitly, a dogmatic fact could be, in some way, not extraneous to the charism of infallibility. Instead, what is not clear is why canonization should be assimilated to a dogmatic fact. The fact that this is stated and repeated is not a sufficient reason; it is not by chance that the ancients warned: *quod gratis asseritur, gratis negatur* (what is gratuitously asserted can be gratuitously denied).

Gratuitous and thus refutable is, therefore, the following reasoning: every canonization is infallible because it is a dogmatic fact insofar as it "authoritatively proposes to the whole Church a model of holiness to be imitated, venerated, and invoked."[63] It seems clear that this is not an argument but an affirmation: as if infallibility itself here is, *per se, liquido pateat* (abundantly obvious).

8. CONCLUSION

It is superfluous to repeat that the present article is neither a formal denial of papal infallibility in the *subiecta materia*, nor a symptom of my adherence to contentious trends. I know, by the grace of God and through my own long academic experience as a teacher of ecclesiology, that the Church is ever Mother and Teacher and that, as such, she is the sole anchor of salvation. I have no certainties that she herself has not communicated and guaranteed to me; nor do I have perplexities, doubts, and reservations — in the order of eternal salvation — that she could not silence and resolve.

---

63   See Frutaz, "La Santità," 119.

The present work, therefore, stands confidently and reverently before her, having the meaning of "methodological doubt": it is not an end in itself; it does not surreptitiously and fearfully conceal the hand that would stir up the hornets' nest, nor does it let what it dare not openly declare emerge out of the mists of indirect discourse. Mine is a doubt that, not opposing any magisterial assertion, wishes simply to be a means for reaching a higher degree of certainty; and, all in all, it is within the bounds of that freedom which the absence of the theological note *immediate de fide* opens to the Christian conscience in looking to the link between papal infallibility and canonization. It is to be hoped — it seems to me, for the seriousness of Catholic theology — that there will not be a sterile polemic over this link, nor the slavish repetition of reasons for or against, but a deeper and more original discussion. It could already be a step forward, for example, if one recognized that the *non immediate de fide* finds a confirmation in the act of canonization itself, which does not insert the new saint into the Creed so that we might "believe in" the saint, but declares *that* he is such, i.e., a saint. And even outside the aforementioned link, it would be no trivial matter if it were established that the meaning of "saint," as understood by the bulls of canonization, is that of "worthy of veneration" and not that of "*comprehensor* in beatitude" — the latter area being more appropriately left to the free and incontestable judgment of God.

It is equally important not to hide behind the distinction between formal and equipollent canonization: what is at stake for both is the infallibility of the one who canonizes, not the manner in which he canonizes. Finally, it would also seem opportune to give an authentic interpretation of the censures that often accompany the bulls of individual canonizations: they are not an excommunication, since they are not consequent to a dogmatic definition; are they then merely a moral or juridical censure of the behavior of the faithful toward the newly-canonized individual? As one can see, the path to a more profound appraisal is wide and open. The essential thing is not to remain behind a corner.

8

The Authority of Canonizations[†]

JOHN R.T. LAMONT

THE CANONIZATIONS OF JOHN XXIII AND JOHN
Paul II, and the announcement of the pending canonization of Paul
VI, have raised some controversy among traditionalists. On the one
hand, objections have been raised to the conduct of the process of
these canonizations and to the claim that these pontiffs exhibited
heroic virtue. On the other hand, there has been a tendency to hold
that traditionalists should accept that all canonizations are infallible,
because this is thought to be the traditional theological view. This
latter tendency seems to have got the upper hand, with the result that
Catholics have largely come to the conclusion that once someone is
canonized, it is the duty of Catholics to accept his sanctity and to
cease questioning his canonization. This essay is intended to reject
this conclusion, and to present an alternative view on the subject of
the duty of Catholics with regard to canonizations.

The view that is being advanced here needs to be carefully explained
at the outset. It is not the claim that Catholics are free to accept or
reject the truthfulness of canonizations that are officially promulgated
by the Supreme Pontiff, as they please. Nor is it the view that canonizations are not authoritative, in the sense of deriving their claim to
acceptance purely from the evidence that is presented for the sanctity of
the person canonized, and not at all from the fact of the official promulgation itself. Such promulgations in themselves give rise to a duty of
belief on the part of Catholics. Nor is it the view that the canonizations
of John XXIII and John Paul II are erroneous because these individuals
are not now enjoying the beatific vision in heaven. The sanctity of these
two pontiffs will not be addressed here. What is being advanced is the
precise claim that not all canonizations need be accepted by Catholics
as infallible acts of the magisterium of the Church.

[†] First published at *Rorate Caeli*, August 24, 2018.

The initial point that needs to be made in this discussion is that the infallibility of canonizations is not taught by the magisterium of the Church. Belief in their infallibility is not therefore required of Catholics. This point is agreed on by theologians, as can be illustrated by the teaching of a standard manual of theology, G. van Noort's *Dogmatic Theology*, vol. II: *Christ's Church*.[1] These authors follow the traditional and very important practice of attaching a theological note to every thesis that they advance. These notes specify the degree of authority possessed by each thesis, and the corresponding obligation to believe that is laid upon Catholics. The highest note is *de fide*: it belongs to propositions that must be believed with the assent of theological faith, and that cannot be knowingly and pertinaciously rejected without committing the sin of heresy. The lowest note is *sententia communis*, which, as Ludwig Ott states, means "doctrine which in itself belongs to the field of the free opinions, but which is generally accepted by theologians."[2]

Van Noort, Castelot, and Murphy specify that the canonizations in question are the final and definitive decrees by which the Supreme Pontiff declares that someone has been admitted to heaven and is to be venerated by everyone. The decree of authority that they attribute to the claim that such canonizations are infallible is *sententia communis*, the common opinion of theologians.[3] Their evaluation of the authority of this claim is the more significant because they themselves agree with the assertion that such canonizations are infallible. There can thus be no intention on their part of minimizing the authority of a claim with which they disagree. The assertion that canonizations are infallible thus belongs to the field of free opinions. It is not one that Catholics have an obligation to accept.

This has been denied by Fr. Benoît Storez, SSPX, who has claimed that doubting the infallibility of canonizations is "temerarious." But to say that a proposition is temerarious is not the same as to say that it departs from the common opinion of theologians. The censure of

---

1   Trans. and rev. by John J. Castelot and William R. Murphy (Westminster, MD: The Newman Press, 1957; repr. Waterloo, ON: Arouca Press, n.d.).
2   Ludwig Ott, *Fundamentals of Catholic Dogma*, trans. Patrick Lynch, ed. James Canon Bastible, rev. Robert Fastiggi (London: Baronius Press, 2018), 11.
3   Van Noort, *Christ's Church*, 117.

temerity adds something to departure from the common opinion of theologians; it adds the assertion that this departure is undertaken without reason. But there do in fact exist serious reasons for questioning the infallibility of canonizations. The first category of reasons are those that have always been raised to the assertion of such infallibility, an assertion which has never been the subject of complete unanimity among theologians. One such reason is the existence of prayers in the canonization ceremony for the truthfulness of the decree of canonization, prayers which were plausibly thought to recognize the possibility of the decrees not being truthful. The second category of reasons arise from the more recent introduction of changes in the process of examining the cause of the one canonized that considerably lessen the reliability of these examinations, such as the abolition of the office of devil's advocate and the reduction in the number of miracles demanded for canonization. Fr. Storez is thus mistaken in asserting that questioning the infallibility of canonizations is temerarious.

The fact that the Church has not taught that canonizations are infallible means that there is no sin in Catholics denying their infallibility for serious reasons, but it does not however imply that they are not infallible. After all, the Church did not teach the doctrine of papal infallibility until 1870, but the pope was infallible prior to 1870 nonetheless. What needs to be established for our purposes is that canonizations, in the sense of the final and definitive decrees by which the Supreme Pontiff declares that someone has been admitted to heaven and is to be venerated by everyone, are not in fact infallible acts of the supreme magisterium. There are two arguments that establish this conclusion.

1. The canonization of saints by the Supreme Pontiff does not satisfy the criteria for an infallible definition as set out by the First Vatican Council.

The criteria for the pope's actually being immune from error are well established, and are set out by Vatican I in its dogmatic constitution *Pastor Aeternus.* An infallible papal definition involves three things: the pope must exercise his authority as successor of Peter in teaching; his teaching must be stated as a matter that concerns faith or morals; and he must assert that his teaching is a final decision that binds the whole Church to believe in its contents upon pain of sin against faith. We can see an example of these criteria in the definition of the doctrine of the Immaculate Conception in the Apostolic Constitution *Ineffabilis Deus*:

> By the inspiration of the Holy Spirit, for the honor of the Holy and Undivided Trinity, for the glory and adornment of the Virgin Mother of God, for the exaltation of the Catholic Faith, and for the furtherance of the Catholic religion, by the authority of Jesus Christ our Lord, of the Blessed Apostles Peter and Paul, and by our own: We declare, pronounce, and define that the doctrine which holds that the most Blessed Virgin Mary, in the first instance of her conception, by a singular grace and privilege granted by Almighty God, in view of the merits of Jesus Christ, the Savior of the human race, was preserved free from all stain of original sin, is a doctrine revealed by God and therefore to be believed firmly and constantly by all the faithful. Hence, if anyone shall dare — which God forbid! — to think otherwise than as has been defined by us, let him know and understand that he is condemned by his own judgment; that he has suffered shipwreck in the Faith; that he has separated from the unity of the Church; and that, furthermore, by his own action he incurs the penalties established by law if he should dare to express in words or writing or by any other outward means the errors he thinks in his heart.

In contrast, the formula for the canonization of John XXIII and John Paul II (substantially the same as the formulas used in earlier canonizations) is as follows:

> For the honor of the blessed Trinity, the exaltation of the Catholic faith, and the increase of the Christian life, by the authority of our Lord Jesus Christ and of the holy Apostles Peter and Paul and our own, after due deliberation and frequent prayer for divine assistance, and having sought the counsel of many of our brother bishops, we declare and define blessed John XXIII and John Paul II to be saints, and we enroll them among the saints, decreeing that they are to be venerated as such by the whole Church, in the name of the Father and of the Son and of the Holy Spirit.

Benedict XVI added the following prayers to the canonization ceremony: "Most Holy Father, Holy Church, trusting in the Lord's promise to send upon her the Spirit of Truth, who in every age keeps the Supreme Magisterium free from error, most earnestly beseeches Your Holiness to enroll these, her elect, among the saints," spoken by the person presenting the saint to the pope; and "Let us, then, invoke the Holy Spirit, the Giver of life, that he may enlighten our minds and that Christ the Lord may not permit his Church to err in a matter of such importance," spoken by the pope himself.

Some authors have claimed that the formula of canonization, or the formula of canonization together with the prayers added to the ceremony by Benedict XVI, suffice to make canonizations an infallible papal act. In considering this claim we need first to keep in mind a basic principle that governs infallible definitions, which is that these definitions have a legal character that results from their strictly binding the minds and actions of the faithful. Thus, they are understood by all theologians as existing only when they are clearly stated and promulgated, according to the ordinary rules of language and communication; a doubtful law does not bind. There cannot be any reasonable doubt about the presence of the criteria for such a definition, if it is to be infallible.

In the case of the formula of canonization, however, the requirements for an infallible definition are not present. The formula invokes the authority of the Supreme Pontiff as vicar of Christ and successor of Peter, but this authority is not confined to the act of making an infallible definition. The crucial fact is that there is no mention of teaching a question of faith or morals, no requirement that the faithful believe or confess the statement being proclaimed, and no assertion that a denial of the proclamation is heretical, subject to anathema, or entails separation from the unity of the Church. The absence of these condemnations is itself an absence of the condition of the intent to bind the whole Church in the sense required for an infallible teaching, because these assertions are what constitute binding the Church in this sense. A binding is done in some particular way; there must be a bond, a constraint, that does the binding. The constraint that applies to infallible definitions is the state of heresy, anathema, and separation from the unity of the Church that is the result of not professing them.

The presence of the word *definimus* in the formula of canonization does not alter this fact. For an infallible definition to occur, it does not suffice to say that a definition is being made; the conditions necessary for a definition must actually be carried out. Nor can we suppose that the use of the Latin word *definimus* necessarily signifies the act of defining a doctrine of the faith. The word has a more general, juridical sense of ruling on some controversy concerning faith or morals. This general sense was recognized by the fathers of the First Vatican Council, and explicitly distinguished by them from the specific sense of *definio* that obtains in infallible definitions.

Nor do the prayers added by Benedict XVI make any difference to the non-infallible character of canonizations. The reference to the Holy Spirit's keeping the magisterium free from error in these prayers is not an assertion that the canonization itself is an infallible act, and is not itself an authoritative declaration, since it is not spoken by the pope. The prayer actually spoken by the pope is not in any way an assertion or guarantee of infallibility. The pope's intending to do something that is not erroneous, and his doing something immune from error, are two different things. The prayers added by Benedict XVI ask God to prevent the decree of canonization from being actually erroneous, not to make them infallible pronouncements. Such a request would be superfluous when the conditions necessary for an exercise of papal infallibility are actually present, and accordingly such prayers are not attached to infallible definitions; the prayers that on some occasions are stated as having preceded such definitions have to do with discerning the possibility and opportuneness of making an infallible definition, not with the infallibility of the definition itself.

2. The act of canonization need not fall within the bounds of the Church's infallibility.

One of the troubling aspects of the common insistence on the infallibility of papal canonizations is that upholders of their infallibility seem to have lost track of what the charism of papal infallibility is for.

It exists to enable the pope to teach and safeguard divine revelation with complete certainty. This is made clear in *Pastor Aeternus*:

> The Roman Pontiffs, according to the exigencies of times and circumstances, sometimes assembling Ecumenical Councils, or asking for the mind of the Church scattered throughout the world, sometimes by particular Synods, sometimes using other helps which Divine Providence supplied, defined as to be held those things which, with the help of God, they had recognized as conformable with the Sacred Scriptures and Apostolic Traditions. For the Holy Spirit was not promised to the successors of Peter that by His revelation they might make known new doctrine, but that by His assistance they might inviolably keep and faithfully expound the Revelation, the Deposit of Faith, delivered through the Apostles.
>
> And indeed, all the venerable Fathers have embraced, and the holy orthodox Doctors have venerated and followed, their Apostolic doctrine; knowing most fully that this See of holy Peter remains ever free from all blemish of error, according to the divine promise that the Lord our Savior made to the Prince of His disciples: "But I have prayed for you, so that your faith may not fail, and so that you, once converted, may confirm your brothers" (Lk 22:32).

The purpose of papal infallibility sets limits to the contents of infallible papal definitions. If a papal statement is not concerned with either a religious truth contained in divine revelation, or some matter that is "so closely connected with the revealed deposit that revelation itself would be imperiled unless an absolutely certain decision could be made about them,"[4] then it cannot be an infallible definition. The upholders of the infallibility of canonizations however do not make any effort to explain how canonizations are connected to the revealed deposit of faith; it is as if they consider papal infallibility to be a prerogative of the papal office that is intended to put the pope above the danger of being discredited by error, rather than a gift made by God to protect the faith He has given to the Church.

One might object that we are not entitled to decide ourselves whether a given papal teaching is concerned with matters of faith

---

4 Van Noort, *Christ's Church*, 110.

and morals; this is something that is for the pope himself to decide. This observation is correct, but it does not provide an objection to the argument that is being offered here. In the case of infallible papal definitions, we can be sure that the teachings concerned are essentially connected to divine revelation because the definitions themselves say so. This assertion is part of what constitutes an infallible definition, as we saw above. It is made in the definitions of both the Immaculate Conception and the Assumption, which incorporate the phrases "is a doctrine revealed by God and therefore to be believed firmly and constantly by all the faithful," and "we pronounce, declare, and define it to be a divinely revealed dogma." It is precisely by including such statements in authoritative pronouncements that the pope decides and determines that the contents of these statements are divinely revealed or essentially connected to divine revelation. Such phrases are not present in the formula of canonization, so this formula provides no basis for claiming that the pope holds that the assertions made by the use of this formula have any connection to divine revelation. Some argument must be offered if we are to accept that canonizations are related to divine revelation, despite the lack of any reference to such a relation in the rite of canonization.

Evidently the saintliness of individuals of the post-Apostolic era cannot be contained in or logically implied by divine revelation itself. So canonizations, if they are to be related to divine revelation, must be so in virtue of being proclamations of dogmatic facts. The classic example of such a dogmatic fact is the assertion that the five condemned Jansenist propositions are contained, according to the ordinary rules for the interpretation of language, in Jansen's work *Augustinus*. This fact obviously is not contained in divine revelation; it is because the condemned propositions themselves contradict divine revelation, and the book in question (contrary to the Jansenist claims) asserts these propositions, that the pope has the power to infallibly teach that the propositions are contained in that book. This power is necessary because the pope's charism of infallibility does not exist simply to proclaim the abstract truth about doctrine, but also to protect the faith of Catholics. If this charism did not extend to discerning and condemning particular concrete heretical statements such as those in Jansen's book, it would not suffice for the purpose of protecting their faith.

It seems to be the case that there are some instances where a given person's being a saint is a dogmatic fact. That is why the argument that is made here is that canonizations do not *as such* fall within the scope of the charism of papal infallibility. The claim is that the factors that make a person's sanctity a dogmatic fact are not always present in canonizations, and hence that canonizations are not by themselves infallible definitions. Some other element is needed to constitute a person's sanctity as a dogmatic fact. This element can take one of two forms: the truth of a canonization can be necessarily connected with the truth of the Church's infallible teaching on faith and morals, or it can be a necessary consequence of the fact that the Church is guided in general by the Holy Spirit.

The former case will arise when the doctrine of a particular saint has been so extensively adopted by the infallible teaching of the Church that denial of his sanctity would cast doubt upon the teachings themselves. Examples would be the doctrines of St. Athanasius, St. Augustine, and St. Cyril of Alexandria. These saints took leading roles in shaping the doctrines of the Church through their personal theological work. To reject their sanctity would thus be to cast doubt on the doctrines themselves. In such a case, therefore, the Church should be considered to be infallible in proclaiming their sanctity.

The latter case will arise when devotion to a saint has been so widespread and important in the Church that the denial of that individual's sanctity would cast doubt upon the role of the Holy Spirit in guiding the Church. Take a hypothetical example that is deliberately extreme, in order to make this point clearly. Suppose a biblical scholar were to produce a document that allegedly established that St. Paul, during the persecution of Nero and after the composition of his epistles, promptly apostatized, betrayed the other Christians of the Roman Church, and ended his days as a pagan living on a state pension under a different name. Independently of any other objections that might be raised to this hypothesis, it would be incumbent upon Catholics to reject it simply because it is incompatible with the veneration of St. Paul that has been so widely embraced and encouraged by the Church. It would be impossible for the Holy Spirit to have permitted this extensive veneration if St. Paul had not in fact been a holy saint and martyr.

These factors therefore can make it the case that a canonization is an infallible action of the Church. But they are not often present in canonizations, so canonizations are not in themselves infallible acts.

However, we should not end with this conclusion. The nature of those canonizations that are dogmatic facts enables us to deepen the discussion of the infallibility of canonizations, and to go beyond a simple rejection of the previous theological consensus about their infallibility. The discussion here has concerned the infallibility of papal decrees of canonization taken in themselves. Its rejection of their infallibility has argued from the criteria that are applied to identify infallible definitions of faith and morals, criteria that bear upon the precise wording of supposed definitions when these are taken in the immediate context of the document in which they are issued.

But this is not the only way to consider canonizations, and it is perhaps not the approach that was taken by Prospero Lambertini (later Pope Benedict XIV) when he first advanced the thesis of the infallibility of canonizations in the 1730s. Rather than consider the papal decrees of canonization taken in themselves, we can consider them in the context of the entire process that led up to them. When we consider this process as it was laid down by Benedict XIV and practiced for many centuries—with its rigorous scrutiny of the life of the candidate, its insistence on waiting for decades or centuries so that extraneous pressures and motivations can disappear and the fullest and most accurate historical evidence concerning the candidate can emerge, its far higher standard for miraculous intercessions by the candidate—we may well conclude that this process as a whole was infallible. We may well think that it is incompatible with the Holy Spirit's guidance of the Church for such a devoted, persevering, sincere, and thorough effort to arrive at the truth about an individual's sanctity to be allowed to fail. But this reason for believing in the infallibility of the former process of canonization as a whole does not extend to the more recent decrees of canonization that have deliberately abandoned this careful and honest search for the truth.

It would indeed seem to be a piece of effrontery on the part of the Church to expect the Holy Spirit to make up for a disregard of honest and reasonable enquiry by a miraculous intervention to avert the consequences of such irresponsibility.

This suggests criteria both for determining when a canonization is not infallible, and for determining when the process of canonization has actually failed and resulted in the veneration of someone who is not enjoying the beatific vision. A canonization would seem to not be infallible when there are serious flaws in the process of canonization itself. Such flaws mean that the Church has failed to take the steps necessary to enlist the aid of the Holy Spirit in preventing a mistaken canonization. The lack of infallibility does not of course mean that the person canonized is not a saint. Padre Pio, for example, was canonized under the seriously flawed process of canonization introduced by John Paul II in 1983, but that does not mean that he is not a saint or that he should not be venerated as such. A canonization would seem to be actually erroneous when the balance of probabilities, given the full evidence about the process of canonization and the life of the person canonized, is very strongly in favor of the process of canonization having been seriously flawed, and also of the person canonized not having exhibited heroic virtue, but instead to have committed serious sins that were not expiated by some heroic penance. The judgment that a given canonization is erroneous of course requires very substantial, thorough, objective, and intelligent investigation, and no such judgments will be ventured in this article.

We have therefore arrived at an even more narrowly defined conclusion than that suggested at the beginning of this paper. We need not hold that the canonizations of John XXIII and John Paul II were infallible, because the conditions needed for such infallibility were not present. Their canonizations are not connected to any doctrine of the faith, they were not the result of a devotion that is central to the life of the Church, and they were not the product of careful and rigorous examination. But we need not exclude all canonizations whatsoever from the charism of infallibility; we can still argue that those canonizations that followed the rigorous procedure of former centuries benefited from this charism. Thus although the conclusion of our inquiry is narrower than anticipated, its lesson is broader. That lesson tells us that a return to the former approach to canonization would mean recovering the guidance of the Holy Spirit in an area of great import for the Church.

9

The Infallibility of Canonizations and the Morals of the Faithful[†]

JOHN R.T. LAMONT

A NUMBER OF DISCUSSIONS OF THE INFALLIBIL-
ity of canonizations have appeared recently in connection with the
canonization of Paul VI. Some of these, including a discussion of
my own,[1] have argued that the act of canonization is not necessarily
an infallible pronouncement, and therefore that the canonization
of Paul VI does not require Catholics to believe that he is a saint
in heaven if they have serious reasons for holding that he was not
a saint. This conclusion has been rejected by many Catholics who
consider themselves to be conservatives or even traditionalists. The
basis for this rejection has not been a conclusive proof of the heroic
virtue of Paul VI, but rather the assertion that canonizations are
always infallible. This rejection is not theologically well-informed,
but it is presented with an air of authority that can take in Catholics
who are not familiar with the theological issues involved. It is thus
worthwhile to provide in more detail the theological reasons that
establish that not all canonizations are infallible, and that Catholics
are not required to accept that canonization is necessarily an infallible
act of the magisterium.

We should begin by explaining the scope of the infallible teaching authority of the Church. This authority extends to all divinely
revealed truths that form part of the deposit of faith, and also to all
those truths whose acceptance is necessary in order that the deposit
of faith be effectively defended or proposed with sufficient authority.
The latter category of truths are termed the secondary object of the
infallibility of the Church.

---

1   See the preceding chapter.

---

†   First published at *Rorate Caeli*, December 27, 2018.

Next, we should define the question being addressed. It is beyond question that the sanctity of some individuals is infallibly taught. It is divinely revealed, for example, that the good thief is a saint in heaven. Other canonizations can undoubtedly be judged to belong to the secondary object of infallibility. The teaching that St. Paul lived a life of heroic virtue after his conversion and is now a saint in heaven is necessary for the credibility of the inspired teaching that the Church has received from him, and hence forms part of the secondary object of infallibility.

The question about the infallibility of canonizations is thus not whether the Church is sometimes infallible in teaching that a given individual is a saint in heaven, but whether the Church is *always* infallible in teaching that a given individual is a saint in heaven. The question arises because it is not evident that the sanctity of every person who has been proclaimed a saint by the Church is divinely revealed or has any connection to divine revelation. If Pope John XXIII is not in fact a saint in heaven, for example, this would make no difference to divinely revealed truth or to the truths that are connected to divine revelation. It would not cast doubt upon the truth of his teachings or the legitimacy of his acts of government, because a pope does not have to be a saint in order to teach truly or govern wisely. Pope John XXIII could have failed to achieve sanctity simply because of an excessive and disordered attachment to the cigarettes that he smoked. If this had in fact been the case, and if the investigation into his sanctity had concluded that he was not a saint for that reason, it would have been completely irrelevant to divinely revealed truth. Of course it is possible to think of other reasons why he might not have been a saint. But this hypothetical example is chosen to make the point that sanctity is not the same as being a good person. Sanctity means showing heroic virtue in *every aspect of life*. It is very difficult and very rare, and it is because it is very difficult and rare that an extremely careful investigation has been required by the Church in the past before a person's sanctity is officially accepted.

There is no magisterial teaching that states that all canonizations are infallible. There has however been a general consensus of theologians in favor of the view that all canonizations are infallible magisterial acts. Advocates of the infallibility of canonizations have appealed to this consensus in support of their claim. There are two aspects of this consensus that need to be considered. The first is the authority of the consensus in itself. The second are the reasons for the infallibility of canonizations that are given by the theologians included in this consensus.

Theologians do not, as theologians, possess any magisterial authority. However, we can reasonably hold that they have the capacity, at least over time and after proper investigation, to determine the content of Catholic doctrine by reflection on pronouncements that do have magisterial authority. If they did not have this capacity, the profession of theologian would be useless, and the judgment of the Church is that it is not useless, but valuable and worth fostering. Accordingly, a theological censure has been devised to condemn propositions that are rejected by the general consensus of theologians. This censure is the term "temerarious." We can therefore ask if the consensus of theologians in favor of the infallibility of canonizations means that denying this infallibility is temerarious, and is therefore to be avoided by Catholics.

The answer to this question is no, for two reasons. The first reason is that the simple fact of the existence of a consensus of theologians in favor of some proposition does not suffice to make the denial of that proposition temerarious. The rejection of a proposition is temerarious only if either the proposition is rejected without providing a serious reason, or the theological censure of "temerarious" has been applied to that proposition by magisterial authority. Neither of these circumstances applies to the assertion that not all canonizations are infallible. Serious reasons have always existed for denying the infallibility of canonizations; these reasons have been proposed by a number of theologians who have argued that canonizations are not in fact infallible. The Church has never taught that the censure "temerarious" applies to the claim that canonizations are not infallible.

The second reason is that a unanimous consensus of theologians does not in fact exist in favor of the infallibility of canonizations. A majority of theologians is not the same thing as a unanimous consensus of theologians, and such a unanimous consensus does not exist. This can readily be ascertained by examining the theological works that argue for this infallibility. If we look at the discussion of the infallibility of canonization in ch. XLIII of the first book of Prospero Lambertini's *De servorum Dei beatificatione et beatorum canonizatione*, we will find several arguments against the infallibility of canonizations, and the names of a number of serious theologians who advanced these arguments. The existence of serious arguments for a theological position, advanced by reputable theologians, means that Catholics are permitted to hold that position unless the position has been condemned by magisterial authority. This point is often not understood by writers who lack a proper grasp of theological method. Such writers will cite a downright pronouncement in favor of their position made by some respected theological authority like Bellarmine, and then conclude that this downright pronouncement settles the question at issue. They do not realize that these downright pronouncements are being made in the course of a theological dispute, in order to counter other downright pronouncements made for an opposing position; and that sometimes their imperious character has the function of disguising a lack of compelling arguments, rather than being the result of such arguments. Such pronouncements are not rulings that settle the matter in dispute.

The question of the infallibility of all canonizations must thus be settled by considering the arguments for holding it. Before considering the arguments for this infallibility that have been advanced by earlier theologians, we should keep in mind the context in which these arguments were advanced. Canonization, as they addressed it, took two forms: equipollent canonization and formal canonization. Equipollent canonization happens when a pope decrees the universal veneration of a person to whom devotion has existed since time immemorial, and whose holiness and miracles are recorded by historians who are worthy of belief. Formal canonization happens when a pope decrees the universal veneration of a person whose heroic virtue and miracles have been established by a juridical process undertaken by the Holy See.

These are still the forms of canonization that exist today (Pope Francis canonized the Canadian saint Marie de l'Incarnation in 2014 through the process of equipollent canonization). The canonizations whose infallibility is now in question are formal rather than equipollent canonizations. The process for formal canonization that is now used is very different from the process that existed when these earlier theologians formed their judgment on the infallibility of canonization. The investigation of the miracles, life, and writings of the person being proposed for canonization was much stricter in the older process. The life and writings were scrutinized by the Promoter of the Faith, more popularly known as the devil's advocate, and any objections raised by him had to be given a satisfactory answer before the person was beatified, let alone canonized. Four miracles *in toto* were required for canonization, and the standards of evidence for accepting that a miracle had occurred were extremely high. In general, the sanctity of the person proposed for canonization had to be proved by human means beyond a reasonable doubt before a decree of canonization would be emitted by the Holy See. The current process for formal canonization has abolished the devil's advocate, reduced the number of miracles required for canonization from four to two, lowered the standards of evidence required for accepting a miracle, and made the scrutiny of a person's life and writings much more lenient.[2] It is now possible for a person to be canonized even if the evidence does not demonstrate his sanctity beyond a reasonable doubt, or, indeed, even if the total available evidence makes it reasonable to believe that the person was not a saint.

This is not to say that the older theologians argued from the thoroughness and reliability of the process of canonization to the infallibility of its results. They did not. But it is inevitable that their approach to the question was influenced by a justified confidence in the honesty and reliability of the investigation of the sanctity of a person proposed for canonization. They did not seriously examine whether or not a canonization based on insufficient or even misleading evidence would be infallible, because they did not suppose that such canonizations would ever occur. The fact that such canonizations are now possible, and in some cases actual, provides a proper reason for revisiting the arguments that they alleged in favor of the

---

2 On these points, see especially chapters 3, 11, and 15. — *Ed.*

infallibility of canonizations, and for examining whether these arguments were as strong as they thought they were.

Nicolau and Salaverri[3] have argued that the formula used in canonizations proves that canonizations are infallible. They cite decrees of canonization pronounced by Pius XI and Pius XII where the decree explicitly states that it is an infallible act ("superno lumine iterum ferventiusque implorato, *infallibilem* Nos, uti Catholicae Ecclesiae supremus Magister, sententiam in haec verba protulimus: *Ad honorem* etc.". . ."Nos universalis Catholicae Ecclesiae Magister, ex Cathedra una super Petrum Domini voce fundata, *falli nesciam* hanc sententiam sollemniter hisce pronunciavimus verbis: *Ad honorem* etc.").[4]

This argument fails to grasp the nature of an infallible definition. In order for a papal teaching to be infallible, it is not enough for it to *say* that it is infallible; it has to actually satisfy the conditions for an infallible statement. Such statements must be exercises of the teaching authority of the Apostolic See, and they must definitively and finally bind all the faithful to assent to the assertions that they are making. In the case of an infallible truth that is divinely revealed, the faithful are required to believe (*credere*) the truth that is being taught. In the case of an infallible truth that belongs to the secondary object of the infallible magisterium, the faithful are required to hold (*tenere*) the truth that is being taught. The term "belief" is used for divinely revealed truths, not because truths belonging to the secondary object of the magisterium do not also need to be believed to be true, but to underline that divinely revealed truths must be believed with an act of the theological virtue of faith.

In the decrees of canonization that are cited, the faithful are not told that they are required to believe or to hold that the person being canonized exhibited heroic virtue, was martyred for the Faith, or is a saint in heaven. No assertion is to be understood as infallibly defined unless this infallibility is manifestly evident (cf. Canon 749). Since this necessary condition of binding the faithful is absent in

---

3   P. Michaele Nicolau and P. Ioachim Salaverri, *Sacrae Theologiae Summa*, vol. I, *Theologia Fundamentalis*, 3rd ed., 725.

4   See Pius XI, *AAS* 25 (1933), 425–26; *AAS* 26 (1934), 539ff.; Pius XII, *AAS* 39 (1947), 209, 249, 281, 329, 377; Pius XII, *AAS* 33 (1941), 105; *AAS* 41 (1949), 137.

these decrees of canonization (and in all decrees of canonization), the content of the decree of canonization itself cannot be given as a reason for the infallibility of canonizations. The assertions of Pius XI and Pius XII to the effect that their decrees of canonization are infallible simply mean that they shared the common opinion of theologians to the effect that canonizations are infallible. Neither the particular claim that the particular canonizations in question are infallibly taught, nor the general assertion that all canonizations are infallibly taught, are themselves being taught with authority in the decrees of canonization that are cited. Of course one might assume that popes would not advance undecided theological positions as certain in their official documents, and it is certainly irresponsible of them to do so; but in this case, this assumption would be mistaken, as our examination shows.

Many supporters of the infallibility of canonizations have argued that it is impossible for a canonization to be in error, because the public veneration of someone in the liturgy who is in fact not worthy of it would be displeasing and dishonoring to God, and the Church's public liturgy is guaranteed to be pleasing and honoring to Him.

This argument is far from convincing. Of course the Church's public liturgy *ought* to be pleasing and honoring to God. But we cannot infer from the fact that it *ought* to be pleasing to God that it always in fact *is* pleasing to God. And it is not difficult to find instances where officially sanctioned liturgical practices are irreverent and hence dishonoring and displeasing to God. Communion in the hand is one example. (The reasons why communion in the hand should not be permitted are set forth in *Memoriale Domini*, the indult of 1969 that addresses this matter. The indult sets out all the reasons why it is an abuse, and actually decrees that communion on the tongue should be retained, before allowing bishops' conferences to permit communion in the hand.[5])

---

5   See www.ewtn.com/catholicism/library/instruction-on-the-manner-of-distributing-holy-communion-2195. [For analysis of the text of this letter and the history surrounding it, see Most Rev. Juan Rodolfo Laise, *Holy Communion. Communion in the Hand: Documents & History; Some Reflections on Spiritual Communion and the State of Grace*, 5th expanded edition (Boonville, NY: Preserving Christian Publications, 2018). —*Ed.*]

This argument can also be applied to beatifications as well as to canonizations, since in a beatification the commemoration in the Mass of the person beatified is officially permitted by the Church. But it is universally accepted that beatifications are not infallible. A good example is the purported saint Simon of Trent. Simon was a Christian child whose dead body was discovered by some Jewish residents of Trent in 1475. The entire Jewish community of Trent confessed under torture to having put Simon to death as part of a ritual murder ceremony. Fifteen Jews were burnt at the stake for having murdered him. A papal commissioner sent by Pope Sixtus IV concluded that there were no grounds for believing in the charges against the Jewish community of Trent, or in the miracles attributed to the intercession of Simon, but he was expelled from Trent by a mob instigated by the local bishop, who continued with the trial and execution of Jews. Pope Sixtus V approved an office for Simon for use by the diocese of Trent, and entered him in the *Roman Martyrology* as a martyr murdered by Jews for the Faith (he was removed from the *Martyrology* in 1965). In this case, a person was officially commemorated in the Mass as a martyr on the basis of evidence obtained by torture; as a result of this commemoration, a grave slander against Jews was given credibility. This was displeasing and dishonoring to God. Nonetheless, it happened.

Better, or at least more representative, arguments for the infallibility of canonizations are set forth in Fr. T. Ortolan's article "Canonisation dans l'Église romaine," in the authoritative *Dictionnaire de théologie catholique*. Fr. Ortolan claims that the infallibility of canonizations is indicated by the fact that no canonization has ever been mistaken, although beatifications in individual dioceses have been found to be in error. Since the evidence upon which canonizations are based is human and fallible, even when the greatest care is taken, this perfect record can be explained only by a special assistance of the Holy Spirit that preserves canonizations from error.

If the premise of this argument is accepted, it has some force. Obviously however it cannot be used when doubt about the infallibility of canonizations is motivated by reasons for thinking that a particular canonized individual was not a saint. If it were to be so used, a circular argument would result: canonizations are infallible because no canonized person has ever been shown not to be a saint, and we can know that every canonized person is a saint because canonizations are infallible.

Fr. Ortolan also gives the most commonly used and most influential argument for the infallibility of canonizations, which is that it is not possible for the Supreme Pontiff to lead the universal Church into error in matters that concern faith and morals; but this is what would happen if he were to canonize someone who was not a saint in heaven. This is the argument offered by Newman for the infallibility of canonizations:

> The infallibility of the Church must certainly extend to this solemn and public act [*sc.* the Canonization of Saints]; and that, because on so serious a matter, affecting the worship of the faithful, though relating to a fact, the Church (that is, the pope) must be infallible. This is Card. Lambertini's decision, in concurrence with St. Thomas, putting on one side the question of the pope's ordinary infallibility, which depends on other arguments. "*It cannot be*," that great author says, "that the Universal Church should be led into error on a point of morals by the supreme Pontiff; and that certainly would, or might, happen, supposing he could be mistaken in a canonization." This, too, is St. Thomas's argument: "In the Church there can be no damnable error; but this would be such, if one who was really a sinner, were venerated as a saint," &c.—Card. Lambert. *de Canon*. Diss. xxi. vol. i. ed. Ven. 1751.[6]

Now it is certainly true that the Supreme Pontiff cannot lead the universal Church into error by any *infallible* act. But to give this as a reason for the infallibility of canonizations is simply to beg the question. Upon examination, this entire argument can be seen to rest upon a begging of the question. Those actions where "*it cannot be* that the universal Church should be led into error on a point of morals by the pope" are actions that are infallible. Inability to be in error is what infallibility means. So if you say that canonizations are

---

6   J. H. Newman, Preface to the Third Edition of the *Via Media*, 27, at www.newmanreader.org/works/viamedia/volume1/preface3.html.

infallible because the pope cannot lead the Church into error through canonizing someone who is not in heaven, you are simply saying that canonizations are infallible because they are infallible.

We can presume that the assertion that popes cannot lead the faithful into error should be understood as saying that popes cannot lead the faithful into error through some official exercise of the papal office. It would not be claimed that popes cannot lead the faithful into error through some disedifying act committed by them as private persons, as, e.g., by keeping mistresses. But the premise that the pope cannot lead the faithful into error by some official act is known to be false. Such acts have not only occurred, but have been pronounced by the Church to have occurred. The most notorious example of such an act is the letter of Pope Honorius to the Patriarch Sergius of Constantinople. In this letter, Honorius gave some endorsement to the monothelite heresy that Sergius was advancing. We need not determine with precision exactly what sort of endorsement he gave, because any sort of endorsement constituted leading the faithful into error. His letter was not an infallible pronouncement, but it was an official reply to a formal consultation, not a private communication, and as such constituted an official papal act. The third ecumenical council of Constantinople in 680–81 condemned this letter and Honorius as a result of it:

> After we had reconsidered, according to our promise which we had made to your highness, the doctrinal letters of Sergius, at one time patriarch of this royal God-protected city, to Cyrus, who was then bishop of Phasis, and to Honorius some time pope of Old Rome, as well as the letter of the latter to the same Sergius, we find that these documents are quite foreign to the apostolic dogmas, to the declarations of the holy Councils, and to all the accepted Fathers, and that they follow the false teachings of the heretics; therefore we entirely reject them . . . we define that there shall be expelled from the holy church of God and anathematized Honorius who was some time pope of Old Rome, because of what we found written by him to Sergius, that in all respects he followed his view and confirmed his impious doctrines.

The acts of this council, including this condemnation, were ratified by Pope Leo II.[7] The anathematizing of heretics by ecumenical councils is a part of their teaching and must be accepted by all Catholics; rejection of this view falls into the Jansenist error that, while denying that the Church can make an error of doctrine, maintains that the Church can make an error of fact in attributing heresy to the writings of a given individual. The heretical nature of the letter of Honorius is thus itself a papal teaching at the highest level.

The situation whose possibility this infallibility-favoring argument denies, viz., that of the faithful's being led into error by the Church through the canonization of a person who is not a saint, deserves further consideration. How is it that this error could be produced by such a canonization? It would not happen by the canonization of a sinner whose misdeeds could not be known through publicly available evidence. In such a case, all that the faithful would know about the supposed saint would be his public actions. Presenting this person as an exemplar of heroic virtue would not lead the faithful into moral error, because they would not know about his misdeeds, and would have only his blameless actions presented to them as models to follow.

In order for a canonization to lead the faithful astray, the sins that excluded the person canonized from sanctity or even from heaven would have to be public knowledge. If the faithful came across evidence of these sins, they could either reject this evidence as not proving that the canonized person actually sinned, or accept it as showing that the purported saint really was a sinner. Only in the latter case would a threat to their morals arise. But they would have a simple remedy available to them for this threat; they could conclude that because the person was a sinner, his canonization must have been erroneous, and that the purported saint is not in fact a model of virtue worthy of emulation. In this latter case, they would also have a remedy available for the evil that arises from the commemoration in the Mass of a person as a saint, when that person is not a saint.

---

7   For more analysis of the case of Honorius and its implications, see Claudio Pierantoni, "The Need for Consistency between Magisterium and Tradition: Examples from History," in *Defending the Faith Against Present Heresies*, ed. idem and John R. T. Lamont (Waterloo, ON: Arouca Press, n.d.), 235–51.

Both priests and faithful can and must refuse to reverence persons of this kind as saints and refuse to celebrate Masses that commemorate them as saints. If they do their duty under these circumstances, then no unpleasing and offensive worship of God will take place.

A real threat to the morals of the faithful will arise only if they accept that canonizations are infallible. In this case, they would have to choose between morals — by accepting sinful conduct as good — and faith — by holding that a magisterial act that satisfies the conditions for an infallible teaching is in fact false.

It is thus the acceptance, rather than the denial, of the infallibility of canonizations that threatens the morals of the faithful. And this threat is being realized right now. If we accept that John Paul II and Paul VI were saints, we must accept that their catastrophic failures in carrying out their duties of state did not interfere with their possession of holiness and exemplification of heroic virtue. It means that Paul VI's protection and promotion of heretical clergy and his illegal suppression of the traditional Latin rite, and John Paul II's inaction in the face of clerical pedophilia — to name only a few of their failures — made no difference to their going straight to heaven after death. Current bishops can thus follow these policies with no qualms of conscience and no fears for their salvation. As is well known, many bishops at the present time are doing just that; and the canonizations of Paul VI and John Paul II play a non-negligible role in their doing so. The faithful, in turn, are hamstrung in criticizing these disastrous policies by these canonizations. This whitewashing of moral failure and dereliction of duty in these popes also produces a general moral confusion and demoralization among all the faithful.

Since the arguments offered by theologians for the infallibility of canonization lack force, and there are now clear examples of canonized persons who did not display heroic virtue in their lives, we should conclude that not all canonizations are infallible acts of the magisterium. In the light of the disastrous consequences that can now result from the acceptance of the infallibility of canonizations, we should add that this conclusion needs to be generally accepted by Catholics.

10

Approaching the Subject of
Canonization with Careful Steps†

FR. JOHN HUNWICKE

AS IF HE HAS NOT YET CREATED ENOUGH DIVI-
sions within the Church militant, Pope Francis intends this month to
perform the highly divisive act of canonizing Paul VI. Even he, judging from what he said in giving this information to the Clergy of the
City, can see that this canonization business has become a silly giggle:
"And Benedict and I are on the waiting list," he quipped. Delightfully
humorous. A very witty joke. Very droll, Sovereign Pontiff.

I share the views of many, however, that the joke is a bad one,
in as far as this projected canonization is fundamentally a political
action to be linked with the apparent conviction of Pope Francis
that he himself is the champion and beneficiary of Paul VI's work
at Vatican II and afterwards. I do not accept that he is, but I do not
intend to discuss these questions of the prudential order. Rather, I
have some genuine questions with regard to important theological
matters antecedent to any canonizations.

I

My mind is not made up regarding the infallibility of an act whereby
the Roman Pontiff "canonizes"; and the probably but certainly related
question of whether a *de fide* assent is required. I assume that every-
body with an interest in this subject knows exactly what the Vatican
I text of *Pastor Aeternus* said and did not say about papal infallibility.
I have also found it useful to have read parts of Prospero Lambertini's
De Beatificatione et Canonizatione, and Liber 1 Caput LXV really is
required reading; it can be found by googling *Benedicti papae XIV
Doctrina de Servorum Dei*, and then scrolling down to pages 55–56

† Published at *Fr Hunwicke's Mutual Enrichment* (http://liturgicalnotes.blog-
spot.com/), October 2 and October 3, 2018.

(42–43 in the printed book which Google copied). It was written *before* the election of the erudite and admirable Prospero Lambertini to the See of Rome as Benedict XIV.

(1) Theologians of distinction can be listed who have taught that canonization is an infallible act of the papal magisterium. But, with regard to those who wrote before 1870, is there not a prior question that has to be asked? The Church had then not *defined* (i.e., put limits, "*fines*," to) the dogma of papal infallibility. The terms of *Pastor Aeternus* were (to the chagrin of Manning and the palpable relief of Newman) extremely limited. Therefore, can we be sure that those pre-1870 theologians really were categorizing canonization as infallible *in the sense of the word "infallible" as defined with all the limitations of the 1870 decree?* Or, because of the limits imposed by that definition, might they have used a different term had they needed to develop their arguments within the confines of what *Pastor Aeternus* lays down? Is this why Lambertini accepts the possibility of arguing that what a Roman Pontiff decrees may be infallible, but still not be *de fide*? It is in logic obvious that a proposition may be true, and may be demonstrably true, without it being incumbent upon anybody to *accept* that truth. But after 1870, I assume, this is changed as far as *ex cathedra* papal pronouncements are concerned, because the scope and function of the term *infallibilis* have been changed to imply and include the notion that a proposition is not merely true but is also *of faith*.

(2) In assessing the arguments of such pre-1870 writers, should we pay attention to the general extent which they assert when talking about the authority of the Roman Pontiff? That is: if a writer is very generous in his estimate of the fields to which papal infallibility extends, he is unlikely to be writing in terms of something like the highly limited 1870 definition. But if an author is very much more sparing and circumspect in associating infallibility with papal interventions, he is more likely to have in mind a concept of infallibility resembling that of Vatican I. As a consequence of this, when, later than 1870, we argue that papal canonizations are infallible, we should not claim *simpliciter* the support of those earlier (pre-1870) theologians, because they are likely to have been using the term in a different sense than that of *Pastor Aeternus*.

(3) And there is another question raised by the definition *and practice* of papal infallibility which the pontificate of Pius IX bequeathed us. It implies an assumption that the Roman Pontiff is acting with the morally unanimous, collegial assent of the whole *ecclesia docens*. I know that, for some traditionalists, collegiality is a dirty word; but Pius IX and Pius XII wrote to the bishops of the entire world seeking their counsel before defining the two Marian dogmas ("Is it definable? Is it opportune to define it?") and ... well ... I'm just an ordinary Catholic ... the *praxis* of those two pontiffs is good enough for me! But do popes seek the counsel of all their Venerable Brethren before canonizing?

(4) Papal infallibility is nothing but one modality within the infallibility of the Church. So is it rational to assign infallibility to some canonizations — those personally enacted by the pope — and not to those enacted by a different authority (the oft-quoted *Quodlibet* IX, q. 8 of St. Thomas is not necessarily limited to papal canonizations)? We know that popes cannot delegate their infallibility. There are the saints on the calendars of *sui iuris* churches, such as that of the Melkite Patriarch of Antioch (after all, it is arguable that, as *a* successor of St. Peter, this Patriarch is, after the Bishop of Rome himself, the senior prelate of the Catholic Church), which include some who lived outside visible unity with the See of Rome in recent centuries and were canonized by Byzantine synods ... and whose names are certainly not on any Roman "list."[1]

I believe the Ukrainian Church includes saints canonized up to the time of the Synod of Brest. And the "two lungs" rhetoric of John Paul II implies that, although the Latin Church is *de facto* very much larger than the Oriental Churches in full communion with Rome, *theologically* these latter are not just almost-irrelevant, tolerated anomalies. What would a rounded and complete understanding of canonization within the Catholic Church have to say about Melkite and Ukrainian praxis? And what would be the bearing of that upon the question of the infallibility of canonization?

---

1   The Melkite Patriarch of Antioch currently celebrates the feast of St. Gregory Palamas, which means that, in some sense, Palamas is acknowledged by the Roman Church which is in communion with the Melkite Church.

(5) Papal infallibility resides in the papal *munus docendi*, the ministry of doctrinally binding the *whole* Church, not part of it: so is there a distinction between those saints who are, by papal authority, to have a compulsory *cultus* in *every* local Church, and those whose commemoration is confined to some localities or is *optional* in the universal Church? If the *sui iuris* Churches not of Latin Rite do not promptly include a Latin saint, when he/she is canonized, on their calendars, and the Roman Pontiff tolerates this, does this mean that he is not imposing that *cultus* on the Universal Church and thus is not using his universal *munus docendi*?

The actual formula of canonization is in fact merely an order that X be placed on the list[2] of saints of the *ecclesia universalis*. What exactly... physically... is this "list"? And furthermore, Lambertini explicitly says that "writing a name down in the *Martyrology* does not yet bring about formal or equipollent canonization" (*descriptio in martyrologio nondum importat canonizationem formalem, aut aequipollentem*). But even if it did, would this mean that the *Martyrologium Romanum*, theologically *and* juridically, applies to *sui iuris* Churches not of the Roman Rite? If it doesn't, does this mean that *ecclesia universalis*, in the context of papal canonization, really means *ecclesia Latina universalis* (because, after all, the Latin Church *is* pretty worldwide)? And if this be true, what then becomes of the observation of Lambertini that an act of "canonization" which lacks complete preceptive universality is not, *in the strict sense*, canonization? Are there other loose ends arising from the fact that Roman documents seem quite often to *sound* as though they are majestically addressing the whole Church, but, when you get down to it, are really pretty obviously addressing the Latin Church (*Sacrosanctum Concilium* being an example of that)?

(6) Finally: St. Thomas held that canonization was *medium inter res fidei, et particulares*; and Lambertini concludes his discussion of this matter by saying that *plures magni nominis auctores* deny that an act of canonization is *de fide*; he gives a fair wind to their arguments; then summarizes the arguments of those, *inferioris notae doctores*, who affirm that it is *de fide*; concludes by saying *utraque opinio in*

---

2   List: *canon* in Greek; *catalogus* in Latin.

sua probabilitate relinquenda videtur, donec Sedes Apostolica de hac re judicium proferat. Lambertini went on to give his own private opinion as favoring the positive thesis (canonizations are *of faith*), but added "but before a judgment of the Apostolic See, it does not seem that the mark of heresy should be branded onto the contrary opinion."

In 1998, the motu proprio *Ad Tuendam Fidem* of John Paul II was accompanied by a *Commentary* written by the Congregation for the Doctrine of the Faith and signed by its august Cardinal Prefect. Paragraph 6 of this, combined with paragraphs 8 and 11, appears to lead to the conclusion that canonizations are to be given the same "full and irrevocable assent" as that required by the Creeds and the doctrinal definitions of Ecumenical Councils and of Roman Pontiffs speaking *ex cathedra*. Have I understood this correctly? But can such a dicasterial "Commentary" be deemed to be that "judgment of the Apostolic See" which was required by Lambertini in order to settle this question?

To be frank with you, I am more impressed by writers who merely call the public rejection of a papal act of canonization "temerarious," than I am by those who invoke the I-word. The I-word surely means, from 1870 onwards, that, as a matter of divine Faith, one must accept something in one's heart. The use of "temerarious" (Suárez; Lambertini) means, I take it, that a public rejection is rash and unsafe and that, accordingly, one should refrain from disturbing the peace of the believing community by publicly attacking an authoritative inclusion of a person on the List of Saints; and, furthermore, that one should preserve an interior awareness of one's own fallibility (after all, *someone* has to decide whether X goes into . . . or does not go into . . . the *canon*, and the decision is certainly way above *my* pay grade). Can anyone claim to be certain that Pope X is *not* in heaven interceding before the Throne of Grace?

Finally: I have a prejudice against potentially causing people problems of conscience by telling them that something is *of divine Faith* when (even if "just possibly") it might not be. After all, a *lex dubia* does not bind. And it potentially damages the authority of the Roman Pontiff to be rash in spraying the I-word too liberally around . . . a point which poor Manning never grasped.

II

There is liturgical evidence, which I do not think has been widely noticed, concerning the authority carried by an act of canonization.

The rites of canonization have tended — this will not surprise you — to vary in the last seventy years. The most recent changes before this (Pope Francis's) pontificate, which took place under Benedict XVI, seemed designed to impose on the rites a *theological meaning which they previously had not so explicitly expressed.* In the form of the rite left by Pope Benedict XVI, before the singing of *Veni Creator Spiritus* the Pontiff asked for prayer that Christ the Lord would not permit His Church to err in so great a matter. And, in the Third Petition the Cardinal Prefect for the Causes of Saints informed the Pontiff that the Holy Spirit "in every time renders the supreme Magisterium immune from error" (*omni tempore supremum Magisterium erroris expertem reddit*). These phrases, added by Pope Benedict, were in formulae *cut out* by Pope Francis when he canonized a number of *beati* in 2014; and subsequently.

It looks to me as though Pope Benedict's additions were intended to strengthen the view that acts of canonization are infallible and require acceptance *de fide.* I wish now to point out that, if the formulae introduced by Benedict XVI *did* affect this debated theological question, then, surely, so does the action of the next pontificate in *removing* them. In the gradual accumulation of evidences and precedents which gradually build up an established judgment of the Magisterium, surely phrases which were introduced into rites by one Pontiff and, very soon afterwards, removed by the next, have less *auctoritas* than established and immemorial formulae which have been used by successive pontiffs for centuries.

Canonization raises questions which, for centuries, interested specialist students of canon law. They interested the future Pope Benedict XIV, Prospero Lambertini. However, they have in the past not been things which concerned non-specialists. Ordinary cardinals, bishops, priests, and laity naturally and very properly just accepted the judgments made by the Sovereign Pontiff in this as in so many other matters. But the situation is not the same now. There has been, in some quarters, an uneasy suspicion for some time that canonizations have turned into a way of setting a seal upon the "policies" of some popes. If these "policies" are themselves a matter of divisive discussion and debate, then the promotion of the idea that canonizations are infallible becomes itself an additional element in the conflict. Canonization, you will remind me, does not, theologically, imply approval of everything a saint has done or said. Not formally, indeed. But the suspicion among some is that, *de facto* and humanly, such can seem to be its aim. This is confirmed by a prevailing assumption on all sides that the canonizations of the "conciliar popes" do bear some sort of meaning or message.

Personally, I feel more confident in my earlier conclusion that to dispute the judgment made in and by an act of canonization would not actually be a sin against *fides*. In other words, I feel happier with the theological implications of Pope Francis's deletions than I did with the implications of what Pope Benedict added. In practical terms, I feel that Pope Francis's excisions from the rite ought to make the canonization of Paul VI just that little bit less of a problem for particularly tender consciences, because the act of canonization does not now come before us weighed down with quite that same degree of authority with which Pope Benedict had wished it to be endowed. And I would regard the observations I made about schismatic canonizations subsequently adopted within the Catholic Church as also pointing in the direction of canonizations (at least *pro eo*) not necessarily being *de fide*.

11

The Canonization Crisis†

CHRISTOPHER A. FERRARA

A PERENNIALLY SMOLDERING DEBATE REIGNITED

Pope Bergoglio's rapid-fire canonizations of John Paul II and John XXIII have understandably contributed to growing concerns among the faithful about the reliability of the "saint factory" put into operation during the reign of John Paul II. John Paul canonized more saints, including large batch canonizations, than the previous seventeen popes combined, going all the way back to 1588, when Sixtus V founded the Congregation for the Causes of the Saints. While Benedict XVI made some effort to slow the output of the factory, it has ramped up production again under Bergoglio, who in five years has cranked out 885 saints, including a batch of 800 Italian martyrs, as compared with 482 saints during John Paul's entire 27-year reign.[1] Five of these Bergoglian additions have been declared saints without even one verified miracle being attributed to them.

Of course, it is undeniable that the Church produces innumerable saints in every age, including martyrs, and that the abundant fruits of the graces she mediates for the elevation of souls to perfection should be recognized in order to edify and encourage the faithful. Canonization, however, is traditionally reserved for those singular cases of sainthood which, after the most careful investigations, are to be held up as models for the veneration of the Church universal because of the particular example each of these remarkable lives provides. It is not only traditionalist commentators who observe that the sheer number of recently proclaimed saints threatens a radical devaluation of the very concept of *canonized* sainthood. Even Cardinal Ratzinger

---

[1]   The number for Francis is 899 as of May 15, 2021, and the exact number of the martyrs of Otranto is 813. — *Ed.*

---

†   Published in two parts in *The Remnant* online, February 26 and October 13, 2018.

suggested as much as early as 1989,[2] when he noted that many of those John Paul II had beatified "don't say much to the great multitudes of the faithful" and that priority should be given to those who "truly carry a message beyond a certain group."

But now the seemingly imminent canonization of Paul VI, following approval of two purported miracles which, based on the information published, seem decidedly less than miraculous (to be discussed below), has provoked widespread incredulity about the canonization process itself, going even beyond the skepticism that greeted the canonizations of John XXIII and John Paul II. How could the very pope who unleashed what he himself lamented — too little, too late — as a "spirit of autodemolition" in the Church, including a "liturgical reform" that led to what Cardinal Ratzinger called "the disintegration of the liturgy,"[3] the same pope who wondered how "the smoke of Satan"[4] had entered the Church during his tumultuous reign, be raised to the altars as a model of Catholic virtue for veneration and *imitation* by all the faithful?

To quote *The Washington Post*: "But for better or worse, Francis's tendency to bypass the normal channels for certifying miracles is generating friction inside the ancient Vatican walls even as it reignites an age-old debate over the nature of Catholic saints."[5] That age-old debate is over two questions yet to be answered definitively by the Magisterium: First, is the infallibility of papal canonizations *de fide* or merely a probable opinion? Second, if canonizations are infallible *de fide*, under what conditions are they such, given the strict conditions for papal infallibility laid down by the First Vatican Council

---

2   See Alan Riding, "Rome Journal; Vatican 'Saint Factory': Is It Working Too Hard?," *New York Times*, April 15, 1989.

3   Joseph Ratzinger, *Milestones: Memoirs 1927–1977*, trans. Erasmo Leiva-Merikakis (San Francisco: Ignatius Press, 1998), 148.

4   Contrary to the scoffing of neo-Catholic commentators who have not troubled themselves with serious research, this reference is not "apocryphal." It has been cited by no less than Monsignor Guido Pozzo, Secretary of the Pontifical Commission Ecclesia Dei (see his lecture "Aspects of Catholic Ecclesiology in the Implementation of Vatican Council II," full text at *Rorate Caeli*, October 14, 2010), and is found in Paul VI, *Insegnamenti*, vol. X (1972), p. 707.

5   Anthony Faiola, "As two more popes are canonized, a question emerges: How miraculous should saints be?," *Washington Post*, April 25, 2014.

respecting dogmatic definitions as opposed to acts of canonization regarding particular people in specific historical circumstances? The two questions can be summarized as one: Are we required to believe that someone is a saint simply and only because the pope has declared him to be so by recitation of the canonization formula, or must the pope base his decision on the prior investigation of verifiable facts, just as dogmatic definitions must be founded on verification of the constant teaching of the Church preceding the definition?

ON WHAT IS THE CLAIM OF INFALLIBLE CANONIZATION BASED?

It seems clear that the Vatican I definition of the dogma of papal infallibility respecting dogmatic definitions cannot be stretched to cover canonizations. The dogmatic definitions of the Extraordinary Magisterium place beyond any possible dispute and thus establish as an article of the Faith only what was already a constant teaching of the Church, not some doctrine newly enunciated by a given pope. But canonizations by their very nature do announce something new respecting a duty of universal veneration for a particular person. To quote John Paul II himself in this regard: "[The Apostolic See] proposes to the faithful for their imitation, veneration, and invocation, men and women who are outstanding in the splendor of charity and other evangelical virtues and, after due investigations, she declares them, in the solemn act of canonization, to be Saints."[6]

Thus, John Paul himself preconditions canonization on a prior investigation, even though it was he who, in 1983, issued the Apostolic Constitution *Divinus Perfectionis Magister*, which largely dismantled the centuries-old investigative machinery for canonization. The result was a "streamlined" process that (a) returns to the local bishop the bulk of the investigation of the candidate, including claimed miracles, without prior permission from Rome; (b) eliminates the fixed adversarial role of the Promoter of the Faith, commonly known as the "Devil's Advocate";[7] (c) reduces the perennial requirement of miracles from four (two for beatification and two more for canonization) to two (one each for beatification and canonization); and (d) converts

---

6   Apostolic Constitution *Divinus Perfectionis Magister*, January 25, 1983.
7   See chapter 3.—*Ed.*

the entire process from the traditional and quite rigorous canonical trial on the merits of the candidate into a committee-style review and discussion practically devoid of adversarial character.[8]

In any case, canonization must be preceded by *some* form of reliable investigation of contingent historical facts. That investigation is either by the "ordinary" process, involving the systematic verification of miracles and virtues, or by the "extraordinary" process of confirming the existence of a longstanding legitimate *cultus* surrounding a particular person and an "uninterrupted reputation for wonders" (the so-called "equivalent" canonization[9]) even if the more exacting ordinary process is not applied. Were it otherwise, we would have to believe the absurdity that someone is to be revered as a saint without any prior investigation whatsoever, simply because the pope says so by means of a recited formula.

Donald S. Prudlo, a highly reputable scholar on the history of canonizations, is clearly vexed by the hastiness and waning quality of pre-canonization investigations since the "saint factory" began its operation. He writes:

> As an historian of sainthood, my greatest hesitation with the current process stems from the canonizations done by John Paul II himself. While his laudable intention was to provide models of holiness drawn from all cultures and states in life, he tended to divorce canonization from its original and fundamental purpose. This was to have an official, public, and formal recognition of an existing cult of the Christian faithful, one that had been confirmed by the divine testimony of miracles. Cult precedes canonization; it was not meant to be the other way around. We are in danger then of using canonization as a tool to promote interests and movements, rather than being a recognition and approval of an extant *cultus*.[10]

---

8 See, e.g., Jason A. Gray, "The Evolution of the Promoter of the Faith in Causes of Beatification and Canonization: A Study of the Law of 1917 and 1983," doctoral thesis, Pontifical Lateran University, Rome, 2015; text available at www.jgray.org/docs/Promotor_Fidei_lulu.pdf.

9 See "Cardinal explains Pope Francis's 'equivalent canonization' of St. Peter Faber," *Catholic Culture*, December 24, 2013.

10 Donald S. Prudlo, "Are Canonizations Based on Papal Infallibility?," *Crisis Magazine*, April 25, 2014.

Exactly so. But, confronted with patent abuses of the canonization process since 1983, reducing it to a "halo award" for favored persons or movements—a trend that has accelerated during this pontificate—Prudlo opts for the view that the process is, in essence, superfluous to the infallibility of canonizations. In responding to the concerns of Roberto de Mattei over Pope Bergoglio's canonization of John Paul II and John XXIII, he concludes:

> It is the act of canonization that is the infallible act of the pope since, as Thomas argues, it is no mere disciplinary decision, but the quasi-profession of faith in the glory of a saint. It is not the investigation, but the inspiration of the Holy Ghost that certifies this reality for us (*Quod.* 9, a. 16, ad 1). Popes are not infallible because of the quality of investigations that precede the definition, they are infallible precisely because of the act they perform in the liturgical setting of canonization.[11]

But if the investigation has no part in "certifying this reality for us," what is the point of the investigation? If the *cultus* of a candidate for sainthood must be confirmed, as Prudlo says, by "the divine testimony of miracles," doesn't there have be a reliable investigation of the miracles attributed to the candidate, ending in the certainty that they are truly miracles? It was reported that during Benedict XVI's slowdown of the "saint factory," he "reads every file page by page, according to the archbishop [Michele di Ruberto, secretary of the Congregation for the Causes of Saints], and *until he is personally satisfied with the miracles* accredited to a candidate, no progress is possible."

Quite simply, if the quality of the investigation has no bearing on the veracity of a canonization, why waste time with an investigation? A pope could simply implore the inspiration of the Holy Ghost and proceed infallibly even when an investigation is clearly flawed or completely absent. But that sounds more like the work of a gnostic Oracle of Rome than a Roman Pontiff acting according to both faith and reason.

---

11   Ibid. [For De Mattei's concerns, see chapter 13.—*Ed.*]

COMPARISON WITH THE INFALLIBLE DEFINITION OF DOGMA

The idea that an inspiration of the Holy Ghost is the real guarantee of canonization is certainly not consistent with the way popes have defined dogmas of the Faith. Of course, the Holy Ghost guides the Church in the matter of dogma, but that guidance has taken place over time as a function of preserving and enunciating the revelation of Christ and the Apostles handed down from century to century, not by momentary *ad hoc* inspirations. Thus, for example, in defining the dogma of the Immaculate Conception, Blessed Pius IX certainly invoked the Holy Ghost, but he also made absolutely certain that "Holy Scripture, venerable Tradition, [and] the constant mind of the Church" supported the definition.[12] His investigation included the findings of a special commission, consultation with the world's bishops — who "with one voice . . . entreated us to define by our supreme judgment and authority the Immaculate Conception of the Virgin" — and a consistory of the College of Cardinals called to address the subject. Pius probably would have laughed at the suggestion that only the inspiration of the Holy Ghost (to which he referred at the moment of the definition) and the recitation of the traditional formula ensured the infallibility of his definition, not *also* the objective and verifiable content of the Faith as confirmed by an exhaustive prior investigation. If such immense investigative care is required for defining as a dogma what the Church has always believed anyway, then how can an adequate investigation of a particular person's alleged sanctity and miracles, which may be hotly contested, not be crucial to a pope's decision to raise him to the altars?

THE "SOLUTION" OF SAINT THOMAS

In his masterful study of this subject, Prudlo cites the solution proposed by Saint Thomas: that the Holy Ghost insures the reliability of canonizations despite the potential for human error or even outright mendacity on the part of investigators and witnesses. But Thomas argues only that "we must piously believe" the pope cannot

---

12 Pius IX, Apostolic Constitution *Ineffabilis Deus* (1854). Incredibly, this monumental papal document is not to be found among the documents of Pius IX archived on the Vatican website. [Confirmed again as of May 2021. — *Ed.*]

err in canonizing and that "Divine Providence preserves the Church assuredly in such things as may be deceived by fallible human testimony."[13] He does not argue, nor has the Church ever taught, that this pious belief is an article of faith not to be questioned or doubted under any circumstances whatsoever.

Furthermore, Prudlo himself explains that there are *three* reasons Thomas concludes that the pope is unable to err in canonizations: "(1) he makes a thorough *investigation* into holiness of life; (2) this is confirmed by the testimony of *miracles*, and (3) the Holy Spirit leads him (for Thomas, the clincher)."[14] But if the guidance of the Holy Spirit is "the clincher," there must be something to clinch in the first place. And that can only be the case for canonization based on *verified* holiness of life and miracles following an investigation into both. Absent that investigation into holiness and miracles, sole reliance on the inspiration of the Holy Ghost would appear to be the rashest of presumptions, at least in ordinary cases. Indeed, the same presumption would justify enunciation of new doctrines not shown *by investigation* to be "the constant mind of the Church," to recall the words of Blessed Pius IX.

In any case, Saint Thomas is not infallible even if he does provide weighty authority for the majority opinion of theologians, at least since the fifteenth century, that papal canonizations are infallible. Indeed, it is not easy to see how formal papal canonization could be subject to error, as this would undermine the entire canon of saints raised to the altars by pontifical act, expose the Church to the charge that she has imposed error in her universal discipline, and favor the opinion of heretics that the Church demands the vain and blasphemous veneration of sinners.

IS THERE ROOM FOR DOUBT?

Nevertheless, the infallibility of papal canonizations has never been defined as a dogma, nor can one find it clearly stated as an explicit doctrine of the universal ordinary Magisterium. For example, as Prof.

---

13   Donald S. Prudlo, *Certain Sainthood, Canonization and the Origins of Papal Infallibility in the Medieval Church* (Ithaca: Cornell University Press, 2016), 141; citing *Quodlibet* IX, q. 8, resp. & ad 2.
14   Ibid. Emphasis added.

de Mattei notes in the article cited above, there is no mention of the infallibility of canonizations, nor even a discussion of the prevailing theological view, in the 1917 *Code of Canon Law*, the 1983 *Code of Canon Law*, or the *Catechism of the Catholic Church*.

In an essay on the subject published in 1848, Father Frederick William Faber, the famous Anglican convert renowned for his scholarship, "unswerving loyalty to the Holy See," and Marian devotion, who authored the definitive *Lives of the Modern Saints*, defended the majority theological opinion in favor of infallibility and argued for the rashness and impiety of attributing error to papal canonizations. But he was also at pains to hedge his discussion with caveats in view of weighty minority views:

> Is it *de fide* that the Church is infallible in the decree of canonization? This is an open question in the Catholic schools....
>
> St. Thomas places the judgment of the Church in canonization as something between a judgment in matters of faith and a judgment on particular facts, and therefore it would follow that the infallibility of the decree is a pious belief, but nothing more, inasmuch as it only pertains to the faith *reductive*[15]....
>
> It is *de fide* that the Church is infallible in the common doctrine of morals; but it is not so certain that the canonization of Saints pertains to the common doctrine of morals.... The Church has never defined her infallibility in this matter to be *de fide*, neither can we collect it from her practice....
>
> It seems then probable that it is *de fide* that the judgment of the Church in canonization is infallible; but beyond this assertion of a strong probability we must not venture to go, especially seeing such great names for the negative opinion.
>
> It is safer to conclude with the wise and learned Lambertini, that each opinion should be left in its own probability, until a judgment shall issue from the Holy See; for when we are treating of setting up a dogma of faith, says the same careful theologian in another place, we must wait for the judgment of the Apostolic See, the mother and mistress of the other Churches, and of the chief pontiff, to whom it exclusively belongs to make definitions of faith, before we

---

15   Reductively, that is, by being traced back to something prior.

venture to brand with the infamous note of heresy those
who follow an opposite opinion.[16]

Likewise, in his own study of the evolution of the papal canonization process and the correlative view of the infallibility of papal canonizations, Prudlo concludes: "Claims of infallibility do not appear
until relatively late in the Middle Ages, usually after the . . . period of
the acquisition of papal hegemony over such cases."[17] But, he notes,
"the seemingly inexhaustible supply of candidates so honored by John
Paul II and the rapidity of advancement advocated by Pope Francis
for some recent figures have also stimulated current arguments." To
say the least! And that is precisely the point: *Current arguments are
permissible* in keeping with the "origins of the theological and historical debate" Prudlo traces to the Middle Ages. Those arguments will
undoubtedly continue on some level unless and until the infallibility
of papal canonizations is removed from the realm of probable theological opinion by either an *ex cathedra* definition or a decisively-worded
encyclical dedicated to the question.

On the subject of current arguments—and quite tellingly in view
of the drive by Pope Bergoglio to canonize with utmost haste every
pope associated with the Second Vatican Council, including even
Pope John Paul I (whom he has already declared Venerable)—we
have a 2014 interview, published by *Vatican Insider*, with Bishop
Giuseppe Sciacca.[18] Sciacca is a renowned canonist who in 2016 was
promoted to the office of no less than Secretary of the Apostolic
Signatura by Bergoglio himself. When asked by the interviewer "Is
the pope infallible when he proclaims a new saint?," Bishop Sciacca
hedged his reply:

---

16   F. W. Faber, *An Essay on Beatification, Canonization, and the Processes of the
Congregation of Rites* (London: Richardson & Son, 1848), 127, 128; paragraph
breaks added. This essay may be found with Google Books. [Note that "probable" in the specialized context of scholastic theology does not mean "likely to
be true," but "provable, sustainable."—*Ed.*]
17   Prudlo, *Certain Sainthood*, 16.
18   This interview, "Are Canonizations Infallible?," was published online at *La
Stampa* on July 10, 2014, www.lastampa.it/vatican-insider/en/2014/07/10/news/
are-canonizations-infallible-1.35731911 (the translation here has been modified in
light of the Italian original, "Canonizzazioni infallibili?").

According to the prevailing doctrine of the Church, when the pope canonizes a saint his judgment is infallible. As is known, canonization is the decree with which the pope solemnly proclaims that the heavenly glory shines upon the Blessed and extends the cult of the new saint to the universal Church in a binding and definitive manner. There is no question then that canonization is an act carried out by the Petrine primate. At the same time, however, it should not be considered infallible according to the infallibility criteria set out in the First Vatican Council's dogmatic constitution *Pastor Aeternus*.

When next asked whether "the pope can make a mistake when he proclaims someone a saint?," Bishop Sciacca offered this nuanced explanation:

> That's not what I said. I am not denying that the decree issued for a canonization cause is definitive, so it would be rash and indeed unholy to state that the pope can make a mistake. What I am saying is that the proclamation of a person's sainthood is not a truth of faith because it is not a dogmatic definition and is not directly or explicitly linked to a truth of faith or a moral truth contained in revelation, but is only indirectly linked to this. It is no coincidence that neither the *Code of Canon Law* of 1917 nor the one currently in force, nor the *Catechism of the Catholic Church* presents the Church's doctrine regarding canonizations.

When queried about the opinion of Saint Thomas on the matter, Bishop Sciacca cautioned that it must be viewed in the context of the Church's much later infallible definition of the strict limits of papal infallibility:

> Of course, I am well aware of that. Thomas Aquinas is the most prestigious author supporting this theory. But it should be said that the use of the concept of infallibility and of language relating to it, in a context that is so far from that of the nineteenth century when the First Vatican Council was held, risks being anachronistic.
>
> St. Thomas placed canonization halfway between things that pertain to the Faith and judgments on certain factors that

can be contaminated by false testimonies, concluding that
the Church could not make mistakes; indeed, he maintained
that "it is pious to believe that the judgment is infallible."

As I said before and I repeat again, *Pastor Aeternus* rigorously defines and restricts the concept of papal infallibility
which could previously also encompass and contain or be
likened to the concepts of "inerrancy" and "indefectibility"
in relation to the Church. Canonization is like a doctrine
which cannot be contested but which cannot be defined as
a doctrine of faith in such a way that all the faithful must
necessarily believe in it.

In other words, while a papal canonization cannot be contested
outright as error, questioning the infallibility of canonizations, or
even arguing against it according to the minority view, does not place
one outside the communion of the Church on account of heresy.
Indeed, Bishop Sciacca—Secretary of the Church's highest canonical
tribunal—rejects the claim that the Church teaches that it is heresy to question the infallibility of canonization. To the interviewer's
question "And what about the words which Pope Benedict XIV, born
Prospero Lambertini, used in the *De servorum Dei beatificatione et
beatorum canonizatione*, about the non-infallibility theory 'smelling
of heresy'?," he responded: "His theory is not binding, as it forms
part of the work he did as a great canonist—but as part of his private studies. It has nothing to do with his pontifical magisterium."
The interviewer, not to be deterred, presses further: "But there was
a doctrinal text issued by the Congregation for the Doctrine of the
Faith in May 1998 which also mentions infallibility in canonizations."
Sciacca replies:

> It is patently clear that the purpose of the [CDF] passage in
> question is purely illustrative and is not intended as a defini-
> tion. The recurring argument according to which the Church
> cannot teach or accept mistakes is intrinsically weak in this
> case. But saying that an act is not infallible does not mean
> to say that the act is wrong or deceiving. Indeed, the mistake
> may have been made either rarely or never. Canonization,
> which everyone admits does not derive directly from faith,
> is never an actual definition relating to faith or tradition…

When the interviewer, with perhaps a touch of impatience, asks: "Sorry, what exactly is canonization then?," the canonist asseverates:

> It is the definitive and irreformable closure of a process, it is the final judgment at the end of a historical and canonical process, which always concerns a factual, historical question. To incorporate it into infallibility is to extend infallibility itself far beyond the boundaries defined by the First Vatican Council.

The reader will notice that both Father Faber and Bishop Sciacca, given the still-unsettled state of the Magisterium, leave room for a measure of doubt on the infallibility of canonizations as a minority view — a view that would constitute theological error at worst, but not heresy, unless the Church formally reprobated it by way of a dogmatic definition (after which it *would* constitute heresy). But they also hold that it would be "rash and indeed unholy" to declare that a canonization is simply erroneous.

PAPAL RELIANCE ON PRE-CANONIZATION INVESTIGATIONS: A CONUNDRUM

So, what exactly inhabits the slim *lacuna* between the permissibility of questioning the infallibility of canonizations and the impermissibility of contesting particular examples as outright papal blunders? This zone of uncertainty seems to arise from the very nature of canonization as the outcome of a prior investigation to determine the existence of historical facts about a particular person, without which canonization cannot occur, as opposed to enunciating doctrinal formulae for the universal Church.

Given the fact-dependency of canonizations, there is no escaping what Prudlo admits is a true and proper "conundrum" with which canonists and theologians, including St. Bonaventure and St. Thomas, had to grapple as the papacy gradually consolidated its authority over a canonization process that for centuries had been a local affair involving, in not a few cases, very dubious "saints":

> Foremost in their minds was the possibility of error as a result of false human testimony. This constantly checked canonists and some theologians from assigning papal infallibility in canonization as a dogma of the faith, especially in the

thirteenth century. The problem of canonizing unworthy figures came up repeatedly, causing the papacy to institute all manner of safeguards to ensure veracity and holiness, such as lengthy investigations of life and miracles. In addition to all of these, the possibility of human frailty remained very much in the forefront of theological writings. It was the central argument against the doctrine in the medieval period. How Church thinkers overcame this conundrum is a central key to understanding the creation of general consensus.[19]

But what necessity is there for "all manner of safeguards to ensure veracity and holiness," including "lengthy investigations of life and miracles," if, as Prudlo argues against de Mattei, "it is not the investigation, but the inspiration of the Holy Ghost that certifies this reality for us" and "popes are not infallible because of the quality of investigations that precede the definition, they are infallible precisely because of the act they perform in the liturgical setting of canonization"?

Moreover, Prudlo's own scholarship tends to undermine his position *contra* de Mattei. As his study notes, Pope Innocent III (r. 1198–1216) declared in his Bull canonizing Homobonus of Cremona that "Two things *are necessary* for one who is publicly venerated as a saint in the Church militant: the power of signs, namely *works of piety* in life, and *the sign of miracles* after death."[20] Innocent also made clear that the papal precept of universal veneration involved in canonization must be supported by more than the bare conviction that a candidate has achieved the beatific vision, as some now argue in a minimalist defense of Francis's canonizations of John Paul II and John XXIII: "While Innocent avers that only final perseverance is absolutely necessary for sainthood simply considered, he maintains that the public veneration of such a person *requires divine testimonies*. Both are required for sanctity, 'for neither are works sufficient by themselves, nor signs alone.'"[21] It is highly significant that, as Prudlo shows, Innocent III is the very pope who "laid down the pattern that would be critical for the elucidation of the qualitative difference in papal canonizations that would arise after his death" — that

---

19 Prudlo, 20–21.
20 In Prudlo, 76, emphasis added.
21 Prudlo, 141.

is, their infallibility — by "reorienting the canonization process from the papal perspective." Part of that reorientation is "the *necessity* of signs and wonders as *a signal precondition for sainthood*, along with the testimony of a life lived according to the virtues."[22] Is it really temerarious to suggest that, absent proof of true signs and wonders, there cannot be a true canonization?

It would appear, then, that Prudlo himself has demonstrated that according to papal teaching some reliable form of factual investigation of the candidate for sainthood, confirming both miracles and virtues, is a prerequisite to papal canonization — that is, the pope's imposition of mandatory veneration of a saint by the whole Church. Although Prudlo concludes that as the process of papal canonization developed "the popes clearly believed they were exercising personal infallibility in their decrees of canonization,"[23] the question remains: On what grounds did they base that belief? Surely, the investigations on which they relied must have had something to do with it.

That being so, how can the quality of the pre-canonization investigation not emerge as an issue? If the quality of the investigation were irrelevant, would not the investigation itself be irrelevant? In which case, we would be left only with the bare assertion that an inspiration of the Holy Ghost guarantees that no papal canonization will ever be in error so long as the pope recites the canonization formula "in the liturgical setting of canonization" (to recall Prudlo's argument *contra* de Mattei). But that kind of infallibility would have to be distinct from the Vatican I definition, which is strictly limited to the pope's solemn proclamation that what the Church has always believed is *de fide*. Thus, a further definition of papal infallibility, embracing the canonizations of particular individuals based on historical facts, would appear to be necessary to end legitimate debate over the matter.

FOUR DUBIA

In the meantime, I do not see why the following specific *dubia* — which of course I have no competence to answer — are not "on the table" respecting canonization:

---

22 Prudlo, 141, emphasis added.
23 Prudlo, 191.

- Could the validity of a canonization, even if it cannot be called an error as such, be doubted if it could be shown that the investigation of the candidate has been compromised by human error, bias, or mendacity?
- Would a papal act of canonization by way of recitation of the canonization formula during the canonization rite be infallible *ex sese* (of or from itself) even if there were no prior investigation of the candidate?
- If the papal act of canonization is infallible *ex sese*, is there any necessity for the investigatory process preceding canonization — developed by the popes themselves to provide safeguards to ensure the veracity of miracles and the holiness of a candidate; and if it is necessary, why is it necessary?
- If a papal act of canonization is not infallible *ex sese*, then is the integrity of the investigatory process preceding it essential to the claim of infallibility, and if not, why not?

These questions can be answered definitively only by the Magisterium. And the need for that answer is urgent. The accelerating operation of the "saint factory" and the clearly expedient move to canonize every pope since the Second Vatican Council on the basis of increasingly slim evidence, while neglecting or completely forgetting the causes of great preconciliar popes renowned for their heroic virtue and plenitude of undeniable miracles — for example, the cause of Blessed Pius IX — has induced a kind of "canonization crisis" in the minds of millions of the faithful.

Is the answer to the crisis blind faith in the infallibility of canonizations, which has never been defined as an article of faith? Or are the faithful permitted to raise today, with greater urgency than ever before, the sorts of questions that have been prompted since the development of the papal canonization process began, yet still without a definitive answer from the Magisterium?

The foregoing *dubia* and this essay as a whole should be understood as an appeal for magisterial clarity by a mere layman who, along with Catholics the world over, is struggling to understand how the infallibility of canonizations can be reconciled with a process that seems increasingly, as Prudlo so rightly observes, to be subject to abuse in order "to promote interests and movements, rather than being a recognition and approval of an extant *cultus*." With all of these concerns in view, we will turn next to a consideration of the problematic character of the alleged miracles attributed to Paul VI as a prime example of why it is reasonable to consider whether the integrity of the investigative process affects the integrity of a canonization, all prior attempts to solve this conundrum notwithstanding.

THE IMPORTANCE OF WELL-ATTESTED GENUINE MIRACLES

On October 14, 2018, Pope Bergoglio, having already authorized Holy Communion for public adulterers and declared the death penalty immoral—flatly contradicting bimillennial Church teaching and practice in both cases—declared that both Paul VI and Oscar Romero are saints that the universal Church must venerate as such. Yet Paul VI unleashed an unprecedented liturgical debacle and the postconciliar revolution in general, over which he spent the rest of his life weeping and wringing his hands while faith and discipline rapidly collapsed all around him. Romero, a complex figure one cannot honestly call a Marxist, was not assassinated on account of hatred of the Faith as such, but rather on account of his public agitation against the government of El Salvador, then in the midst of a civil war with Marxist revolutionaries.[24] Nor has it ever been determined with certainty which side of the conflict was responsible for his murder, for which no one has ever been prosecuted or even identified definitively as a suspect.[25]

What are we to make of these canonizations—the latest in the output of what the press mocks as the "saint factory"[26] put into operation by John Paul II? In considering this question, I venture the opinion of a layman who cannot see how the infallibility of canonizations can be anything but dependent upon the integrity of the investigative process that precedes the papal canonization decree.

---

24 See "Is Romero a martyr of the Faith?," at the website of the SSPX District of the USA, February 6, 2015.

25 See "Oscar Romero, assassinated during El Salvador's civil war, to be made Catholic saint," Thomson Reuters media service, March 7, 2018.

26 See Peter Popham, "Vatican halts John Paul II's 'saint factory,'" *Independent*, October 23, 2011.

Above, I noted the decisive role the divine testimony of miracles plays in canonization. I quoted Donald Prudlo, an expert on the history of canonizations, who observes that because "the problem of canonizing unworthy figures came up repeatedly" with local canonizations by bishops, once Rome had assumed control over canonizations in the late twelfth century "the papacy institute[d] *all manner of safeguards to ensure veracity and holiness,* such as lengthy investigations of life *and miracles.*" In that regard Prudlo cites Pope Innocent III, who declared that "two things *are necessary* for one who is publicly venerated as a saint in the Church militant: the power of signs, namely *works of piety* in life, and *the sign of miracles* after death." As Prudlo is at pains to note: "While Innocent avers that only final perseverance is absolutely necessary for sainthood simply considered, he maintains that the public veneration of such a person *requires divine testimonies.* Both are required for sanctity, 'for neither are works sufficient by themselves, nor signs alone.'"

Viewing the canonizations of Paul VI and Romero under the aspect of the purported medical miracles attributed to their intercession — an indispensable element of the process as it has developed under papal authority — one cannot fail to note that, based on the information made publicly available, none of them satisfies all of the traditional criteria[27] for verification of a miracle as a divine testimony of sanctity. Those criteria are (1) a *cure* that is (2) instantaneous, (3) complete, (4) lasting, and (5) scientifically inexplicable, meaning not the result of treatment or natural processes of healing but rather an event originating outside the natural order. (Once such a medical miracle is verified according to these criteria, it must further be determined that it occurred "solely through the intercession of that particular candidate for sainthood"[28] as opposed to prayers in general or prayers to other intercessors.)

It should be obvious that no purported miracle failing to meet even one of these criteria could rationally be considered a divine testimony of the candidate's sanctity. If there is no cure as such then there is

---

27 As noted even by the USCCB: see Jeannine Marino, "How the Church Recognizes Saints" at the USCCB website.

28 See Heidi Schlumpf, "Why does the church require miracles for sainthood?," *U. S. Catholic,* December 9, 2011.

no miracle at all. If the cure is merely partial, it is not miraculous. If the cure is not instantaneous but only gradual, then non-miraculous natural processes of healing or medical treatment could account for it. If the cure is only temporary and the condition returns, nothing miraculous has occurred.

PAUL VI'S "MIRACLES"

Let us look, then, at the "miracles" attributed to the intercession of Paul VI and Oscar Romero. As to Paul, the first purported miracle, which supported his beatification, "concerned an unborn which was found to have a serious health problem that *could mean* brain damage. Doctors advised that it be aborted, but the mother entrusted her pregnancy to Paul VI. The child was born healthy."[29] The purported miracle has been more fully described thus:

> The attributed miracle involves an unborn child, who was found to have a serious health problem that posed a high risk of brain damage, in the 1990s in California. The child's bladder was damaged, and doctors reported ascites (the presence of liquid in the abdomen) and anhydramnios (absence of fluid in the amniotic sac). Physicians advised that the child be aborted, but the mother entrusted her pregnancy to the intercession of Pope Paul VI, who succeeded St. John XXIII on June 21, 1963, and served until his death on August 6, 1978.
>
> The mother took the advice of a nun who was a friend of the family and had met Paul VI. The mother then prayed for Paul VI's intercession using a fragment of the pope's vestments that the nun had given her.
>
> Ten weeks later, the results of the medical tests showed a substantial improvement in the child's health, and he was born by Caesarean section in the 39th week of pregnancy. He is now a healthy adolescent and considered to be completely healed.
>
> The Italian postulator said it is not possible to give more details about the case in order to "respect the privacy" of the family and the boy concerned.[30]

---

29 See Patsy McGarry, "Vatican approves second miracle needed for canonisation of Pope Paul VI," *The Irish Times*, February 6, 2018.

30 "Pope Confirms Miracle Attributed to Paul VI's Intercession," *National Catholic Register*, May 10, 2014.

Where exactly is the miraculous cure? What is described is a good outcome from the aggressive fetal treatment typical in such cases, including an analogous case in which the neonate, in even greater danger from such conditions, was treated in the womb and delivered alive.[31] He was later reported to be "a 5-year-old [who] develops normally, but still remains under regular neurological, cardiologic, and ophthalmologic control." Indeed, the alleged beneficiary of the miraculous intercession of Paul VI was likewise monitored until he was "a healthy adolescent and considered to be completely cured." There is not even a claim of an instantaneous medical cure in the Vatican's ambiguous explanation of "substantial improvement" of the child's condition *in utero* and the avoidance of a *risk* of brain damage, not a cure of the same.

The second purported miracle attributed to Paul's intercession involves another ambiguously described fetal crisis: "the healing of an unborn child who was suffering from *a potentially fatal disease*. Shortly after Pope Paul VI's beatification, the child's mother travelled to Brescia, the former Pontiff's hometown, to pray for healing. The child was eventually born in good health."[32] How is that outcome different from the innumerable other cases when a child in danger in the womb is, against the odds, born healthy despite a grave prognosis? The medical literature and our common experience are replete with such cases. Again, where exactly is the *miraculous cure* of a seemingly incurable condition? Here too there is only a *potentially* fatal disease, another risk avoided, not the instantaneous cure of an otherwise fatal condition.

In both cases, one has the unmistakable sense of a stretching of the medical facts to reach the desired result: It's a miracle! Proceed immediately to canonization! (We are not even considering here the *other* indispensable requirement, heroic virtue. Suffice it to note that "heroic" does not seem applicable to a weeping pope who rued the

---

31 See the study "Successful intrauterine treatment and good long-term outcome in an extremely severe case of fetal hemolytic disease," *Journal of Ultrasonography,* June 2014, 14(57): 217–22.

32 "Cardinals approve miracle attributed to Pope Paul VI," *Catholic Herald,* February 6, 2018. This article appears to have been removed from the *Herald's* website but can be found with the Wayback Machine of the Internet Archive.

results of his own reckless permissions for unheard-of innovations in the Church, which he nonetheless obstinately refused to admit were his own catastrophic blunders.)

ROMERO'S "MIRACLE"

As for the one miracle attributed to the intercession of Oscar Romero — only one sufficing, given his prior designation as a "martyr" — here too, curiously enough, we encounter yet another ambiguous pregnancy-related medical emergency.[33] In this case we are informed that the purported miracle is that after giving birth, a woman named Cecilia developed HELLP syndrome, a condition related to preeclampsia which involves hemolysis, elevated liver enzymes, and low platelet count. In an effort to address threatened organ failure and other problems seen in the worst cases of this condition, she was placed in an induced coma — falsely described in some accounts as "slipping" into a coma as if to increase the drama. The claim is that after prayers to Romero, the woman saw a "dramatic recovery" over the next 72 *hours* and was discharged from the hospital a few days later, fully recovered from the effects of HELLP syndrome.

But recovery from HELLP syndrome after an induced coma, which constitutes aggressive medical treatment under the standard of care, is precisely what has happened in other such cases.[34] There is nothing miraculous about a very good medical outcome from very good medical treatment. As the husband said of the outcome in the second analogous case cited in the last footnote: "It's a miracle. I thought I was losing both of them." There is no sign that Oscar Romero or any other purported Catholic saint was involved in that happy result. In fact, overall the mortality rate for HELLP syndrome is reported

---

33 See "Papa approva miracolo per Romero," *Super Martyrio*, March 7, 2018.
34 See Leesa Smith, "Mum's first cuddle with stillborn son three weeks after waking from coma," kidspot.com.au, July 3, 2017; Claire Bates, "Mother loses 41 pints of blood due to severe pre-eclampsia but returns home with baby girl after making miracle recovery," *Daily Mail.com*, October 24, 2012. It is ironic that the latter article uses the word "miracle" but intends to speak of nothing supernatural; colloquially it seems to mean "really, really improbable and amazing."

to be only 1.1–3.4% with good treatment,[35] and only 25% globally,[36] including many cases where no treatment at all occurred. Moreover, the fetal mortality rate from HELLP syndrome is much higher[37] than the maternal mortality rate, but the child in the Romero case had already been born normally without his purported intercession. Was that normal birth, with much greater odds against survival, a "miracle" too?

The criteria for an authentic medical miracle supporting beatification or canonization have elsewhere been described thus: "1. Serious medical condition; 2. Condition not likely to disappear on its own; 3. Instantaneous; 4. Lasting; 5. Complete; 6. No other disease or incident can occur which may have caused the condition to disappear; 7. No medical treatment relative to the cure."

That description appears in an article on the two miracles attributed to the intercession of the Fatima visionaries Jacinta and Francisco in connection with their beatification by John Paul II and their canonization by Francis.[38] The first miracle involved the recovery of a paraplegic, who was able to walk normally again, and the second the recovery of a brain-damaged boy who had fallen 20 feet, landed on his head, fractured his skull and lost brain tissue, yet walked out of the hospital following prayers to the visionaries, with no signs of brain damage or loss of physical or mental function. In other words, both cases involve actual *cures* of otherwise incurable conditions, not merely the avoidance of a risk of harm or recovery after aggressive treatment.

With good reason did the post-Tridentine Church institutionalize strict verification of purported medical miracles as scientific knowledge advanced. Urban VIII (r. 1623–1644) and later Prospero Lambertini, who became Benedict XIV (r. 1740–1758), established the framework under which, via the function of the "devil's advocate" (*promotor fidei*), which Lambertini had exercised before his pontificate, the Church "leaned toward refuting miraculousness by means

---

35 See Michael Tsokos, "Pathological Features of Maternal Death from HELLP Syndrome," *Forensic Pathology Reviews* 1:275–90.

36 See https://www.preeclampsia.org/public/hellp-syndrome.

37 See "Neonatal Outcome after Preterm Delivery in HELLP Syndrome," *Yonsei Medical Journal*, June 30, 2006, 47(3):393–98.

38 See "Second Miracle of Fatima Shepherd Children," *The Miracle Hunter*, updated May 1, 2017.

of natural explanations."[39] Accordingly, "especially since Pope Urban VIII's reforms in the first half of the seventeenth century, medical judgment was given an increased role in evaluating claims of miracles." But even as early as the thirteenth century—the very century in which the debate over the infallibility of canonizations was at its height, as I showed earlier—"a chief expression of such skepticism has been the consultation of physicians to examine proposed miraculous healings and decide if they had natural causes."[40]

Natural explanations are plainly available for the "miracles" attributed to the intercession of Paul VI and Oscar Romero, none of which actually involved an outright and instantaneous *cure* in the first place as opposed to avoiding a medical risk, however serious, and reaching a good outcome while under aggressive, state-of-the-art medical treatment.

THE ABOLITION OF THE *PROMOTOR FIDEI*

It appears, then, that these imminent canonizations are yet another hasty product of the high-speed assembly line in the "saint factory" established by John Paul II. Not only did John Paul reduce the number of required miracles from four (two for beatification and two more for canonization) to only two (a mere one each for beatification and canonization), but the traditional role of the *promotor fidei* has effectively been eliminated so that there is no longer a truly adversarial procedure in the Congregation for the Causes of Saints, involving an institutionalized *contradictorium* by an official we know as the "devil's advocate." As one scholar on the subject writes:

> The observations of the Promoter of the Faith and the responses of the advocate have disappeared, as the Promoter of the Faith receives the cause for study only after the position [brief advocating sainthood] has been completed. In the current law, the Promoter of the Faith does not participate in a formal *contradictorium* with an opposing party, but rather presents his opinion regarding the cause when it is evaluated by the theologians. As the Roman phase is studied, it must

---

39 Fernando Vidal, "Miracles, Science, and Testimony in Post-Tridentine Saint-Making," *Science in Context* 20.3 (2007):481–508, at 481.
40 Ibid. at 482, 485.

be considered whether the Promoter of the Faith exercises even an informal role in the *contradictorium*. . . .

From these observations it can be concluded that there is not a clear *contradictorium* in the current legislation, since the party who stands in the second position in opposition to the cause remains obscure.[41]

As a defender of the "streamlined" process writes regarding this practical elimination of the "devil's advocate":

Pope John Paul II changed that role to a great degree. . . . but contrary to popular belief . . . it was not eliminated. . . . His authority to "veto," or cancel, a cause is gone. He does not provide a list of objections and complaints, he provides a report of what his findings are, but that report does not mandate there be a satisfactory answer to each objection. Thanks to Pope John Paul II, the process of canonization was transformed from a type of trial by fire form of scrutinization to a committee or business type meeting.[42]

In other words, the devil's advocate *has* been eliminated — not only his decisive veto, but his role as such. He is now, at most, just another member of a committee whose function is essentially to "make saints" as requested by generating the appropriate findings, including the finding that cures readily explicable by natural means, and indeed frequently observed without any invocation of a purported saint, are "miracles."

Earlier, I posed four *dubia*, given that the infallibility of canonizations remains only a probable theological opinion and not an article of faith. These questions, I noted, "can be answered definitively only by the Magisterium." The Church has never declared that they may no longer be discussed. Quite the contrary, they have never ceased to be matters for debate. From which follows a fifth *dubium*, as suggested by the problems we have identified with the supposed miracles:

If the integrity of the investigatory process is essential to the infallibility of a canonization, and if the process examines purported medical miracles, is not the quality of evidence in

41   Gray, "Evolution of the Promoter of the Faith," 262, 309.
42   Amelia Monroe Carlson, "No! The Church did not eliminate the 'Devil's Advocate' position," *Catholic365.com*, November 16, 2016.

support of the alleged miracles also an essential element, such that dubious miracles readily explainable by natural means, including modern aggressive medical treatment, would tend to undermine confidence in the validity of the canonization and give grounds for reasonably doubting its validity?

I can only agree with the view expressed by Peter Kwasniewski:

> With the greatly increasing number of canonizations; the removal of half of the number of miracles required (which are sometimes waived); the lack of a robust *advocatus diaboli* role; and, at times, the rushed manner in which documentation is examined or even passed over (as, apparently, has been the case with Paul VI), it seems to me not only that it has become impossible to claim that today's canonizations always require our assent, but also that there may be canonizations about which one would have an obligation to withhold assent.[43]

What Kwasniewski is saying is that in recent decades the very nature of canonization appears to have changed to such an extent that we may no longer be dealing with the same thing that gave us the likes of Pope St. Pius X and that we would be violating conscience if we blindly accepted every result of the current process. What seems to have replaced the traditional exceedingly rigorous process is a kind of weighty honorific bestowed by a committee predisposed to grant it without serious opposition.

In short, we no longer have the *reasonable* perception of an iron-clad, infallible determination that every candidate approved by the "saint factory" is not only in attainment of beatitude but also a model of virtue for the universal Church, one who *must* be venerated by all the faithful because of his splendid example of conformity to the divine will. Who can say that with any honesty concerning Paul VI? As Kwasniewski observes:

> Paul VI did not helplessly watch the Church's "autodemolition" (his own term for the collapse after the Council); he did not merely preside over the single greatest exodus of Catholic laity, clergy, and religious since the Protestant

---

43 See p. 229.

Revolt. He *aided and abetted* this internal devastation by his own actions....

Many Catholics are rightfully anxious about Pope Francis. But what he has done in the past five years is arguably small potatoes compared with what Paul VI had the audacity to do: substituting a new liturgy for the ancient Roman Mass and sacramental rites, causing the biggest internal rupture the Catholic Church has ever suffered. This was the equivalent of dropping an atomic bomb on the People of God, which either wiped out their faith or caused cancers by its radiation. It was the very negation of paternity, of the papacy's fatherly function of conserving and passing on the family heritage. Everything that has happened after Paul VI is no more than an echo of this violation of the sacred temple. Once the most holy thing is profaned, nothing else is safe, nothing else is stable.[44]

Finally, in concluding this series, I can only adopt as my own the limited conclusion expressed by John Lamont: "We need not exclude all canonizations whatsoever from the charism of infallibility; we can still argue that those canonizations that followed the rigorous procedure of former centuries benefited from this charism.... A return to the former approach to canonization would mean recovering the guidance of the Holy Spirit in an area of great import for the Church."[45]

Perhaps that conclusion is wrong. But let the Magisterium, in a definitive and binding pronouncement, tell us so. Let it declare, in other words, that any and all canonizations pronounced by a pope are infallible *ex sese* even if the preceding investigation is patently flawed or corruptly motivated, which would mean that the investigation is ultimately superfluous. Until then, neither Paul VI nor Oscar Romero will figure in this poor Catholic's invocation of the saints. I reserve the right in conscience, not to deny, but to doubt where doubt is still permitted rather than doing violence to reason itself.

---

44 See pp. 231–32.
45 See pp. 161–62.

12

True and False Saints in the Church[†]

ROBERTO DE MATTEI

AMONG THE ANNIVERSARIES OF 2018 THERE IS
one that has gone unnoticed: the sixty years since the death of Venerable Pius XII, after a nineteen-year reign, at Castelgandolfo on
October 9, 1958. Yet today his memory still lives on, especially, as
Cristina Siccardi notes, as an icon of holiness worthy of the Vicar
of Christ, and for the vastness of his Magisterium in the context of
tragic events, like the Second World War, which erupted six months
after his election to the Papacy on March 20, 1939. The death of
Pius XII closed an era, which today is referred to contemptuously as
"pre-conciliar" or "Constantinian." With the election of John XXIII
(October 28, 1958) and the calling of the Second Vatican Council,
a new era in the history of the Church opened: that which had its
moment of triumph, on October 14, 2018, with the canonization of
Paul VI, after that of Pope Roncalli.

Blessed Pius IX is still awaiting canonization and Pius XII has still not
been beatified, but all the Council and post-Council popes have been
canonized, with the exception of John Paul I. It seems that what they
want to canonize, through its main actors, is an age, which, however,
is perhaps the darkest the Church has ever experienced in Her history.

Immorality spreads through the entire body of the Church, starting
from the highest levels. Pope Francis has refused to admit the reality
of the tragic scenario brought to light by Archbishop Carlo Maria
Viganò.[1] Doctrinal confusion is total, to the point that Cardinal

---

1   De Mattei refers here to the historic "First Testimony" of the Archbishop in
which he disclosed the intricate web of complicities behind the McCarrick scandal,
culminating in the pope. For the definitive edition and related documents, see *A
Voice in the Wilderness: Archbishop Carlo Maria Viganò on the Church, America,
and the World*, ed. Brian M. McCall (Brooklyn, NY: Angelico Press, 2021).

---

†   First published in *Corrispondenza Romana*, October 17, 2018; English translation by Francesca Romana, published at *Rorate Caeli*, October 18, 2018.

Willem Jacobus Eijk, Archbishop of Utrecht, has publically stated that "the bishops and, above all, the Successor of Peter fail to maintain and transmit faithfully and in unity the deposit of faith contained in Sacred Tradition and Sacred Scripture."[2] This drama has its roots in the Second Vatican Council and the Post-Council, and those primarily responsible were the popes who have governed the Church over the last sixty years. Their canonization proclaims heroic virtues in the governing of the Church. The Council and Post-Council have denied doctrine for the sake of "the pastoral," and for the sake of this "pastoralism" they have refused to define truth and condemn error. The only truth which is proclaimed solemnly today is the impeccability of the conciliar popes—and them alone. The intent seems to be that of suggesting as infallible their political and pastoral choices rather than the canonizing of men.

But what credit must we give to these canonizations? Even if most theologians maintain that canonizations are infallible acts of the Church, we are not dealing with a dogma of faith. The last great exponent of the "Roman Theological School," Monsignor Brunero Gherardini (1925–2017), voiced all his doubts about the infallibility of canonizations in the publication *Divinitas*.[3] For the Roman theologian the decree of canonization is not infallible as the conditions of infallibility are lacking, starting with the fact that the canonization does not have, as direct or explicit object, a truth of faith or morals contained in Revelation, but only a fact indirectly linked to dogma, without strictly being a "dogmatic fact." Indeed, neither the codes of canon law of 1917 and 1983, nor the old or new catechisms of the Catholic Church,[4] make clear the doctrine of the Church on canonizations.

Another accomplished contemporary theologian, Father Jean-Michel Gleize, of the Fraternity of St. Pius X, admits the infallibility of canonizations in general, but not of those after the Second Vatican Council, for the following reasons: the reforms after the Council entailed

---

2 See Cardinal Willem Jacobus Eijk, "Pope Francis Needed to Give Clarity on Intercommunion," at *National Catholic Register*, May 7, 2018.
3 See chapter 7.—*Ed.*
4 That is, the *Catechism of the Council of Trent* promulgated by Pius V and the *Catechism of the Catholic Church* promulgated by John Paul II.—*Ed.*

certain insufficiencies in the procedure and introduced a new collegial intention, two consequences which are incompatible with the certainty of the beatifications and the infallibility of the canonizations. Moreover, the judgment that is expressed in the process allows for an ambiguous conception at least, and thus allows for doubt about the sanctity and heroic virtue. Infallibility is based on a rigorous complex of investigations and verifications. There is no doubt that after the reformed procedure established by John Paul II in 1983, this process in the verification of the truth has become more fragile and there has been a change in the concept of sanctity itself.

Other important contributions have recently been published along the same lines. Peter Kwasniewski notes at *OnePeterFive* that the worst change in the canonical process is in the number of miracles required:

> In the old system, *two* miracles were required for *both* beatification *and* canonization — that is, a total of four investigated and certified miracles. The point of this requirement is to give the Church sufficient moral certainty of God's "approval" of the proposed blessed or saint by the evidence of His exercise of power at the intercession of this individual. Moreover, the miracles traditionally had to be *outstanding* in their clarity — that is, admitting of no possible natural or scientific explanation. The new system cuts the number of miracles in half, which, one might say, also cuts the moral certainty in half — and, as many have observed, the miracles put forward often seem to be lightweight, leaving one scratching one's head: was that *really* a miracle, or was it just an extremely improbable event? [5]

Christopher Ferrara, for his part, in an accurate article in *The Remnant*, after stressing the decisive role that the testimony of miracles plays in the canonizations, noted that none of the miracles attributed to Paul VI and Monsignor Romero satisfy the traditional criteria for the verification of the divine in a miracle: "Those criteria are (1) a *cure* that is (2) instantaneous, (3) complete, (4) lasting, and (5) scientifically inexplicable, meaning not the result of treatment or natural processes of healing but rather an event originating outside the natural order." [6]

---

5   See chapter 14; for this citation, pp. 228–29. — *Ed.*
6   See chapter 11; for this citation, p. 199. — *Ed.*

John Lamont, who dedicated a wide and convincing study to the theme of the authority of canonizations on *Rorate Caeli*, concludes his investigations with these words:

> We need not hold that the canonizations of John XXIII and John Paul II were infallible, because the conditions needed for such infallibility were not present. Their canonizations are not connected to any doctrine of the faith, they were not the result of a devotion that is central to the life of the Church, and they were not the product of careful and rigorous examination. But we need not exclude all canonizations whatsoever from the charism of infallibility; we can still argue that those canonizations that followed the rigorous procedure of former centuries benefited from this charism.[7]

Thus, canonization not being a dogma of faith, there is no positive obligation for Catholics to lend assent to it. The exercise of reason demonstrates plainly that the Conciliar papacies have been of no advantage to the Church. Faith transcends reason and elevates it, but does not contradict it, since God, Truth in essence and the source of all truth, is not self-contradictory. Hence we may in good conscience maintain our reservations about these canonizations.

The most devastating act of Paul VI's pontificate was the destruction of the Old Roman Rite. Historians know that the *Novus Ordo Missae* was not Monsignor Bugnini's *Ordo*, but the one prepared, wanted, and carried into effect by Pope Montini, causing, as Kwasniewski writes, an explosive internal rupture: "This was the equivalent of dropping an atomic bomb on the People of God, which either wiped out their faith or caused cancers by its radiation."

The most commendable act of Pius XII's pontificate was the beatification (1951) and subsequently the canonization (1954) of Pope Pius X, after a long and rigorous canonical process and four inconfutable miracles. It is thanks to Pius XII that the name of Pius X shines in the firmament of the Church and represents a sure guide in the midst of the confusion of our times.

---

7 See above, pp. 161–62. — *Ed.*

13

On the Proposed Canonizations of Popes John XXIII and John Paul II†

INTERVIEW WITH ROBERTO DE MATTEI

PROFESSOR DE MATTEI, THE IMMINENT CANON-
izations of John XXIII and of John Paul II raise, for various reasons,
doubts and confusion. As a Catholic and as a historian, what judgment
do you express?

I can express a personal opinion, without pretending to solve this
complex problem. First of all, I am perplexed, generally speaking, by
the ease with which, in the past few years, canonization processes
begin and conclude. The First Vatican Council defined the primacy of
jurisdiction of the pope and the infallibility of his Magisterium under
certain conditions, but certainly not the personal impeccability of the
Sovereign Pontiffs. In the history of the Church, there have been good
and evil popes, and those solemnly elevated to the altars [as saints] were
few in number. Today, one has the impression that, in place of the
principle of the popes' infallibility, there is a desire to substitute that
of their impeccability. All popes, or rather, all the most recent popes,
starting from the Second Vatican Council, are presented as saints. It is
not by chance that the canonizations of John XXIII and John Paul II
have left in the shadows the canonization process for Pius IX and the
beatification process for Pius XII, while the cause of Paul VI moves
forward. It almost seems that a halo of sanctity must envelop the conciliar and postconciliar eras, to "infallibilize" an historic age which saw
the primacy of pastoral praxis assert itself over doctrine in the Church.

Do you hold, instead, that the last popes were not saints?

Allow me to explain myself using the example of one pope whom
I know better, as a historian: John XXIII. Having studied the Second

---

† First published by *Catholic Family News*, April 14, 2014, shortly before the
canonization ceremony on April 27.

Vatican Council, I examined in depth his biography and consulted the acts of his beatification process. When the Church canonizes one of the faithful, it is not that she wants to assure us [merely] that the deceased is in the glory of Heaven; rather, She proposes them as a model of heroic virtue. Depending on the case, the saint will be a *perfect* religious, pastor, father of a family, and so on. In the case of a pope, to be considered a saint he must have exercised heroic virtue in performing his mission *as Pontiff*, as, for example, was seen in the cases of St. Pius V or St. Pius X. Well, as far as John XXIII is concerned, I am morally certain, after careful consideration, that his pontificate was objectively harmful to the Church, and so it is impossible to speak of sanctity for him. Dominican Father Innocenzo Colosio, one who understood sanctity and is considered one of the greatest historians of spirituality in modern times, affirmed this prior to me, in a famous article in the *Rivista di Ascetica e Mistica* (*Ascetical and Mystical Review*).

If, as you think, John XXIII was not a pontiff-saint, and if, as it seems, canonizations are an infallible papal act, we find ourselves facing a great contradiction. Is there not a risk of falling into sedevacantism?

The sedevacantists apply an excessive meaning to papal infallibility. Their reasoning is simplistic: if the pope is infallible and does something evil, it means that the seat is vacant. The reality is much more complex and the premise that every action, or almost every action, of the pope is infallible, is mistaken. In reality, if the upcoming canonizations cause problems, sedevacantism causes infinitely greater problems of conscience.

And yet, the majority of theologians, especially the surest, those of the so-called "Roman School," support the infallibility of canonizations.

The infallibility of canonizations is not a dogma of the Faith; it is the opinion of a majority of theologians, above all after Benedict XIV, who expressed it moreover as a private doctor and not as Sovereign Pontiff. As far as the "Roman School" is concerned, the most eminent representative of this theological school in our times is Msgr. Brunero Gherardini. And Msgr. Gherardini expressed, in the review

Divinitas directed by him, all of his doubts on the infallibility of canonizations.[1] I know in Rome distinguished theologians and canonists — disciples of another illustrious representative of the Roman School, Msgr. Antonio Piolanti — who harbor the same doubts as Msgr. Gherardini. They hold that canonizations do not fulfill the conditions laid down by Vatican I to guarantee a papal act's infallibility. The judgment of canonization is not infallible in itself, because it lacks the conditions for infallibility, starting from the fact the canonization does not have as its direct or explicit aim a truth of faith or morals contained in Revelation, but only a fact indirectly connected with dogma, without being a "dogmatic fact" properly speaking. The field of faith and morals is broad, because it contains all of Christian doctrine, speculative and practical, human belief and action, but a distinction is necessary. A dogmatic definition can never involve the definition of a new doctrine in the field of faith and morals. The pope can only make explicit that which is implicit in faith and morals, and is handed down by the Tradition of the Church. That which the popes define must be contained in the Scriptures and in Tradition, and it is this which assures the infallibility of the act. That is certainly not the case for canonizations. It is not an accident that the doctrine of canonizations is not contained in the codes of canon law of 1917 and of 1983, nor the catechisms of the Catholic Church, old and new. Referring to this subject, besides the aforementioned study of Msgr. Gherardini, is an excellent article by José Antonio Ureta appearing in the March 2014 edition of the magazine *Catolicismo*.[2]

Do you hold that canonizations lost their infallible character following the changes to the canonization procedure as promulgated by John Paul II in 1983?

This position is supported in the *Courrier de Rome* by an excellent theologian, Fr. Jean-Michel Gleize.[3] One of the arguments on which Fr. Löw, in the article on canonizations in the *Enciclopedia cattolica*,

---

1 See chapter 7. — *Ed.*
2 See chapter 2. — *Ed.*
3 See "Canonization doubts for John XXIII & John Paul II," October 18, 2013, https://sspx.org/en/news-events/news/canonization-doubts-john-xxiii -john-paul-ii-2637.

bases his thesis on infallibility is the existence of a massive complex of investigations and findings, followed by two miracles which precede the canonization. There is no doubt that after the reform of the procedure willed by John Paul II in 1983, this process of ascertaining the truth has become much weaker and there has been a change of the very concept of sanctity. The argument, however, does not seem to me decisive because the canonization process has deeply changed throughout history. The proclamation of the sanctity of Ulrich of Augsburg by Pope John XV in 993 — considered the first canonization by a pope — was done without any investigation on the part of the Holy See. The process of thorough investigation dates back mainly to Benedict XIV: he was responsible, for example, for the distinction between formal canonization, according to all the canonical rules, and equivalent canonization, when a Servant of God is declared a saint by virtue of popular veneration. St. Hildegard of Bingen was hailed as a saint after her death, and Pope Gregory IX, starting in 1233, began the investigation for the canonization. However, there was never a formal canonization. Nor was St. Catherine of Sweden, daughter of St. Bridget, ever canonized. Her process was held between 1446 and 1489 but never concluded. She has been venerated as a saint without ever being canonized.

What do you think of the thesis of St. Thomas, also echoed in the article on canonization in the Dictionnaire de théologie catholique, *according to which the pope, if he were not infallible in a solemn declaration like a canonization, would deceive himself and the Church?*

We must first dispel a semantic misconception: a non-infallible act is not a wrong act that necessarily deceives, but only an act subject to the possibility of error. In fact, this error may be most rare, or may never have happened. St. Thomas, balanced, as always, in his judgment, is not infallible to the end. He is rightly concerned to defend the infallibility of the Church and he does so with a theologically reasonable argument. His argument can be accepted in a broad sense, but admitting the possibility of exceptions. I agree with him that the Church as a whole cannot err. This does not mean that every act of the Church or act on behalf of the Church, such as the act of canonization, is in itself necessarily infallible. The assent to be given to acts of canonizations is that of ecclesiastical faith, not divine. This means that a member of the faithful believes because he accepts the principle that the Church does not normally err. The exception does not cancel out the rule. An influential German theologian, Bernhard Bartmann, in his *Manual of Dogmatic Theology* (1962), compares the veneration (*cultus*) of a false saint to homage paid to a false ambassador of a king. The error does not detract from the principle that the king has true ambassadors and, correspondingly, that the Church canonizes true saints.

So then, in what sense can we speak of the Church's infallibility in canonizations?

I am convinced that it would be a serious mistake to reduce the infallibility of the Church to the Extraordinary Magisterium of the Roman Pontiff. The Church is not infallible only when She teaches in an extraordinary way, but also in her Ordinary Magisterium. But just as there are conditions for the infallibility of the Extraordinary Magisterium, there also exist conditions for the infallibility of the Ordinary Magisterium. And the first of these is its universality, which is proved when a truth of faith or morals is taught in a consistent manner over time. The Magisterium can infallibly teach a doctrine with an act of definition by the pope, or with a non-definitive act of the Ordinary Magisterium, provided that this doctrine is constantly held and passed down (transmitted) by tradition and by the ordinary and universal Magisterium. The instruction *Ad Tuendam Fidem* of the Congregation for the Doctrine of the Faith of May 18, 1998 (no. 2) confirms that. By analogy, one could argue that the Church cannot err when she confirms truth, over time, related to faith, dogmatic facts, liturgical usages. Canonizations may also fall into this group of connected truths. You can be sure that St. Hildegard of Bingen is in the glory of the saints, and can be proposed as a model, not because she was solemnly canonized by a pope, seeing as in her case there has never been a formal canonization, but because the Church recognized her *cultus*, without interruption, since her death. *A fortiori* for those saints who have never been formally canonized, like St.

Martin of Tours or St. Patrick, the infallible certainty of their glory in a diachronic sense (developed over time) stems from the universal *cultus* that the Church has bestowed on them and not by a judgment of canonization in itself. The Church does not deceive, in its universal Magisterium, but one can admit a mistake on the part of ecclesiastical authorities constricted in time and space.

Would you like to summarize your opinion?

The canonization of Pope John XXIII is a solemn act of the Sovereign Pontiff, which derives from the supreme authority of the Church and should be regarded with respect; but it is not a judgment infallible in itself. The exercise of reason, supported by a careful examination of the facts, shows quite clearly that the pontificate of John XXIII was not of benefit to the Church. If I had to admit that Pope Roncalli exercised virtue in a heroic way while carrying out his role of Pontiff, I would undermine at the core the rational presuppositions of my faith. When in doubt, I adhere to the dogma of faith established by the First Vatican Council, according to which there can be no contradiction between faith and reason. Faith transcends reason and elevates it but does not contradict it, because God, Truth itself, is not contradictory. I feel in conscience able to maintain all my reservations about this act of canonization.

14

Animadversions on the
Canonization of Paul VI†

PETER A. KWASNIEWSKI

MANY WHO HAVE STUDIED THE LIFE AND PON-
tificate of Pope Paul VI are convinced that he was far from exemplary
in his conduct as pastor; that he not only did *not* possess heroic virtue, but *lacked* certain key virtues; that his promulgation of a titanic
liturgical reform was incompatible with his papal office of handing
on that which he had received; that he offers us a portrait of failed
governance and tradition betrayed. In short, for us, it is impossible
to accept that a pope such as this could ever be canonized. Not sur-
prisingly, then, we are vexed about Pope Francis's "canonization" of
Giovanni Battista Montini on Sunday, October 14, 2018 and have
grave doubts in conscience about its legitimacy or credibility.

But are we allowed to have such doubts? Surely (people will say),
canonization is an infallible exercise of the papal magisterium and
therefore binding on all — indeed, the very language used in the ceremony indicates that! — therefore we must accept that Paul VI is a
saint in heaven, honor him and imitate him, and embrace all that he
did and taught as pope.

Not so fast. In reality, the situation is more complicated. In this
tempestuous time, it is just as well that we should come to know the
complexity of it, rather than seeking refuge in naïve simplifications.
In this essay, I will cover seven topics: the status of canonizations,
the purpose of canonizations, the process of canonization, what is
objectionable in Paul VI, what is admirable in Paul VI, the limits of
canonization's meaning, and practical consequences.

---

† First published at *OnePeterFive* under the title "Why We Need Not (and
Should Not) Call Paul VI 'Saint,'" October 12, 2018; revised and expanded for
inclusion herein.

THE STATUS OF CANONIZATIONS

While historically the majority of theologians have defended that canonizations must be infallible — especially neoscholastic theologians who tend to be extreme ultramontanists[1] — the Church herself has, in fact, never taught this as binding doctrine.[2] The exact status of canonizations remains a legitimate subject of theological debate, and it is all the more debatable given the changing expectations, procedures, and motivations for the act of canonization itself (points to which I shall return).

The infallibility of canonizations is *not* taught by the Church, nor is it necessarily implied by any *de fide* doctrine of the Faith. Catholics are therefore not required to believe it as a matter of faith and may even, for serious reasons, doubt or question the truthfulness of a certain canonization. This conclusion is defended by John Lamont in two incisive articles.[3]

In attempted refutation, many have quoted the lines from the CDF's "Doctrinal Commentary on the Concluding Formula of the *Professio Fidei*," signed by then-Cardinal Ratzinger and then-Archbishop Bertone on June 29, 1998, which says the following:

> With regard to those truths connected to revelation by historical necessity and which are to be held definitively, but are not able to be declared as divinely revealed, the following examples can be given: the legitimacy of the election of the Supreme Pontiff or of the celebration of an ecumenical council, the canonizations of saints (dogmatic facts), the declaration of Pope Leo XIII in the Apostolic Letter *Apostolicae Curae* on the invalidity of Anglican ordinations.

---

1 For example, arguing that all papal disciplinary acts that bear on the entire Church must be inerrant and certainly favoring the common good — a position that one might have defended earlier in history, but which, at the present moment, is nothing less than grossly risible.

2 It is therefore harmful when popularizers write things like this: "Beatification requires one attested miracle and allows the beatified person to be venerated by his local church. Canonization requires two attested miracles and allows veneration of the saint by the universal Church. Canonization is an infallible statement by the Church that the saint is in heaven" (https://www.catholic.com/qa/what-is-the-difference-between-saints-and-blesseds). This is to state too much, unless some qualifications are added.

3 See chapters 8 and 9.

However, documents of the CDF have magisterial weight only insofar as they are acts of the Supreme Pontiff, which they become when he officially authorizes their publication. This "Doctrinal Commentary," unlike many other documents from the CDF (such as a "Notification" published five days earlier), *lacks* the concluding formula: "The Supreme Pontiff approved this and ordered it to be published." And surely this lack was not accidental, as if they forgot to show it to John Paul II, or he was too busy to sign it; rather, it shows that this document is a commentary furnished by Cardinal Ratzinger and Archbishop Bertone, expressive of their opinions (which are, of course, worthy of consideration both intrinsically and circumstantially), but not something requiring *obsequium religiosum*, religious assent of mind and will.[4] Hence, even after this Doctrinal Commentary, the infallibility of canonizations remains a theologically debatable issue. And it must be said that we are being given more reasons today than ever before to question certain things that may once have been taken for granted.

THE PURPOSE OF CANONIZATIONS

Traditionally, canonization is not merely a recognition that a certain individual is in heaven; it is the recognition that this member of the Church lived a life of such heroic virtue (above all, the theological virtues of faith, hope, and charity), had fulfilled in so exemplary a fashion the duties of his state in life (and this would include, for a cleric, the duties of his office), and had so practiced asceticism as befits a soldier of Christ, that public veneration (including liturgical) should be offered to him by the *universal Church*, and his example should be followed as a model to imitate (cf. 1 Cor 11:1). This indeed is how Catholics, lofty and lowly, have always understood its significance in and for the life of the Church:

> A canonization . . . is a formal papal decree that the candidate
> *was holy* and is now in heaven with God; the decree allows
> *public remembrance* of the saint at liturgies *throughout the
> Church*. It also means that churches can be *dedicated* to the
> person without special Vatican permission. . . . "In addition

---

4   For an illuminating discussion of this concept, see Jeremy Holmes, "On non-infallible teachings of the Magisterium and the meaning of 'obsequium religiosum,'" *Catholic World Report*, December 30, 2017.

to reassuring us that the servant of God lives in heaven in communion with God, miracles are the divine confirmation of the judgment expressed by church authorities about *the virtuous life*" lived by the candidate, Pope Benedict said in a speech to members of the Congregation for Saints' Causes in 2006.[5]

Or again, in the words of a different author:

A canonization is supposed to be not only a declaration that so-and-so is enrolled among the saints, but that the manner of their life (and how they carry out the obligations relevant to their state in life) is worthy of imitation. This has never meant that every thing a saint does has to be approved of; canonization was never meant to be the canonization of a saint's every word and deed. But, to borrow the language of the *Catechism*, it nevertheless was meant to identify that saint's life as a "sure norm" for Christian living.[6]

The *Catechism of the Catholic Church* expresses the same point of view:

By canonizing some of the faithful, i.e., by solemnly proclaiming that they practiced heroic virtue and lived in fidelity to God's grace, the Church recognizes the power of the Spirit of holiness within her and sustains the hope of believers by proposing the saints to them as models and intercessors. (n. 828)

We can see all of these features shining in the "classic" saints, to whom there is much popular devotion.

In recent pontificates, we have seen a shift take place in why individuals—at least, certain individuals—are canonized. Donald Prudlo observes:

As an historian of sainthood, my greatest hesitation with the current process stems from the canonizations done by John Paul II himself. While his laudable intention was to provide models of holiness drawn from all cultures and states in life,

---

5 Cindy Wooden, "Holy confusion? Beatification, canonization are different," *Catholic News Service*, April 15, 2011, emphases added. This article had appeared at http://www.catholicnews.com/services/englishnews/2011/holy-confusion-beatification-canonization-are-different.cfm, but was inexplicably removed by CNS. A cache can be located with the Internet Archive Wayback Machine.
6 Boniface, "Thoughts on the Canonization of Paul VI," *Unam Sanctam Catholicam*, October 26, 2018.

> he tended to divorce canonization from its original and fun-
> damental purpose. This was to have an official, public, and
> formal recognition of an existing cult of the Christian faith-
> ful, one that had been confirmed by the divine testimony of
> miracles. Cult precedes canonization; it was not meant to be
> the other way around. We are in danger then of using canon-
> ization as a tool to promote interests and movements, rather
> than being a recognition and approval of an extant *cultus*.[7]

Prudlo is making the obvious point that beatification and canonization
are supposed to be responses of the Church to a strong popular devotion shown to a particular individual, whose earthly sanctity and heavenly glory God has validated, so to speak, by working several demonstrable miracles. It is not supposed to be the Vatican rubber-stamping
particular individuals the Vatican happens to want to promote. There
is no serious popular *cultus* of Paul VI, nor has there ever been, and
it is doubtful that papal fiat can create a *cultus ex nihilo*.[8]

In reality, we see that Pope Francis has carried to its extreme the
"politicization" of the process, whereby the individual to be beatified
or canonized is instrumentalized for an agenda. As Fr. John Hunwicke
points out:

> There has been, in some quarters, an uneasy suspicion for
> some time that canonizations have turned into a way of
> setting a seal upon the "policies" of some popes. If these
> "policies" are themselves a matter of divisive discussion and
> debate, then the promotion of the idea that canonizations
> are infallible becomes itself an additional element in the con-
> flict. Canonization, you will remind me, does not, theolog-
> ically, imply approval of everything a saint has done or said.
> Not formally, indeed. But the suspicion among some is that,

---

7 Donald S. Prudlo, "Are Canonizations Based on Papal Infallibility?," *Crisis*,
April 25, 2014.
8 The number one requirement for beatification and, *a fortiori*, canonization, is
evidence of popular veneration. The next most important characteristic is a life of
evident heroic virtue as discerned by a rigorous process of investigation, for in the
absence of such virtue, the man or woman being raised to the honors of the altar
would serve as a snare and a scandal to the faithful, or at least those who take him
as a model to be emulated. Paul VI in particular has lacked substantive popular
veneration and, moreover, presents ambiguous and conflictive traits in his public
life and the exercise of his office that make him singularly ill-suited for emulation.

de facto and humanly, such can seem to be its aim. This is confirmed by a prevailing assumption on all sides that the canonizations of the "conciliar popes" do bear some sort of meaning or message.[9]

Similarly, Fr. "Pio Pace" writes:

We must dare say it: by canonizing all the Vatican II popes, it is Vatican II that is canonized. But, likewise, canonization itself is devalued when it becomes a sort of medal thrown on top of a casket. Maybe a council that was "pastoral" and not dogmatic is deserving of canonizations that are "pastoral" and not dogmatic.[10]

Most keenly, Prof. Roberto de Mattei observes:

For the papolater, the pope is not the vicar of Christ on earth, who has the duty of handing on the doctrine he has received, but a successor of Christ who perfects the doctrine of his predecessors, adapting it to changing times. The doctrine of the Gospel is in perpetual evolution, because it coincides with the Magisterium of the reigning pontiff. The "living Magisterium" replaces the perennial Magisterium; it is expressed by pastoral teaching that changes daily, and has its *regula fidei* (rule of faith) in the subject of the authority and not in the object of the transmitted truth.

A consequence of papolatry is the pretext of canonizing all and each of the popes of the past, so that retroactively, each word of theirs, every act of governing, is "infallibilized." However, this concerns only the popes following Vatican II and not those who preceded that Council.

At this point arises a question. The golden era of the history of the Church is the Middle Ages, and yet the only medieval popes canonized by the Church are Leo IX, Gregory VII, and Celestine V. In the twelfth and thirteenth centuries, there were great popes, but none of these were canonized. For seven hundred years, between the fourteenth and twentieth centuries, only Pope Pius V and Pope Pius X

---

9   See above, pp. 180–81.

10   "Paul VI: a 'Pastoral' Canonization," *Rorate Caeli*, February 27, 2018. See also the insightful article by Lee Fratantuono, "Calendar Clues: Pope Francis and the *Lex Orandi* of Papal Maximalism," *OnePeterFive*, April 26, 2021.

were canonized. Were all the others unworthy popes, sinners? Certainly not. But heroism in the governing of the Church is *an exception, not the rule*, and if all the popes were saints, then nobody is a saint. Sanctity is such an exception that it loses meaning when it becomes the rule.[11]

This last paragraph is particularly worth emphasizing: while the Church had canonized three popes in a period comprising over 600 years of papal reign,[12] in recent years, she has "canonized" three popes from a period of scarcely over 50 years — a half-century that just happens to coincide with the preparation, execution, and aftermath of the Second Vatican Council. Must be the "new Pentecost" effect! If this is not enough to make a cynic of someone, I'm not sure what would be.[13]

THE PROCESS OF CANONIZATION

In order to expedite the making of saints, John Paul II introduced many significant changes in the canonization process that had been stably in place since the work of Prospero Lambertini, who later became Pope Benedict XIV (1740–1758). This process was based, in turn, on norms going back to Pope Urban VIII (1623–1644), and many centuries earlier in its fundamental principles. It was none other than Paul VI who, in this area as in so many others, initiated a simplification of the procedures in 1969, and John Paul II who completed a massive overhaul in 1983.

Studying a comparison of the old process and the new process is illuminating.[14] After noting the obvious fact that the old process is

---

11   De Mattei, *Love for the Papacy and Filial Resistance to the Pope in the History of the Church* (Brooklyn, NY: Angelico Press, 2019), 140–41. De Mattei is evidently restricting the term "Middle Ages" to the period after the year 1000. Moreover, Victor III and Urban II, the two popes after Gregory, are Blesseds.
12   The three popes are St. Celestine V (d. 1294), St. Pius V (d. 1572), and St. Pius X (d. 1914). This is surely not for lack of many heroic individuals in that 600-year period — but, as we have said, if there was no popular *cultus* yielding indisputable miracles, the Church was not going to go rifling through the archives to find whatever candidates for honors she could and push their causes.
13   See my article "The One and Only Pentecost: Against the Neo-Joachimite Heresy," *New Liturgical Movement*, May 21, 2018.
14   See "Canonization: Old vs. New Comparison" at www.unamsanctamcatholicam.com/theology/81-theology/555-canonization-old-vs-new.html.

considerably more involved and thorough, *Unam Sanctam Catholi-cam* proffers this evaluation:

> The difference between the old and new procedures is not in their length, but in their *character*. In the pre-1969 proce-dure, you will note the care with which the integrity of the process itself is safeguarded. The Sacred Congregation must attest to the validity of the methodology used by the diocesan tribunals. The *Promotor Fidei* must sign off on the canonical form of every act of the Postulator and the Congregation. The validity of the inquiries into the candidate's miracles [is] scrutinized. *There is a very strict attention to form and methodology in the pre-1969 procedure which is simply lack-ing in the post-1983 system. . . .* Essentially, while the modern canonization procedure maintains the nuts-n'-bolts of the pre-1969 system, the aspect of "checks and balances" that characterized the pre-1969 procedure is weakened. The rigid oversight is missing in the [modern] system.[15]

The role of the *promotor fidei*, the so-called "devil's advocate," was obliterated. In the old system, this person's crucial role was:

> . . . to prevent any rash decisions concerning miracles or vir-tues of the candidates for the honors of the altar. All docu-ments of beatification and canonization processes must be submitted to his examination, and the difficulties and doubts he raises over the virtues and miracles are laid before the congregation and must be satisfactorily answered before any further steps can be taken in the processes. It is his duty to suggest natural explanations for alleged miracles, and even to bring forward human and selfish motives for deeds that have been accounted heroic virtues. . . . His duty requires him to prepare in writing all possible arguments, even at times seemingly slight, against the raising of any one to the honors of the altar. The interest and honor of the Church are concerned in preventing any one from receiving those honors whose death is not juridically proved to have been "precious in the sight of God."[16]

---

15 Ibid. This way of putting it is rather understated; see chapter 3 for a closer look.
16 William Fanning, *"Promotor Fidei," The Catholic Encyclopedia*, vol. 12 (New York: Robert Appleton Company, 1911); see https://www.newadvent.

This paragraph bears repeated reading. "Rash decisions concerning miracles or virtues must be prevented . . . *all* documents must be submitted . . . apparent virtues and alleged miracles must be argued against . . . the Church's interest and honor must be defended at all costs. . . ." The far-reaching simplification of the process, together with the chaos that often seems to reign in the Vatican in its free-wheeling postconciliar years, has meant that nothing comparable to the above stringent "devil's advocate" role has been seen since 1983.

Among other things, it was taken for granted that *all* of the documentary archives associated with a proposed blessed or saint should be reviewed carefully for doctrinal, moral, and psychological issues that might be red flags. In this connection, I must share some disturbing information. A person who works at the Vatican in the Congregation for the Causes of Saints told me personally that orders were received from "on high" that the canonization process for Paul VI should be sped along as quickly as possible — and that, as a result, the Congregation did not examine all of the documents by or about Paul VI housed in the Vatican archives. This glaring lacuna is all the more grave when we recall that Paul VI was accused of being an active homosexual, a charge that was taken seriously enough to be officially denied:

> Roger Peyrefitte, who had already written in two of his books that Paul VI had a longtime homosexual relationship, repeated his charges in a magazine interview with a French gay magazine that, when reprinted in Italian, brought the rumors to a wider public and caused an uproar. He said that the pope was a hypocrite who had a longtime sexual relationship with a movie actor. Widespread rumors identified the actor as Paolo Carlini, who had a small part in the Audrey Hepburn film *Roman Holiday* (1953). In a brief address to a crowd of approximately 20,000 in St. Peter's Square on 18 April [1976], Paul VI called the charges "horrible and slanderous insinuations" and appealed for prayers on his behalf. Special prayers for the pope were said in all Italian Catholic churches in "a day of consolation." The charges have resurfaced periodically. In 1994, Franco Bellegrandi, a

---

org/cathen/12454a.htm. To learn more about the "devil's advocate," see chapter 3.

former Vatican honor chamberlain and correspondent for
the Vatican newspaper *L'Osservatore Romano*, alleged that
Paul VI had been blackmailed and had promoted other gay
men to positions of power within the Vatican. In 2006, the
newspaper *L'Espresso* confirmed the blackmail story based
on the private papers of police commander General Giorgio
Manes. It reported that Italian Prime Minister Aldo Moro
had been asked to help.[17]

As incredible as such a story may seem, we have far less reason today to
write it off considering what we now know about decades of clerical
sexual abuse and the powerful influence of the lavender mafia in the
hierarchy of the Church. The well-documented evidence that Pope
Francis has promoted and protected many such criminals during his
pontificate has shattered naïve piety in this respect.[18]

The alleged inadequacy of the documentary investigation into Montini is grave for another reason: Paul VI's undeniable involvement in
secret negotiations with Communists and his endorsement of *Ostpolitik*, under which many injustices were committed.[19] One would think
a desire for transparent truth about every aspect of Montini would
have led to an exhaustive examination of the relevant documents.
However, this seems to have been purposefully bypassed. It goes
without saying that such a lack of due diligence, all by itself, would
be sufficient to cast into doubt the legitimacy of the canonization.

An equally bad change to the process is the reduction of the
number of miracles required. In the old system, *two* miracles were
required for *both* beatification *and* canonization — that is, a total of
four investigated and certified miracles. The point of this requirement
is to give the Church sufficient moral certainty of God's "approval"
of the proposed blessed or saint by the evidence of His exercise of
power at the intercession of the one called upon for aid in desperate

---

17 Although not a scholarly source, this summary from Wikipedia's entry on
Paul VI accurately presents the allegations and the principal names involved.
Historian Yves Chiron, in his comprehensive biography of Paul VI, investigates
these claims and judges them to be false.

18 See Lamont and Pierantoni, *Defending the Faith*, 138–45 et passim.

19 See George Weigel, "The *Ostpolitik* Failed. Get Over It," *First Things*, July
20, 2016. Again, we see that Bergoglio, by his negotiations and compromises
with Communist China, is simply following in Montini's footsteps.

circumstances. Moreover, the miracles traditionally had to be *out-standing* in their clarity—that is, admitting of no possible natural or scientific explanation.

The new system cuts the number of miracles in half, which, one might say, also cuts the moral certainty in half—and, as many have observed, the miracles put forward often seem to be lightweight, leaving one scratching one's head: was that *really* a miracle, or was it just an extremely improbable event? The two miracles for Paul VI are, to be frank, underwhelming.[20] I mean, it's lovely that two babies were "healed" or "protected," but that we are dealing with a naturally inexplicable supernatural intervention by the force of Paul VI's prayers is by no means obvious. Four robust miracles, like the restoration of sight to the blind or the raising of the dead (and without any medical intervention in sight), would carry conviction.

With the greatly increasing number of canonizations; the removal of half of the number of miracles required (which are sometimes waived[21]); the lack of a robust *advocatus diaboli* role; and, at times, the rushed manner in which documentation is examined or even passed over (as, apparently, has been the case with Paul VI), it seems to me not only that it has become impossible to claim that today's canonizations always require our consent, but also that there may be canonizations about which one would have an obligation to withhold assent.

WHAT IS OBJECTIONABLE IN PAUL VI?

Beyond the general consideration of the status of canonizations, the purpose that should animate them, and the procedures by which they are securely or insecurely conducted, we must also consider the particular merits of the case at hand. Why, specifically, do traditional Catholics object to the possibility of the canonization of Paul VI?

During his pontificate, Montini presented a conspicuous *lack* of heroic virtue in shouldering his solemn responsibilities as shepherd

---

20 See chapter 11.
21 Or redefined: see John Thavis, "John XXIII the missing miracle," June 2, 2014, at https://legatus.org/news/john-xxiii-the-missing-miracle. Pope Francis waived the requirement of a second miracle for the "canonization" of John XXIII. We can see in this a fine example of the crass abuse of pontifical power that Francis depends on for his ideological consolidation.

of the universal flock. Instead, he displayed a habitual incapacity for effective discipline, as he wavered between extreme indulgence and extreme sharpness (e.g., rarely punishing the most obnoxiously heretical theologians of his day but treating Archbishop Marcel Lefebvre as if he were worse than Martin Luther, or empowering Annibale Bugnini with continual papal access and support over the course of the postconciliar liturgical reform, then suddenly banishing him to Iran[22]). The contradictory signals he gave — encouraging modernism, then curtailing it; intervening in controversial matters and then withdrawing, back and forth, like Hamlet (a character to whom he compared himself in a private note from 1978) — only compounded the confusion and anarchy of the period. What was needed was a pilot with a steady hand in the midst of the storm, not a self-doubting semi-modernist suffering an existential crisis.

In his execution of the liturgical reform, Paul VI gave ample evidence of operating under rationalist Pistoian principles incompatible with Catholicism[23] and of gross negligence in reviewing materials.[24] His *Ostpolitik* dealings with Communists, including his disobedience to Pius XII, are well known. Although Paul VI maintained the traditional teaching on contraception, at the same time the manner in which he failed to respond to media manipulation of the Pontifical Commission on Birth Control, refused to discipline dissenters from *Humanae Vitae*, and allowed those who upheld the papal teaching to be marginalized, all conspired to undermine that encyclical's reception. The irrational harshness of his dealings with traditional Catholics was shameful, as when he turned down the petition of a group of

---

22 If Bugnini had not been a Freemason, this exile would be difficult to understand; if he *were* a Freemason, however, as seems far more likely, then his punishment should have been worse. See the interviews mentioned in note 33.

23 I am referring to the Synod of Pistoia (1786), whose Enlightenment-flavored efforts to "reform" Catholicism were soundly condemned by Pope Pius VI in his Bull *Auctorem Fidei* of 1794.

24 There seem to have been quite a number of things he signed off on without being familiar with their details. See my article "Who Was Captain of the Ship in the Liturgical Reform? The 50th Anniversary of an Embarrassing Letter," *New Liturgical Movement*, June 24, 2019; cf. Gregory DiPippo, "Paul VI's Dislike of the Liturgical Reform," *New Liturgical Movement*, April 19, 2018; Fr. John Zuhlsdorf, "A Pentecost Monday lesson: 'And Paul VI wept,'" *Fr. Z's Blog*, May 21, 2018.

over 6,000 Spanish priests[25] who wished to continue celebrating the immemorial Roman Rite of St. Pius V (while he later granted this permission to priests in England and Wales — once more showing the stuff out of which Hamlets are made). He abused his papal authority by discarding what should have been revered and by treating as forbidden what could never be abrogated.

The pope has a solemn obligation to uphold and defend the traditions and rites of the Church; he has no moral authority to modify them past recognition. No pope in the 2,000-year history of the Catholic Church altered traditions and rites as Paul VI did across the board, fueling the fires of iconoclasm and sacrilegious experimentation. This alone should make him forever suspicious in the eyes of any orthodox believer. Either this pope was the great liberator who delivered the Church from centuries, perhaps millennia, of bondage to harmful forms of worship — in which case the Holy Spirit had fallen asleep on the job and the Protestants were correct all along that the true Church of Christ had disappeared or gone "underground" — or he was the great destroyer who tore down what Divine Providence had lovingly built up and who sold the Church into a slavery to intellectual fashion more humiliating than the physical bondage suffered by the Israelites.

Paul VI did not helplessly watch the Church's "autodemolition" (his own term for the collapse after the Council); he did not merely preside over the single greatest exodus of Catholic laity, clergy, and religious since the Protestant Revolt. He *aided and abetted* this internal devastation by his own actions. By pushing ahead at breakneck speed a radical liturgical and institutional "reform" that left nothing untouched, he multiplied a hundredfold the destabilizing forces at work in the 1960s. Anyone who enjoyed the functionality of reason

---

25   Namely, the "Hermandad Sacerdotal Española de San Antonio Mª Claret y San Juan de Ávila," which was formed by the "Hermandad Sacerdotal Española," founded in 1969 by Spanish priests to defend Tradition in the face of the changes in the Church, and another similar group, based in Catalonia, called "Asociación de Sacerdotes y Religiosos de San Antonio Maria Claret." They sent a letter to the Vatican in 1969 petitioning the continued use of the old Roman missal — and Paul VI refused them flatly. Unfortunately, as Spanish and Italian traditionalism was characterized by absolute obedience to Rome, the Novus Ordo was thereafter accepted without cavil, and to this day tradition has difficulty making inroads into either of these cultural spheres.

would have been able to see that it was dangerous, not to mention impious, to change so much, so fast. But no: Paul VI was a willing votary of the ideology of modernization, a high priest of progress, who boldly went where none of his predecessors had ever gone before.

Ironically, it is none other than Pope Francis, the willful canonizer of Paul VI, who has demonstrated past all doubt the self-destructive trajectory of postconciliar Catholicism, when its own tendencies are acted on without restraint, rather as Theodore McCarrick acted on his own tendencies without restraint. The lust for novelty and the lust for victims are psychological twins.

Many Catholics are rightfully anxious about Pope Francis. But what he has done in the past five years is arguably small potatoes compared with what Paul VI had the audacity to do: substituting a new liturgy for the ancient Roman Mass and sacramental rites, causing the biggest internal rupture the Catholic Church has ever suffered. This was the equivalent of dropping an atomic bomb on the People of God, which either wiped out their faith or caused cancers by its radiation. It was the very negation of paternity, of the papacy's fatherly function of conserving and passing on the family heritage. Everything that has happened after Paul VI is no more than an echo of this violation of the sacred temple. Once the most holy thing is profaned, nothing else is safe, nothing else is stable.

At this point, someone may object: "So what if Paul VI wasn't very good at being pope? Surely he could still have been a holy man on the inside. He was living in a tempestuous period, when everyone was confused, and he was doing his best. We should admire his intentions and his great desires, even if we might criticize in retrospect certain decisions and actions. Sanctity isn't a blanket approval of everything a person says or does."

The problem with this objection is that it fails to recognize that how a Catholic lives out his primary vocation in life is part and parcel of his sanctity. How a bishop of the Church—and all the more, a pope—exercises his ecclesiastical office is not incidental, but *essential* to his sanctity (or lack thereof). Imagine it this way: could we canonize a man who, in spite of beating his wife and neglecting his children, was dutiful in attending daily Mass, praying the Rosary, and giving alms to the poor? It would be absurd, because we would rightly say: "A married man with children has to be holy *as* a husband and father, not *in spite of* being a husband and father." It is no less absurd to say: "Such-and-such a pope was negligent, irresponsible, indecisive, rash, and revolutionary in his papal decisions, but his heart was in the right place, and he was always striving for the glory of God and the salvation of men." A pope is a saint because he "poped" well: he showed heroic faith, hope, charity, prudence, justice, fortitude, temperance, etc. *in his very activity of governing the Church.* This is the precise doctrine of the canonist and one-time *Promotor Fidei* Prospero Lambertini (subsequently Pope Benedict XIV), whom everyone acknowledges to be the single greatest authority on the subject.[26]

If we are supposed to *venerate* Paul VI, then inconsistency, ambiguity, pusillanimity, injustice, reckless change, negligence, indecisiveness, false signaling, despondency, wishful thinking, irritability, scorn, and contempt for tradition, coupled with an abysmal record of episcopal appointments, are not merely virtues, but virtues one can exercise to such a heroic degree that they are actually sources of sanctifying grace, deserving of general admiration, veneration, and emulation. Sorry, I'm having none of it. Such things have always been, and will always be, vices. Montini was a terrible ruler of the Church, and if the virtuous fulfillment of one's responsibilities in one's state in life is constitutive of admirable and venerable sanctity, we may conclude that it is impossible to imagine a worse role model for any ruler than Montini.

Here I shall quote at length my colleague at New Liturgical Movement, Gregory DiPippo:

> This particular canonization is an absolute *unicum* in the history of the saints and of the canonization process. With John XXIII, and especially with John Paul II, the popular *cultus* is undeniable, and even in the debased modern process, this is still regarded as a most important indication of sanctity. In St. Peter's basilica, there are *always* people praying at the altars in which their relics are kept, basically from the moment the church opens to the moment it closes. John Paul II had to be moved out of the grottoes because there were always so many people praying at his tomb that they made it difficult

---

26 See the texts from Lambertini given in the Appendix.

for people to move through the grottoes. But nobody is even bothering to pretend that there is a hint of popular devotion to Paul VI. Nobody is saying "Look at all his *evidently* heroic exercises of the virtues of fortitude, prudence, justice, etc." Nobody is saying "Look at all of these marvelous things that came from his reign, and the ways the Church thrived because of his accomplishments!" Were they to say so, he himself would be the strongest witness against them — in his own words: "The Church finds herself in a period of anxiety, of self-criticism, one could say of self-destruction. It is like an internal upheaval, serious and complex — as if the Church were flagellating herself," he said. Again: "In many areas the Council has not so far given us peace but rather stirred up troubles and problems that in no way serve to strengthen the Kingdom of God within the Church or within souls." Most famously: "The smoke of Satan has entered by some crack into the temple of God; doubt, uncertainty, problems, restlessness, dissatisfaction and confrontation have come to the surface . . . doubt has entered our consciences."

In the second millennium, there were one hundred twenty-five popes, of whom a grand total of eight have been formally canonized as of today. (One of them, Celestine V, was pope for five months.) And yet for *this* particular canonization, no one has *anything* to say in its defense apart from "It's an infallible exercise of the Magisterium."

Paul VI was not just incompetent as an administrator; he was grossly imprudent.

Read the decree permitting Communion in the hand, in which he outlines the reasons why Communion in the hand is a terrible idea — and then proceeds to permit it. He also notes that it had arisen as an act of defiance against the authority of the Holy See — and still permits it. He also notes that the majority of the world's bishops when petitioned were solidly against any innovation in regard to how Communion would be distributed — and he still permits it, the great trumpeter of "collegiality." I guess this would be like Pope Francis shoving synodality into the Synod report and then, a couple of weeks later, telling the USCCB to hold off on voting standards for itself.

Read his decree permitting religious orders to do the Office in the vernacular, in which he says to them that if they do the Office in the vernacular, they will collapse. Of course, he watched them all move to the vernacular, and watched them all collapse.

Read the transcript of his colloquium with Archbishop Lefebvre in 1976, in which Lefebvre says "Why can't we just have churches that do the old rite, since everyone else is permitted to do everything else?," and Paul replies that we cannot permit the kind of divisions within the Christian community that such a permission would entail—he, the promulgator of a liturgy whose own creators bragged that it was a feature, not a bug, that the new liturgy would be essentially the creation of the individual celebrant and celebrating community, and lamented that they were not permitted to go far enough in that direction!

"Because Paul VI approved things we do not like (e.g., the liturgical reform), he cannot be a holy person." This is *not* the line of reasoning. The line of reasoning is that Paul VI routinely did things which gravely damaged the Church (like approve Communion in the hand), and by doing so, demonstrated a grave lack of the virtues of prudence and fortitude, precisely because they were things which he himself publically noted would be damaging to the Church even as he did them. For the rest, he issued a few documents which certainly might have been useful to the Church, had he not lain down like a dog and allowed every heretic to trample on them. This is not the behavior of a saint, and there is no other sainted prelate of any kind who behaved like this as a matter of routine. Things like this are not outliers in his papacy; they are the *story* of his papacy. And again, this is the reason why apparently no one can formulate any defense of his canonization other than "Suck it up, canonization's infallible!," nor can anyone point out any specific example of his heroic exercise of all of the virtues which the process itself solemnly assures us must have taken place.

Again, the difficulty is not just about this pope's enthusiastic promotion and promulgation of a massive liturgical reform of unprecedented rupture from tradition; it's about the continual stream of horrible things which Paul VI did, things which by any objective standard have done enormous damage to the Church, which anyone could see at the time would do damage to the Church, and which he himself on more than one occasion *said* would do damage to the Church, but then did anyway. I pointed out that the canonization process itself claims to be based on the recognition of the heroic exercise of the virtues, and thus presents the Saint to the Church as a universally valid model for the Christian life. The only "virtue" anyone has identified thus far in the person of Paul VI in his governance of the Church is "he wasn't morally depraved."

It becomes evident, then, that there really is nothing to be said on behalf of Paul VI's sanctity other than "canonization's infallible. Suck it up." This would make Paul VI the only formally canonized prelate in the history of the Church of whom there is nothing *else* to say. It is totally unreasonable to ask people to look at that and *not* have some suspicion that something has gone very badly wrong. Perhaps I am wrong. Perhaps it is totally normal for there to be a sainted model of the Christian virtues in whom no one cares to identify any given virtue and in which one can identify several vices. But it is not "temerarious" or "disobedient" to look at this particular canonization and fear that something, somewhere, has gone badly wrong. One way or the other, the credibility of the process itself is completely shot.

Canonization touches on a great deal more than the person being in heaven, as the Church's own decrees have stated, going back to the time of Innocent III. It proposes to identify, in the case of one who did not die as a martyr, a person whose life is such an outstanding model of all of the virtues that he is worthy to be both venerated and imitated by all of the Christian faithful, and above all, those who occupy high rank in the Church. A formal recognition by decree that such a degree of virtue has been identified in the proposed Saint is still a part of the process to this day. In the case of Paul VI, however, this is manifestly absurd. To canonize such a man as he was is scandalous, nor is there any other saint whose canonization, however dodgy, rests on nothing *other* than the papal fiat. No one is claiming that there was nothing to say on behalf of St. Bonaventure, Francis of Paola, Leopold III apart from "The pope has said it infallibly, so you must believe it." Either way, something precious and important has been broken, perhaps irreparably.[27]

---

27 In correspondence on social media.

Those who wish to read more about the flaws of Paul VI as pope should consult the following: "The Enigma of Pope Paul VI" by John Knox [Msgr. F. D. Cohalan][28]; "The Papacy of Paul VI" by Henry Sire[29]; "50 Years Ago: Dietrich von Hildebrand Confronts Pope Paul VI"[30]; "Liturgy, Abuse and *Humanae Vitae*: Some Connections?"[31]; "Archbishop Lefebvre, Pope Paul VI, and Catholic Tradition" by Neil McCaffrey[32]; and two interviews with Fr. Charles Murr, personal secretary to Cardinal Gagnon during the latter's investigation of the Vatican under Paul VI.[33]

At this point it may be opportune to note that those who espouse the infallibility of any and all canonizations but who also recognize that, in keeping with Church tradition, canonization is and must be far more than a declaration that someone is in heaven — for it unavoidably implies that the one canonized shall be honored by the faithful for a virtuous life well-lived in fulfillment of the duties of state and shall be imitated as a model of the same[34] — will necessarily

---

28   First published in *National Review* in 1969; republished at *OnePeterFive* on October 20, 2015.

29   An excerpt under this title from H. J. A. Sire's book *Phoenix from the Ashes: The Making, Unmaking, and Restoration of Catholic Tradition* (Kettering, OH: Angelico Press, 2015), pp. 363–73, was published at *Rorate Caeli* on October 19, 2015.

30   See *Rorate Caeli*, June 20, 2015.

31   See the article of that title by Fr. Hugh Somerville Knapman, OSB, at *Dominus Mihi Adjutor*, August 1, 2018. See also "The Pennsylvania Truth: John XXIII, Paul VI, and John Paul II were no saints," *Rorate Caeli*, August 15, 2018.

32   See *Rorate Caeli*, October 7, 2015; also published in *And Rightly So: Selected Letters and Articles of Neil McCaffrey*, ed. Peter A. Kwasniewski (Fort Collins, CO: Roman Catholic Books, 2019), 210–14.

33   See "New Interview with Fr. Charles Murr on Mother Pascalina, Bugnini, Paul VI, and Other Major Figures," *Rorate Caeli*, October 10, 2020; "Rooms broken into, dossiers stolen, death threats, armed guards, assassinations… Fr. Charles Murr on Vatican intrigues surrounding Cardinals Baggio, Benelli, Villot, and Gagnon," *Rorate Caeli*, December 18, 2020.

34   It is sometimes said: "Canonization only means that someone's soul is in heaven." If that's all it means, then — if I may borrow Flannery O'Connor's reaction to the idea that the Eucharist is no more than a symbol — to hell with it. If canonizing a pope doesn't mean we are supposed to admire how he "poped" with an heroic exercise of virtues and thus deem him to be a model for future popes, what good is it? What's the point? To canonize someone who lived a mediocre or mixed life simply because he died piously with last rites and is

end up in sedevacantism. It belongs above all to the pope, by his very office, to receive, defend, and pass on faithfully the immemorial traditions of the Church, a thing Paul VI most definitely did not do. Either Bergoglio is pope and the attempted canonization of Paul VI is without effect, or canonizations can never be without effect and therefore Bergoglio is not the pope. To this author, at least, the sedevacantist/sedeprivationist thesis is far more problematic than the non-infallibility thesis.

WHAT IS ADMIRABLE IN PAUL VI?

Do traditionally-minded Catholics admire Paul VI for anything? Yes, of course: no serious Christian's life is utterly bereft of good works, and we would be foolish not to acknowledge Montini's. But that good is not sufficient to cancel out the many and serious problems discussed in the preceding section. Indeed, the history of Montini's pontificate is as vivid a demonstration as one could wish to have of the difference between the person and the office. In the case of saintly popes, the grace of office seems to take up and enfold the person and transform him into a luminous icon of St. Peter and of Christ whose vicar he is. In the case of bad popes or mediocre popes, the grace of office is something that occasionally flares up, that comes out of hiding in emergency situations, but does not transform the incumbent in the same way. The latter is what we see with Paul VI, as an editorial at *Rorate Caeli* astutely expressed it:

> Pope Paul VI is described by most historians as a kind of tragic figure, trying to control the whirlwind of events surrounding him, but unable to do much. It is probably because of this, because it seemed that Montini often bent to the opinions of the world, because it seemed that he frequently accepted the fabricated notions and texts which committees of false

---

presumed to be in heaven is not at all in accordance with Church tradition. Such a "minimalist" canonization runs altogether against the interests and common good of the Church, seeming to favor the errors and the lack of virtue of the candidate, and thereby favoring their spread. At very least, it makes a mockery of beatification and canonization, since, on the new low standards, we could beatify and canonize a few hundred thousand people just by demonstrating they received the last rites with faith and that someone else experienced a recovery from COVID-19 by praying to them.

sages delivered to him (with very small modifications), that the moments in which he did not bend shine so clearly with the simple brightness of Peter. The *Nota Praevia* to *Lumen Gentium*, the vigorous defense of the traditional Eucharistic doctrines (in *Mysterium Fidei*) and of the teachings on Indulgences (in *Indulgentiarum Doctrina*), the *Credo of the People of God* are pillars which remain standing in a crumbling edifice, signs of supernatural protection. Amidst the moral collapse of the 1960s, and against the commission set up by his predecessor to reexamine the matter, Peter spoke though [Pope] Paul in *Humanae Vitae*: "it is never lawful, even for the gravest reasons, to do evil that good may come of it."[35]

If such good actions and teachings had been habitual, normal, and characteristic of Paul VI, and had been imbued with the panoply of Christian virtues St. Thomas discusses in the Second Part of the *Summa*, and if, on top of this, a popular *cultus* had arisen around a beloved pontiff, culminating in many indisputable miracles, then—and *only* then—would we have had reason to elevate Paul VI to the altars.

It is worthwhile to point out that, as time will show and as we have already begun to see, the good for which Paul VI was responsible is *not at all* the point of his canonization. In fact, all of the things listed above as "good moments" are contrary to the prevailing trends of the Bergoglio party. We are therefore ringside witnesses of the most cynical case of *"promoveatur ut amoveatur"* ever seen in Church history—that is, promoting someone to another, usually more distant position in order to remove them from their current more influential position.[36]

THE LIMITS OF CANONIZATION'S MEANING

There is, as usual, a divine irony in all of this. Even if the canonization of Paul VI turns out to have been legitimate—one may have one's serious doubts, obviously, but one cannot rule out this possibility altogether—it would not, strictly speaking, accomplish what its

---

35 See "*Humanæ Vitæ* at 50, I: 'never lawful,'" *Rorate Caeli*, July 21, 2018.
36 See my article "Two strategies enemies within Church will use to abandon *Humanae Vitae*," *LifeSite News*, August 14, 2018.

political proponents seek from it. By canonizing Paul VI, they intend to canonize his entire Vatican II program and, above all, the liturgical reform. But, as Shawn Tribe of the *Liturgical Arts Journal* noted:

> Anyone who would try to use the canonization of Paul VI to seriously propose that therefore all of the ecclesial and liturgical reforms that took place around his pontificate are therefore canonized and cannot be questioned (let alone reformed/rescinded) is either being intentionally and deceitfully manipulative or is woefully misinformed and uncatechized. Personal sanctity does not equate to infallibility; saints are often found at cross purposes with other saints; not every utterance/policy/decision/opinion of a saint stands the test of time nor the eventual judgment of the Church, nor is it dogmatic — not to mention that the Conciliar and liturgical reforms are not the personal possession of Paul VI but rather of a whole host of people and figures.[37]

Gregory DiPippo extends the same argument:

> The canonization of a Saint does not change the facts of his earthly life. It does not rectify the mistakes he may have made, whether knowingly or unknowingly. It does not change his failures into successes, whether they came about through his fault or that of others....
>
> The intrinsic merits or demerits of the postconciliar reform, and its status as a success or a failure, will not change in any way, shape, or form if Pope Paul VI is indeed canonized. No one can honestly say otherwise, and no one has the right to criticize, attack, silence, or call for the silencing of other Catholics if they contest that reform. If that reform went beyond the spirit and the letter of what Vatican II asked for in *Sacrosanctum Concilium*, as its own creators openly bragged that it did; if it was based on bad scholarship and a significant degree of basic incompetence, leading to the many changes now known to be mistakes; if it failed utterly to bring about the flourishing of liturgical piety that the Fathers of Vatican II desired, none of these things will change if Paul VI is canonized. Just as the canonizations of Pius V and X, and the future canonization of XII, did not place

---

37 On social media.

their liturgical reforms beyond question or debate, the canonization of Paul VI will not put anything about his reform beyond debate, and no one has any right to say otherwise.[38]

PRACTICAL CONSEQUENCES

Given the foregoing, what are the practical consequences for clergy, religious, and laity who doubt the validity of this canonization?

This topic deserves a separate fuller treatment, but briefly, anyone with such a doubt or difficulty is permitted to suspend judgment while the Church is in a state of manifest crisis.[39] He should refrain from praying to Paul VI and refuse to participate in his liturgical or devotional *cultus*. No one is required to invoke Paul VI publicly, to respond to such invocation, to offer Mass in his honor, or to comply with or offer financial support to efforts to promote his *cultus*. Indeed, to force oneself to venerate a man of whose sanctity, moral probity, and fidelity to the papal office one stands in severe doubt would be to violate one's conscience and to dishonor God. Far better to remain silent and, if circumstances permit and prudence dictates, to help other Catholics to see the real problems raised by this canonization as well as certain other beatifications and canonizations of the postconciliar period.

We are all obliged to pray for the salvation of our Holy Father and for the liberty and exaltation of our Holy Mother the Church on earth. This prayer implicitly includes the intention that the papacy, the Roman Curia, the Congregation for the Causes of Saints, and the very process of beatification and canonization all be reformed in due season, so that they may better serve the needs of Christ's faithful and give glory to Almighty God, who is "wondrous in His saints" (Ps 67:36).

---

38 See "What Would the Canonization of Paul VI Mean for the Liturgy and Liturgical Reform?," *New Liturgical Movement*, December 29, 2017; cf. my articles "Do New Saints Vindicate the New Mass?," *OnePeterFive*, October 22, 2020, and "We shouldn't take holiness as blanket approval: Even saints have their blind spots," *LifeSite News*, December 8, 2020.

39 See my article "Have There Been Worse Crises Than This One?," *OnePeterFive*, January 31, 2021.

15

Walking into a Trap[†]

JOSEPH SHAW

DR. JOHN LAMONT MADE THE THEOLOGICAL case against the infallible nature of decrees of canonization on *Rorate Caeli* a couple of years ago.[1] Recently I stirred up Twitter by repeating some of Dr. Lamont's arguments, and it didn't surprise me at all to see a fair amount of resistance, from traditionally-inclined Catholics, to the idea that canonizations are fallible.

This follows very naturally from the fact that a lot of old books and old authorities say that canonizations are infallible. What one has to remember is that St. Alphonsus Liguori and the other writers who are commonly cited on the issue used the term "infallible" in a far looser way than Vatican I's definition, and when the term is used today it is the Vatican I definition which tends to be uppermost in our minds. Again, since the time of St. Alphonsus and the rest, the process of determining the sanctity of individuals has been vastly "speeded up" — that would be a polite term for the reform of 1983. Before then, saints generally needed four miracles to be canonized; after 1983, they have needed only two; and so on.[2]

I am not going to repeat Dr. Lamont's arguments, however. No one outside Twitter has ever seriously suggested that the infallibility of canonizations was itself a doctrine of the Church which requires the assent of Catholics. So Catholics can agree to differ, as theologians in fact always have.

---

1 See chapters 8 and 9. — *Ed.*
2 Not only have the number of miracles required for canonization been reduced, but the criteria for identifying miracles are loosely applied in practice: see chapter 11. — *Ed.*

---

† An earlier version of this essay was published at *LMS Chairman* on July 31, 2020, and at *Rorate Caeli* on August 1, 2020. The author has revised and expanded it for inclusion herein.

Instead I wish to point out something else, which has its own importance. The process of canonization has always required money — researchers have to be paid — and many of those canonized have supporters with deep pockets. Having rich supporters does not in itself show that a person is not holy — even Christ had some rich friends, after all. But joined to an (*ahem*) streamlined process, there is a potential problem.

Among those being touted for canonization, there are bound to be celebrity Catholics backed by rich and powerful institutions determined to gain the prestige of having a founder or member canonized, even if the candidate falls below the moral standards of sanctity. We have seen how some of these institutions operate. Marcial Maciel Degollado was investigated for drug abuse as early as 1956, but he and his order, the Legionaries of Christ, not only survived this and later accusations, but continued to extend their influence and increase their prestige, not just for years, but for decades. They paid off some witnesses, denounced others, and greased the wheels of the Holy See with envelopes of cash. Using somewhat different methods, the Dominican priest Thomas Philippe survived not just being suspected of wrongdoing, but actually being removed from active ministry, in the 1950s, and teamed up with Jean Vanier to continue to abuse women up to his own death in 1993 and Vanier's in 2019.[3]

It says something about the capacity of ecclesial institutions to discern who is holy and who is a career criminal that one after another of the founders of successful religious orders and other institutions are found, often after their deaths, to have been evil men. A few years ago the suggestion that Vanier was anything other than a saint would have been shouted down by thousands of people genuinely moved and influenced by his work and writings. I don't blame them. Vanier was clever, and he was careful. Are we quite sure that no one as morally corrupt as he has been more careful, or more lucky?

We were fortunate that Maciel was exposed before his death, and Vanier shortly after his own. It is true that even the expedited

---

3   See Lianne Laurence, "Serial female sex-abuser Jean Vanier supported assisted suicide, waffled on abortion," *LifeSite News*, February 24, 2020; Peter Kwasniewski, "L'Arche founder Jean Vanier's abuse of women shows the 'mystery of iniquity' in our fallen world," *LifeSite News*, February 24, 2020.

canonization process provides an opportunity for accusations to be aired, but it is not beyond the realm of possibility that abuse-enabling institutions which manage to keep a lid on complaints for several decades — as we know many have — should not continue their success after the death of their abuser-in-chief, long enough to rush through a canonization process. Not much time is required. The speed record so far, in modern times, is held by Pope John Paul II, who was beatified six years and one month after his death, and canonized a little less than three years after that.[4]

It may be suggested that I am assuming what ought to be proved: that the canonization process is not infallible. The difficulties, from a human point of view, of exposing fraudulent sanctity are irrelevant to canonizations, it might be said, if the process is guaranteed by the Holy Ghost. If these difficulties are increased by speeding up the process and removing some of the traditional safeguards, what difference does it make? The Holy Ghost will overcome them just the same.

What difference would it make, indeed? Come to that, why bother having an investigation at all? Why not simply get the pope to take names of candidates for canonization out of a hat? This would, after all, not only be faster than even the current system, but also vastly cheaper.

The reason why such a procedure would be ridiculous gives us a clue about the status of canonizations. In the absence of a formal process of canonization, people could be made — and once were made — the subjects of public veneration by popular acclaim. By this means, indeed, some extremely dubious candidates enjoyed local cults, and many such cults had to be suppressed in later times. These included alleged victims of Jewish ritual murders, such as Simon of Trent and "Little St. Hugh" of Lincoln. We can be grateful for the skepticism of serious investigators at the time, who at least prevented these candidates from being formally canonized. What the investigators, including the traditional *advocatus diaboli*, were and are concerned to do, is to prevent the faithful being imposed upon by cunning frauds or popular hysteria. Careful historical investigation can never exclude the possibility of error altogether, but it can at least

---

4 He died on April 2, 2005; was beatified on May 1, 2011; and canonized on April 27, 2014.

make a judgment one way or the other *reasonable.* In a similar way, a diocese or the Holy See appoints investigators to look into alleged miracles and apparitions, to see if they are "worthy of belief."

If the investigators are rushed, under-resourced, subject to intolerable political pressure, or incompetent, they will perform this vital function less well than they would otherwise have done. That is an undeniable fact of life. In response to this reality, our predecessors in the Faith went to a great deal of trouble to make the process as rigorous as possible, even at great cost of time and expense, and on occasion public conflict, inevitably excluding some worthy candidates from the possibility of public veneration because, for one reason or another, they could not be investigated in the required way, or failed to meet all the very demanding criteria. That was a price popes over many centuries thought worth paying for a high degree of *certainty*: the highest possible level of confidence in an historical investigation anyone could hope to achieve. If the process is speeded up and some of the safeguards are removed, the level of assurance we can have about its conclusions falls. How could it not?

Painful as it is, it is necessary today not only to make the general point that canonizations are not infallible, but to distinguish between pre-1983 and post-1983 investigations — and to begin to do this loudly and clearly. For while in the past the process was fallible but extremely cautious and thorough, it is now fallible, and not nearly so cautious and thorough as before. It seems to me inevitable that, at some point, some fraudulent celebrity priest, some abusive charismatic layman, or some founder of a cultlike religious order, is going to be canonized. In fact, I would be very surprised if this has not already happened. Who could even read a short account of the life and work of all the people canonized since 1983? There are thousands of them. They represent a vast field for a well-resourced anti-Catholic media to look in for hidden scandal.

One fine day in the next ten years, credible allegations will be made against a *beatus* or canonized saint. Remember, you read it here first. And if we are not careful, the people defending the indefensible will be conservative and traditional Catholics — those maintaining the pious belief that canonizations are infallible, and who want to defend the system as a whole, and indeed the very concept of heroic virtue and sanctity.

Liberal Catholics, by contrast, will just walk away from the shambles. After all, they don't even believe in supernatural virtue, let alone miracles. For them, it will be embarrassing, if they happened to have promoted the individual concerned, but they will not be concerned about the destruction of the confidence ordinary Catholics can repose in the sanctity of canonized saints in general. On the contrary, if this confidence is destroyed, it will enable them to attack all those saints they do not like with greater force than before, and even to demand an end to the *cultus* of the saints, with its awkward implication that heroic virtue is truly attainable.

This is worth considering. The saints who defended the traditional teaching and liturgy of the Church — which is to say, more or less all of them — are an endless source of irritation for liberal Catholics. Even worse are those who did what liberals assure us is impossible: in difficult circumstances, by God's grace, to resist carnal temptations and live in fidelity to their state of life and vows. To manage this problem, liberals have, over the decades, sought to minimize the saints' influence: they have removed their statues from churches, they have abolished or failed to observe their feasts, they have ridiculed the *cultus* of relics and the practice of pilgrimages, and they have discouraged the reading of the lives of the saints, or rewritten them to suit their own agenda. The white-robed army of martyrs, the heroic confessors, the kings, monks, and penitents, the Doctors and the great popes, are a standing rebuke to the liberal attempt to remake the Church, and a ceaseless source of inspiration to the open-minded to rediscover the Church's ancient Tradition. The liberal Catholic project is fundamentally hostile to the entire *concept* of sanctity as traditionally understood. Don't expect liberal Catholics to defend that concept if some recently canonized individuals turn out to have been abusers.

It is not difficult to imagine how things would play out. Were some unworthy person canonized, and then exposed, those who hold that canonizations are infallible would be forced to defend him for as long as humanly possible. This may well be the kind of person they would least like to defend had he *not* been canonized, but it will be the *conservatives* defending the indefensible, not the liberals, even if it had been the latter pushing for the canonization in the first place. Thus it will be those Catholics most queasy about the accelerated canonization process, the ones most leery about canonizing every pope since Vatican II, the ones least comfortable about the scramble to find people to canonize who tick various ethnic and ideological boxes — these will be the people who are going to be left to defend the "St. Jean Vanier" or the "St. Marcial Maciel" to be revealed in the future. As the details gradually emerge, as they tend to do, they will be utterly humiliated, and forever associated with the crimes of the accused.

My friends, you are walking into a trap.

APPENDIX

Prospero Lambertini on Papal Sanctity

FOR IF...IN ORDER TO BE HEROIC IT IS NECESsary that one conduct oneself heroically in exercising those virtues which one has the occasion to exercise, all the more must this be said of those virtues which one must exercise not only because the occasion arises, but because of the office that one has assumed. And to start with a servant of God who in his lifetime was the Supreme Pontiff, we must note first of all that the Supreme Pontiff is the shepherd and ruler of the whole Church, and also the bishop of the church of Rome, the metropolitan of the Roman province, the primate of Italy, and the patriarch of the West.... This being premised, we may infer that in the cause of a servant of God who during his lifetime had received the Supreme Pontificate, one must investigate before all else whether and in what way he fulfilled these offices; and since the Supreme Pontiff is also a ruler possessing secular power, and has both swords in that territory which is legally subject to him, one must certainly not fail to investigate the matters pertaining to the rank of a secular ruler, and without which secular government cannot be rightly conducted.[1]

---

1 *De beatificatione et canonizatione*, Bk. III, ch. 32: "Si enim, ut quis sit heros, ex alibi dictis praecipue necesse est, ut heroice se gesserit in earum virtutum exercitio, quarum exercendarum habuit occasionem; a fortiori idem dicendum erit de virtutibus, quas non modo ex oblata occasione, sed ex assumpto munere debuit exercere. Initioque ducto a Dei Servo, qui dum viveret, Summus Pontifex fuit, praenoscere opus est, Summum Pontificem Pastorem esse, et Moderatorem universae Ecclesiae, praeterea esse Episcopum Urbis Romae, Metropolitanum Provinciae Romanae, Primatem Italiae, et Occidentis Patriarcham [...] Quo proinde posito, infertur, in causis Servorum Dei qui dum viverent Summum Pontificatum adepti sunt, praeter alia inquiri debere an, et quomodo praedicta munera impleverint; et quia Summus Pontifex est etiam Princeps Ditionis saecularis, et in terris sibi pleno iure subiectis habet utrumque gladium, omitti certe non debebit inquisitio de iis, quae ad dignitatem Principis saecularis pertinent, et sine quibus recte Principatus saecularis administrari non potest" (1–2).

The Venerable Servant of God Cardinal Bellarmine made a study for the Supreme Pontiff Clement VIII about the principal duty of the Supreme Pontiff.... After stating that among all his duties, the solicitude for all the churches must hold first place, he says that the Supreme Pontiff must be sure to put good bishops at the head of all the churches, and see to it that they fulfil their task and, if necessary, force them to do so.[2]

In the *Liber Diurnus* of the Roman pontiffs published by Lucas Holstenius on the basis of an ancient manuscript, there is a profession of faith which used to be made by the man elected as Supreme Pontiff. In this profession of faith, not only were heretics condemned by an anathema, but the man chosen also promised that he would preserve with the greatest diligence all that his apostolic predecessors had ordained in their synods and decrees, and that he was ready to die for the faith of Christ. "We declare that, faithful to what has been ordained by our predecessors, we will never adopt any novelty contrary to the Catholic and Orthodox faith, and that we will sooner die, if need be, by the help of God's grace, rather than in any way to give our consent to persons who are so audacious as to introduce such things." No one can fail to see, from the terms of this oath, that the investigation [for the sanctity of a pope] must turn above all on his zeal for preserving and promoting the Catholic faith, for enforcing ecclesiastical discipline, and for restoring and upholding the rights of the Apostolic See. This is further shown by those Roman pontiffs who have been numbered among the saints, and who are honored throughout the Church; there is none of them who did not excel in zeal for the Catholic Faith and for ecclesiastical discipline.[3]

---

2   Ibid., 3: "Venerabilis Dei Servus Cardinalis Bellarminus nonnulla exposuit Summo Pontifici Clementi VIII de Officio primario Summi Pontificis [...] Postquam autem retulit inter omnia eius officia sollicitudinem omnium Ecclesiarum primum locum tenere debere, ait eum curare debere ut singulis Ecclesiis bonos Episcopos praeficiat, curetque, eos suo muneri satisfacere et si opus sit cogat."
3   Ibid., 3–4: "In *Libro Diurno Romanorum Pontificum* ex antiquissimo Codice manuscripto in lucem edito studio Lucae Holstenii extat formula Professionis Fidei, quae ab electo in Summum Pontificem fiebat; in qua non modo Haeretici anathemata condemnabuntur, sed electus pollicebatur, se toto mentis studio conservaturum esse quae Apostolici Praedecessores per Synodos et Decreta statuerant, et se pro Fide Christi mori paratum: *Profitemur etiam, Nos secundum illa, quae*

a Praedecessoribus statuta sunt numquam aliquid novi contra Catholicam atque Orthodoxam Fidem suscepturos, vel talia temerarie praesumentibus, si opportunum fuerit, etiam mori, Dei gratia nos corroborante, quoquo modo consensum praebituros. Ex qua iuramenti formula, nemo est qui non videat praecipuum indaginis momentum esse constituendum in zelo conservandae et dilatandae Fidei Catholicae, Ecclesiasticae Disciplinae institutendae, et instaurandae et Iurium Sedis Apostolicae vindicandorum. Confirmari id posset exemplis Romanorum Pontificum inter Sanctos relatorum, qui Cultum habent in Ecclesia universali; nemo enim ex illis est, qui zelo Catholicae Fidei, et Ecclesiasticae Disciplinae non excelluerit."

THE CONTRIBUTORS

PHILLIP CAMPBELL holds a BA in European History from Ave Maria University and a certificate in Secondary Education from Madonna University. He teaches history for Homeschool Connections and is the author of the popular "Story of Civilization" series by TAN Books, as well as *Heroes and Heretics of the Reformation, Power from on High*, and other works of Catholic historical interest. Phillip is also the founder of Cruachan Hill Press, an independent publishing firm specializing in works of Catholic history and spirituality. He is the creator of the blog and website *Unam Sanctam Catholicam*.

THOMAS CREAN is a friar of the English Province of the Dominicans. He has a doctorate in sacred theology from the International Theological Institute in the archdiocese of Vienna, and he has taught philosophy and theology in Austria and Ireland. His most recent book, co-authored with Alan Fimister, is *Integralism: A Manual of Political Philosophy*, published by Editiones Scholasticae in 2020. He is also the translator of Humbert of Romans's *De Oratione* (Arouca Press, 2020).

ROBERTO DE MATTEI, a student of philosopher Augusto del Noce and historian Armando Saitta and a disciple of Professor Plinio Corrêa de Oliveira, served as chair of Modern History in the Faculty of Letters at the University of Cassino (1985–2009), and, since 2005, as Associate Professor in the European University of Rome. He is President of the Lepanto Foundation, and was Founder and Director of the Lepanto Cultural Centre (1986–2006). De Mattei directs the magazine *Radici Cristiane* and the *Corrispondenza Romana* news agency. Between 2003 and 2011 he was Vice President of the Italian National Research Council (CNR). He is the author of many books, which have been translated into several languages — most recently in English, *Saint Pius V: The Legendary Pope Who Excommunicated Queen Elizabeth, Standardized the Mass, and Defeated the Ottoman Empire* (Sophia, 2021).

WILLIAM MATTHEW DIEM holds degrees from Christendom College, VA (BA, MA), the Pontifical Faculty of the Immaculate Conception, DC (STL), and the Pontifical University of St. Thomas Aquinas, Rome (STD). He has taught Theology at Christendom College (Virginia) and the University of St. Thomas (Texas). His research focuses on the thought of Aquinas and his school.

CHRISTOPHER A. FERRARA is a civil rights attorney and the author of six books and thousands of articles and essays on subjects ranging from the current crisis in the Catholic Church to political philosophy to scientific controversies. His book *Liberty, the God that Failed* has been hailed as "an intellectual landmark in Catholic ecclesiastical history" (Graham Ward, Regius Professor of Divinity, University of Oxford) and "a tour de force — a marvelous achievement" (Patrick McKinley Brennan, John F. Scarpa Chair in Catholic Legal Studies, Villanova University). His study of the current crisis in the Catholic Church, *The Great Façade* (co-authored with Thomas E. Woods Jr.) has been praised as "a spirited brief against the fantasies of recent decades, and an appeal to Catholics and the Church to return to what they have been, in order to become what they most truly are" (James Kalb, author of *Against Inclusiveness*).

BRUNERO GHERARDINI (1925–2017) was ordained a priest on June 29, 1948 in Pistoia, for the diocese of Prato and studied theology with Cornelio Fabro at the Lateran. In 1958 he was called to the Holy See, where he served as an official of the then Sacred Congregation for Seminaries. From 1968, for thirty-seven years, he was full professor of ecclesiology and ecumenism on the theological faculty of the Pontifical Lateran University, of which he was also dean. Until his death he was a consultant to the Congregation for the Causes of Saints. From 1994 onwards he was a canon of the patriarchal basilica of St. Peter's in the Vatican, where he resided. After the death of Msgr. Antonio Piolanti (1911–2001), Gherardini was postulator of the cause of canonization of Blessed Pius IX, for ten years until 2011. In the year 2000, he took over direction of the journal *Divinitas*, founded by Piolanti in 1954. Gherardini participated for over half a century in theological debate, especially in the field of ecclesiology and the interpretation of the Second Vatican Council. He authored more than eighty books and hundreds of articles.

JOHN HUNWICKE, a priest of the Personal Ordinariate of Our Lady of Walsingham, was for nearly three decades at Lancing College, where he taught Latin and Greek language and literature, and was Head of Theology and Assistant Chaplain. He has served three curacies and been a parish priest, and was a Senior Research Fellow at Pusey House in Oxford. Since 2011, he has been in full communion with the See of St. Peter.

PETER A. KWASNIEWSKI (BA in Liberal Arts, Thomas Aquinas College; MA and PhD in Philosophy, Catholic University of America) is an author and speaker on Catholic Tradition, especially in its liturgical dimension. After teaching at the International Theological Institute in Austria and the Franciscan University of Steubenville's Austrian Program, he joined the founding team of Wyoming Catholic College in 2006, where he taught theology, philosophy, music, and art history, and directed the choir and schola until 2018. He has published over a thousand articles on Thomistic thought, sacramental and liturgical theology, the history and aesthetics of music, Catholic Social Teaching, and issues in the contemporary Church, and has written or edited twelve books, including most recently *Reclaiming Our Roman Catholic Birthright* (Angelico, 2020), *The Holy Bread of Eternal Life* (Sophia, 2020), and *The Ecstasy of Love in the Thought of Thomas Aquinas* (Emmaus Academic, 2021).

JOHN R.T. LAMONT is a Canadian Catholic philosopher and theologian. He studied philosophy and theology at the Dominican College in Ottawa and at Oxford University, and has taught philosophy and theology in Catholic universities and seminaries. He is the author of *Divine Faith* (Ashgate, 2004) and of a number of academic papers.

JOSEPH SHAW is a British academic and the current chairman of the Latin Mass Society of England and Wales. Educated at Ampleforth

College and the University of Oxford, he is currently a tutorial fellow in philosophy at St. Benet's Hall, Oxford. His main areas of interest are practical ethics, the philosophy of religion, and medieval philosophy. In 2015, he was elected a fellow of the Royal Society of Arts. His publications include *The Case for Liturgical Restoration: Una Voce Studies on the Traditional Latin Mass* (Angelico, 2019) and *How to Attend the Extraordinary Form* (Catholic Truth Society, 2020). He blogs at *LMS Chairman* and *LifeSite News*.

JEAN-FRANÇOIS THOMAS is a member of the Society of Jesus. After completing his formation in France and the United States, Fr. Thomas was a missionary in Romania and then in the Philippines, and has taught philosophy in several seminaries and universities in France and abroad. He published a work of spirituality, *Les mangeurs de cendre* (*The Ash-Eaters*, Via Romana, 2017) and is pursuing research in art history.

JOSÉ ANTONIO URETA, co-founder of Fundación Roma (Chile) and advisor of its pro-life and pro-family project Acción Familia, is a senior researcher at Société Française pour la Défense de la Tradition, Famille et Propriété (Paris) and author of *Pope Francis's Paradigm Shift: Continuity or Rupture in the Mission of the Church?* (Spring Grove, PA, 2018).

INDEX OF PROPER NAMES

www.ingramcontent.com/pod-product-compliance
Lightning Source LLC
LaVergne TN
LVHW091803050125
800531LV00005B/531/J